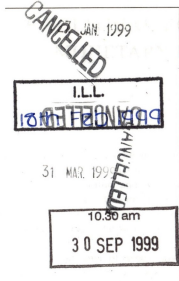
Is moneta
gradual e
so widel
expected
and slow
institutio
political

The bc
academic
far beyor
wider int

- Effe
- Lega
- The
- Bud
- Inter

Drawing
non-tech
eral sens
Economy
fessional:

Francesco Giordano is Vice President and Senior International Economist at Credit
Suisse First Boston, previously he held positions at San Paolo Bank and MMS
Standard and Poors. **Sharda Persaud** is EMU Economist at Banque Paribas.
Previously she worked as Senior Economist at San Paolo Bank, and at The European
Economics and Financial Centre.

THE POLITICAL ECONOMY OF MONETARY UNION

Towards the euro

*Francesco Giordano and
Sharda Persaud*

London and New York

First published in 1998
by Routledge
11 New Fetter Lane, London EC4P 4EE

Simultaneously published in the USA and Canada
by Routledge
29 West 35th Street, New York, NY 10001

Typeset in Times by
J&L Composition Ltd, Filey, North Yorkshire
Printed and bound in Great Britain by
Creative Print and Design (Wales), Ebbw Vale

British Library Cataloguing in Publication Data
A catalogue record for this book is available from the British Library

Library of Congress Cataloging in Publication Data
Giordano, Francesco, 1966–
The political economy of monetary union : towards the euro /
Francesco Giordano and Sharda Persaud.
p.   cm.
Includes bibliographical references and index.
1. Monetary unions–European Union countries.   2. Monetary
policy–European Union countries.   3. Europe–Economic
integration.
I. Persaud, Sharda, 1971–   .   II. Title.
HG925.G555   1998
332.4′566′094–dc21   97–29026
CIP

ISBN 0–415–17442–2 (hbk)
ISBN 0–415–17443–0 (pbk)

TO SUSANA AND ANDREW

CONTENTS

FIGURES AND TABLES

Figures

Tables

ABBREVIATIONS

BIS	Bank of International Settlements
BDA	Bundesvereinigung Deutscher Arbeitgeberverbände (national grouping of 1000 employers' associations in Germany)
BDI	Federation of German Industry
CDU	Christian Democratic Party in Germany
CAP	Common Agricultural Policy
CEEC	Committee of European Economic Co-operation
CMEA	Council for Mutual Economic Assistance
EAGGF	European Agricultural Guidance and Guarantee Fund
EC	European Community
ECB	European Central Bank
ECOFIN	Economic and Financial Committee
ECSC	European Coal and Steel Community
ECU	European Currency Unit
EDF	European Development Fund
EEA	European Economic Area
EEC	European Economic Community
EFTA	European Free Trade Association
EIB	European Investment Bank
EMCF	European Monetary Co-operation Fund
EMI	European Monetary Institute
EMS	European Monetary System
ERDF	European Regional Development Fund
ESF	European Social Fund
EMU	Economic and Monetary Union
ERM	Exchange Rate Mechanism
ESF	European Social Fund
EU	European Union
FDI	Foreign Direct Investment
GATT	General Agreement on Tariffs and Trade
GDP	Gross Domestic Product

ABBREVIATIONS

GNP	Gross National Product
IGC	Intergovernmental Conference
IMF	International Monetary Fund
NAFTA	North American Free Trade Agreement
NAIRU	non-accelerating inflation rate of unemployment
NATO	North Atlantic Treaty Organisation
OECD	Organization for Economic Co-operation and Development
SEA	Single European Act
SDP	Social Democratic Party (UK)
TUC	Trade Union Congress
VAT	value added tax
WEU	Western European Union
WTO	World Trade Organisation

1

INTRODUCTION

I insist that no emotion, not even love, can replace the rule of
institutions controlled by reason.

(Popper 1945)

Institutions, together with the usual constraints of economic
theory, determine the opportunities in a society.

(North 1990)

Eminent US economist Paul Krugman distinguishes three categories of economics books: Greek letter books (which in-house we call pitch forks, following the shape of the Greek letter phi), these are mathematical, technical
and complex, but conclusions are often fuzzy and difficult; up and down economics, as you read in the financial press, largely focused on the very latest
piece of news or move in the stock market; and airport lounge economics,
where the need to attract attention prevails over the rigour of the content and
authors often fall into the temptation of predicting permanent gloom or a
coming golden age (Krugman 1994). The following pages are an attempt to
present a book which does not belong to any of the three categories above.

The book is written by people involved in financial markets. Most chapters
were, in one form or another, previously presented in San Paolo Bank's
monthly publication the *Euro Newsletter*. The book tries to put together three
things, firstly the experience that we have gained from working in the markets. Financial markets are often accused of reacting – often without sense of
measure – only to the latest set of news and with a limited perspective.
Nevertheless, financial markets are producers and consumers of a great
deal of information. Government policies are dissected, political crises
spotted in the making, changes in economic circumstances reacted to in real
time. Much of the information supply by financial companies is not of great
depth and there is also a tendency in repeating everyone else's line either in
gloom or joy. Markets have a powerful role as wardens of policy orthodoxy
and though not everyone might agree on this, they often find wisdom in a
multitude.

Secondly, although it is not an academic book, the book draws on academic work and we think it might prove interesting to academics. Throughout we have made an attempt to present some of the recent areas of research
and some of the most influential opinions which are attracting the attention

of academic economists. The treatment is generally non-technical, but it summarises some of the leading ideas and conclusions, particularly for their implications in terms of political choices. Economics is probably one of the professions where the cleavage between academics and its applied branches is greatest. In what follows, we try to set many of the recent areas of academic debate against the background of day-to-day policy decisions and financial market behaviour.

Last, but not least, this book attempts to address a number of political issues. It is a book on Economic and Monetary Union (EMU), but not only on the pros and cons of monetary union. It sets out what we consider to be some of the main economic and political problems faced by Europe in the next few years, describing their recent evolution and the policy options open to us. For this reason, it describes the specific experiences of a number of countries in facing problems such as public deficits, unemployment and interest rate policy.

In writing this book we have been driven by three leading ideas. The first, as in the opening sentence by Douglass North above, is that institutions matter. The choices on labour market institutions, on how monetary policy should be run, and central bank status designed, for example, make a difference to the economic performance of a country. In this sense, we believe that governments should be actively involved in their design. Governments are faced with alternative options. We think that it is important to stimulate a debate on these options and to diffuse ideas on how economics sets out to address the problems. We do not share the view that governments should at all times be 'hands off' and let markets find the best outcomes.

Secondly, we think that there is scope for economic policy to improve economic outcomes. Under certain conditions, both monetary and fiscal policy can effectively be used to stabilise the economy during economic cycles. In some circumstances, they might also promote economic growth or lower unemployment. Past experience, particularly from the 1970s, has warned that an indiscriminate use of pro-growth economic policies is the cause of inflation and does not affect growth in the long term. This calls for restraint and for institutions that prevent excesses, but not for the end of stabilisation policy.

Finally, globalisation is an issue which appears in the book at regular intervals. This refers largely to the evolution and rising power of international capital markets. Financial innovation and a progressive move towards greater capital mobility have steadily increased the size and role of international capital flows. The Bank of International Settlements (BIS) shows that turnover in financial derivatives rose from about US$50 trillion to over US$ 300 trillion in the ten years up to 1995 (BIS 1996). This is likely to have enhanced the allocation of capital towards its most profitable uses. Also, however, 'on the economic side, public officials have discovered that it has become increasingly costly to defend economic policies against market pressures, given the unimpeded flow of international financial transaction'

(Kapstein 1996). Apart from finance, globalisation also recurs frequently in the analysis of recent trends in unemployment and labour markets. We try to discuss briefly the implications of a more global labour market.

Monetary union will be the end of a long process. European integration started from the post-war period and talk of monetary union started early, only a few years after the set up of the European Community (1958). The reasons behind the introduction of the single currency are, therefore, not straightforward. Many are historical and political motivations, such as the attempt to increase Europe's role as an economic power house. Others are economic, the single currency saves money and makes business decisions easier. The economic reasons are, however, difficult to quantify and not everyone agrees that EMU will stimulate growth and prosperity. It is more important, in our opinion, to say that monetary union is a further step in a process of greater integration in Europe which, we think, is largely irreversible and mostly desirable.

The common market is already well established and, within Europe, few consider going back on that decision. An effort to make domestic arrangements in legal, tax and regulatory areas uniform throughout Europe has been made and significant progress can be reported there. Several private companies have become pan-European in character. At least at the professional level, labour markets have started to operate with a European mentality. Overall, both questions of economic opportunity and political trends suggest that greater European integration will continue in areas such as trade, business regulation and policy, defence, etc. That Europe should think and act as one also in matters of domestic monetary policy and exchange rate policy seems to be a natural – albeit large – step forward. This does not necessarily mean that Europe is heading towards a Federal state, but it implies that, in the future, the frontiers of domestic sovereignty will have to be shifted further back to leave room for greater pan-European rule.

EMU has in a sense been a policy imposed from above, by politicians, onto a confused public, in many cases suffering the consequences of striving to meet the EMU criteria in a period of low growth. The details of EMU implementation, and the consequences for nations, are very open to misinterpretation and political diatribe. There is a tendency for politicians to explain EMU either as a magical panacea for all ills, which will also reduce the need for future trips to bureau de change, or as a Eurocratic nightmare which will submerge national identity. It is therefore sometimes difficult to 'separate the wood from the trees'. Here we try to look at the economic and not the political picture. EMU has something of its own momentum, and is a natural progression from the common market. The step to EMU has no real predecessors, and therefore it is difficult to predict exactly what effects it might have, and how it would operate. In this sense it is an educated gamble. We try here to define the picture a little further, using the ideas and examples of economic theory and empirical evidence.

Many economic problems will, under EMU, need to be seen as European problems. Much of EMU success will depend not only on how the introduction of the euro is devised, but on how Europe will be able to address rising budget deficits, high unemployment or currency fluctuations. These themes – and some others – are discussed below.

Chapter 2, on monetary union, contains a review of the main areas of debate relative to monetary union. We present a brief history of the main steps which have been taken towards monetary union and in particular the landmark Maastricht Treaty which set up a timetable and conditions for the single currency. Some of the main problems faced by Europe in the run up to 1999 – when the single currency is introduced – are also discussed. In particular, we highlight the need for some arrangement for the currencies whose participation in EMU is delayed. The need to agree on a system for preventing governments of member countries from running high budget deficits also calls for specific provisions. Chapter 3 is a brief discussion on the experience of Germany after the 1990 monetary unification which followed the fall of the Berlin Wall and German unification. Integration in Germany has taken longer than expected and has caused larger problems than people believed. While the differences with EMU are large, some interesting lessons can be learned from the German experience.

Chapter 4 deals specifically with the issue of public deficits and debts. The reasons why large deficits and debts have adverse economic and financial consequences are discussed, together with some suggestions on the reasons why the problem was exacerbated over the last few years. Attempts to regulate or control deficits and debts are also described. We conclude that reducing budget deficits has become a priority as people have become less tolerant of large government intervention in the economy and of taxation. Budget imbalances also affect economic growth and financial stability. Nevertheless, while macroeconomics clearly point to the need to limit budget deficits, the amount of taxation, social services and income redistribution are still choices which remain in the realm of politics. Here we note that programmes aimed at reducing budget deficits have adverse effects on growth which require a large amount of co-ordination with interest rate policy.

In Chapter 5, we discuss central bank independence. This has been an area of great academic debate and policy action, which has led to most central banks in the industrialised world, including the future European central bank, becoming independent from government control. Independence seems desirable as a way of controlling inflation. Transparency and accountability are, however, needed as non-elected central bankers become depositories of considerable power. Similar conclusions are reached in Chapter 6, which is also on the theme of central banks and deals with the way in which monetary policy is conducted. We note that monetary targeting Bundesbank-style is faced with a number of problems, resulting from financial innovation and markets globalisation. In the face of this, central banks need to become more eclectic: in deciding interest rates, they have to look at a broader range of indicators and take a more discretionary attitude.

Chapter 7 looks at why unemployment has remained so high in Europe. Most of European unemployment is structural and seems to stem from the particular characteristics of the labour market. We look at some of the main explanations for Europe's high and persistent unemployment, in comparison with countries with difference experiences such as the US. Chapter 8 looks in greater detail at the case of Germany, where a lack of wage flexibility has been blamed for a substantial increase in the unemployment rate.

Chapter 9 looks at the increases in currency volatility experienced after the breakdown of the Bretton Woods system. Currency markets are very difficult to predict, and fluctuate widely making it difficult for firms and other economic agents to plan ahead. This uncertainty should be reduced under EMU, as EU countries will fluctuate together against outside currencies, but not against each other. This should enforce a more stable economic environment reducing the adverse effects of shocks on investment, production and unemployment. Chapter 10 looks into possible currency regimes, including Exchange Rate Mechanism (ERM) II, for countries which do not join EMU at the first wave. Argentina's currency board – possibly the strictest form of currency pegging – is evaluated as an option. Chapter 11 looks at the recent history of UK involvement with Europe, and some of the UK's EU complaints over the years. Chapter 12 looks at various proposals for Italian institutional reforms, in a search for greater government stability.

Acknowledgements

Susana Garcia Cervero, of the European University Institute, Florence, Italy, has given invaluable contribution to Chapters 5 and 7. We would also like to thank Carlo Monticelli and Marcello Pericoli of the Bank of Italy as well as Giovanni Mallen, Eugenio Namor, Vourneen O'Connell and Anna Salter of San Paolo Bank.

We are grateful for permission to reproduce the following copyright material: *The European Union* 3rd edition (*Economics Today* edited by Andrew Leake) by S.F. Goodman, published by Macmillan Press Ltd, 1996, pp. 247–8; *From Salisbury to Major* by Brendan Evans and Andrew Taylor, published by Manchester University Press, 1996, p. 250; *Two Decades in British Politics* edited by Bill Jones and Lynton Robins, published by Manchester University Press, 1992, reprinted 1994, p. 244; *Money, Information and Uncertainty* 2nd edition by C.A.E. Goodhart, published by Macmillan Press Ltd, 1989, p. 422; *The New European Economy – the politics and economics of integration* 2nd revised edition by L. Tsoukalis, published by Oxford University Press, 1993, material reprinted by permission of Oxford University Press.

2

MONETARY UNION: TO BE OR NOT TO BE?

History, motivations and prospects

Introduction

EMU is fast becoming a reality. 1995 and 1996 saw many crucial advances along the road to EMU, both in terms of official progress in panning out the details of the introduction of the single currency and in terms of financial market movements signalling rising expectations that EMU will take place. The December 1995 EU Madrid summit saw extensive discussion of technical reports by both the European Commission (the 'Green Paper', European Commission 1995b) in June, and the European Monetary Institute in November 1995, on the procedures for the introduction of the single currency (see Box 2.1). The name of the new currency, the euro, was agreed together with details and timing for the conversion of domestic currencies. Another important decision was the 'one-to-one' conversion between the ECU and the 'euro'. Late 1996 saw vigorous attempts by many governments to meet the deficit criterion with 1997 data, in their 1997 budgets. These attempts and lower than expected European growth in 1995 and 1996 seem to have reduced the perception of the gap between core and non-core countries and to have increased the probability of a wider EMU.

The Dublin summit in December 1996 saw the ratification of the European Commission proposals on the legal arrangements for the introduction of the 'euro'. Arrangements for ERM II – an exchange rate agreement for countries that do not join EMU in the first wave – were also agreed. Expectations of EMU starting on time in 1999, and with enough countries to make it a viable entity, has induced substantial spread tightening between core and non-core yields on long-term government bonds and has tightened the 'delta' or spread between the theoretical and actual ECU market (a technical indicator of improved investor expectations on the prospects for EMU). Meanwhile, there remains evidence of concern – particularly from German investors – about committing funds beyond the date of implementation of EMU due to fears that the new currency will perhaps be weaker than the deutsche mark. Worries that a wider EMU could mean a weaker euro, and a less stable union, have brought the question of ensuring fiscal rectitude after

6

the birth of EMU to the fore. Some agreement has been reached on the 'Stability Pact' – an attempt to impose fiscal discipline on countries joining EMU – but it remains to be seen how the implementation of this monitoring and punishment system will be in reality. Below, we present some historical remarks on the process which has led to the project of monetary union. Also, we review the main reasons why, we believe, monetary union will go ahead, highlighting some of the main areas of discussions for EMU implementation. In particular, the aforementioned Stability Pact and interim arrangements for the currencies of countries which join EMU at a second stage (if any).

Historical remarks

The main aim of the six-country European Community set with the Treaty of Rome in 1957 was clearly the foundation of a common market, an area of free circulation of goods and uniform trade relations with the rest of the world. However, awareness that monetary matters could be critical was raised early on. In 1969, at the Den Haag meeting, European Heads of State agreed on the desirability of monetary union (following the 1968 Barre plan). The Werner Report – published in 1970 – presented a detailed plan for the introduction of monetary union for the first time. The report set the objective of complete economic and monetary union by 1980. It was fairly ambitious as far as policy co-ordination was concerned: economic policy was to become the responsibility of a new body, the Centre for Economic Policy, while a standing conference of central bank governors would manage monetary policy. The plan also recognised the need for economic convergence before the move to full monetary integration. There were also provisions for financial compensation for regional imbalances which could result from the fact that countries lost control over fiscal and monetary policy. While there was a common feeling on this issue – largely due to the desire to challenge the dominant position of a weakening dollar – the plan for its implementation was met with very different views. The French insisted on immediate implementation, while the Germans put greater emphasis on the need for economic convergence, a familiar theme. The plans were shelved as a result of the financial turmoil following the 1971 collapse of the Bretton Woods system (see Chapter 9, see also Halwood and MacDonald 1986). This sanctioned the termination of the convertibility of the dollar into gold and started the period of 'dollar standard' (Smithsonian agreement). In fact, the 1970s saw very little progress towards European monetary integration. From 1972, the European countries pegged their rates against each other – while also pegging against the dollar – in the so-called 'Snake in the Tunnel'. Bilateral exchange rate fluctuations were limited to within 2.25 per cent bands, with participating currencies moving up and down together within a wider 4.5 per cent band against the dollar. However, the oil shocks and consequent high inflation rates caused balance of payment problems and the system did not last long. In 1974 France left the system (briefly rejoining it in 1975), after Italy and the UK had already quit. The Snake remained just a DM area. Germany's greater dislike – relative to the other participating countries – of inflation in the presence of an external shock such as the oil crisis proved fatal.

The Exchange Rate Mechanism (ERM)

In 1979, there was a new drive towards exchange rate co-ordination. Germany's Chancellor Schmidt proposed and then agreed with the French a new system of pegged exchange rates – the ERM – in which currencies would fluctuate within set bands and with an obligation for all countries to intervene to defend currencies at the margin of the bands. Germany's motivation, as now, was twofold: to protect its competitiveness relative to its European partners in the presence of a weakening dollar, while forcing others to follow more stringent anti-inflationary policies. France joined with a desire to strengthen its anti-inflationary drive, but also with strong political motivation, while Italy joined, despite doubts from many sides – including the central bank which feared the political and economic costs of being left out. The main foe of the agreement was the Bundesbank, which fought, and obtained clear limits to its obligation to intervene. The system worked reasonably smoothly – though with numerous devaluations – during a decade characterised by convergence of inflation rates. The system seemed increasingly solid until German unification, higher DM interest rates, a Europe-wide recession and doubts over progress in deepening European integration caused severe problems, which ended in 1992–3 with the exit of the lira and sterling and the widening of the bands to 15 per cent from 2.25 per cent.

A new drive towards EMU

In the late 1980s, monetary union proposals returned to the fore. The Delors report on EMU (Committee for the Study of Economic and Monetary Union 1989) was set up in June 1988 by the European Council of Hanover under the Chairmanship of the President of the European Commission. The Committee included all governors/presidents of EC central banks and some independent experts. The Delors report listed three conditions for monetary union: total convertibility of currencies, liberalisation of capital flows – with full integration of financial markets – and the locking of exchange rates. The report also noted that action should be taken in a number of areas to avoid or limit economic imbalances. These included competition policies and other measures to strengthen the single market; common policies where the market mechanism could not operate adequately; and macroeconomic policy co-ordination, particularly via rules to regulate budgetary policies 'uncoordinated and divergent national budgetary policies would undermine monetary stability' (op. cit.). For a comprehensive discussion of this and other issues see Kenen 1995. This report set three stages for the implementation of EMU. The first stage would involve a number of preparatory steps towards monetary union. The main steps would include the completion of the internal market and the reform of the Community's Structural Funds with the aim of reducing regional disparities. On the monetary side, the main provisions required the removal of all obstacles to financial integration, the entry of all the EC currencies in the Exchange Rate Mechanism of the European Monetary System (EMS) and the removal of impediments to the use of the private ECU. The first stage started in July 1990. By the same date, capital controls had to be removed in all countries and an intergovernmental conference was called to design subsequent stages to take place in Maastricht in December 1991. The Maastricht conference focused largely on implementation and again on the different priorities between France and Germany. France insisted in obtaining a binding commitment to a precise timetable. Germany emphasised the need for increased convergence and strict rules for admission. The peripheral countries – Italy in particular – struggled to introduce some flexibility in the otherwise prohibitive criteria. The result was a compromise, with a clear and binding timetable, but also the well known five Maastricht criteria (see Box 2.1). The second stage started in 1994 and instituted the EMI (European Monetary Institute), which will turn into the ECB (the European Central Bank) with the third stage (monetary union proper due to begin in 1999). The second stage also forced countries to respect limits on national budget deficits, excessive deficits did not imply sanctions, but were simply to be reported to the Council by the Commission. Countries also had to comply with certain legal obligations (e.g. independence of central banks). 1995–6 saw substantial advances in working out the details of EMU, including the timetable for the transition phases, and the stages involved in the introduction of the euro. The Appendix to this chapter shows the outline of the EMI's paper setting out the details for the introduction of the single currency – the euro – and the phasing out of domestic currencies.

Box 2.1 The Maastricht criteria as stated in the Treaty

'The criterion on price stability . . . shall mean that a Member State has a price performance that is sustainable and an average rate of inflation, observed over a period of one year before the examination, that does not exceed by more than 1.5 per cent that of, at most, the three best performing Member States in terms of price stability.'

'The criterion on the government budgetary position . . . shall mean that at the time of the examination the Member States in not the subject of a

Council decision . . . that an excessive deficit exists.' This decision is conducted by examining '. . . compliance with budgetary discipline on the basis of the following 2 criteria:

a whether the ratio of the planned or actual government deficit to GDP exceeds a reference value [3 per cent in the attached Protocol], unless either the ratio has declined substantially and continuously and reached a level that comes close to the reference value; or, . . . unless the ratio is sufficiently diminishing and approaching the reference value at a satisfactory pace.

b whether the ratio of government debt to GDP exceeds a reference value [60 per cent in the attached Protocol], unless the ratio is sufficiently diminishing and approaching the reference value at a satisfactory pace.'

'If a Member State does not fulfil the requirements under one or both of these criteria, the Commission shall prepare a report. The report . . . shall also take into account whether the government deficit exceeds government investment expenditure and . . . all other relevant factors, including the medium term economic and budgetary position of the Member State.'

'The criterion on participation in the ERM . . . shall mean that a Member State has respected the normal fluctuation margins provided for by the ERM . . . without severe tensions for at least the last 2 years before examination. In particular, the Member State shall not have devalued its currency's bilateral central rate against any other Member State's currency on its own initiative for the same period.'

'The criterion on the convergence of interest rates . . . shall mean that, observed over a period of one year before examination, a Member State has had an average nominal long-term interest rate that does not exceed by more than 2 per cent that of, at most, the 3 best performing Member States in terms of price stability. Interest rates shall be measured on the basis of long-term government bonds or comparable securities . . .'

(European Commission 1992)

Will EMU fly?

Amidst all the political talk about EMU it is important to understand the underlying motivations for countries to become a part of EMU. For non-core countries the adoption of a core inflation credibility and shelter from the full consequences of currency fluctuations are obvious advantages, but for the core countries such as France and Germany, the motivations are less clear.

Reasons for monetary union

The likelihood of monetary union in 1999 will depend largely on the consensus and on the reciprocal trust between France and Germany, especially as politicians seem considerably more enthusiastic than their electorates on going ahead with EMU. Nevertheless, there are a number of compelling reasons why Germany, France and other core countries might decide to go ahead. Some of these reasons were mentioned above when briefly discussing the origin of EMU. They can be broadly divided into political and economic reasons:

Political arguments for EMU

The political arguments are that a single currency would deepen the European alliance with a step which is almost entirely irreversible. The underlying idea is that closer European ties would increase the relative weight of Europe in many issues at the international level – not only as far as economic decisions are concerned – as Europe would be acting as a whole rather than as single states. Defence and international policy could be two important areas. In this sense monetary union would be seen as the ancestor of a deeper political union. Note, though hardly mentioned, this was a reason often present in politicians' minds and one that the French in particular have promoted for many years.

To assess the political justifications for EMU it is also important to remember that the Maastricht Treaty matured soon after German unification. At this time, there was concern in Europe over the imbalance caused by the size of a unified Germany and fears that widening the union eastward could slow the drive towards its deepening. A desire to appease these concerns is one reason why Germany signed a binding agreement setting a precise date, a move they had consistently refused before. This point can be illustrated by a quotation from Balladur in November 1989.

> The two Germanies will be united economically even more than today and union will be a powerful force of disequilibrium in their favour. That will raise the problem of the place and role of Germany in Western Europe ... Let us stop cultivating the illusion that we can bind the Federal Republic of Germany irreversibly into Western Europe.
>
> (Marsh 1994)

11

This highlights the mood preceding the Maastricht debate. Binding Germany irreversibly to Europe is what Mitterrand set out to do. Kohl himself defended the 'political interpretation' of EMU saying 'we are giving up sovereignty in favour of the political unification of Europe' (*Suddeutsche Zeitung* 1990). If the political motivation was dominant at the time of the treaty, it is key to assess its current validity.

Obviously, the justifications for EMU which are linked to German unification are much less compelling now than they were when the Maastricht Treaty was written. But the issue of whether Germany prefers to deepen the existing community or widen it with looser links remains open. Recent indications suggest that the 'deepening' strategy is still dominant among the current political leadership. In summary, the more general ambition of Germany and France to create political economies of scale by achieving closer European ties is still present and should be the driving force behind the progress to a single currency. A core union would include a population of over 150 million with a GDP of over two-thirds the size of the US. This would increase the relative political weight of the countries involved in EMU in the international arena. Though this is the main priority, the question of widening a successful union out towards eastern Europe remains a background ideal. This is illustrated in the Intergovernmental Conference, the deliberations over the Maastricht II Treaty, which planned for a wider union extending eastward.

Economic reasons

According to supporters of EMU – in terms of economic consequences – the single currency is a positive-sum game. The economic reasons behind EMU (following the line of the European Commission's study in 1990 which presents a survey of the literature on the issue) are mainly:

1   The efficiency gains stemming from the elimination of exchange rate uncertainty and transaction costs. Monetary union is a natural complement of the single market, reducing the uncertainty associated with fluctuating exchange rates, and making prices fully transparent. The removal of exchange rate risk could also improve the return on capital and have a positive impact on investment and growth. The effects of these microeconomic gains are hard to quantify, but they provide the most significant economic reason in the long term

2   Increased anti-inflation credibility, as member states with higher historical inflation should be able to borrow the inflation credibility of the countries which have achieved higher price stability. In this sense, the emphasis in the Maastricht Treaty on the independence of the central banks is of key importance. High credibility should reduce the output costs of maintaining inflation at a frictional level

3   The system of incentives and controls within the union – with the so-called Stability Pact system of monitoring and punishments – should increase the effort to limit budget deficits, still leaving countries with their fiscal independence. The lower interest rates and risk premia for countries with higher inflation histories should more than compensate for their loss in seigniorage. Seigniorage is the difference between the value of the resources which can be obtained in exchange for notes/coins and the cost of their production. Seigniorage can be an important way of financing large public debts in some countries, and according to the European Commission the revenue effects in 1988 were over 2 per cent of GDP in Greece and Portugal and 1 per cent in Italy and Spain

4   The increased role of the new currency as an international means of payment would also offer gains to the member countries. Its likely role as an international reserve currency would also imply a seigniorage gain at the union level. The reasons highlighted have to be weighed against the loss of monetary and exchange rate policy as an instrument to adjust to shocks at the national level. Transitional costs – though by their nature temporary – should also be considered. Initial estimates by the European Banking Federation in 1994 showed that conversion to the euro by the banking sector would cost a total of ECU 8–10 billion (about £6–7.5 billion), about 2 per cent of annual operating costs over a 3–4 year period. This however assumes a 'big bang' introduction rather than a gradual introduction of the euro. This could easily mean a doubling of that initial estimate. The retail sector faces costs also, with double pricing systems needed, but all these would be one-off costs in 1999, or before

EMU: two scenarios and policy proposals

A core-only or wider union?

With EMU expected to go ahead, there seem to be two possible scenarios concerning its implementation, i.e. a core-only or a wider EMU including perhaps Spain and Italy. Our scenarios are based on the recent European Commission forecasts as far as assessing countries' compliance with the Maastricht criteria is concerned, although we put relatively little emphasis on whether countries strictly respect them. Eventually, criteria could be interpreted in a flexible way and the final decision could be largely political.

A core union would involve only the countries which already belong to the DM area (Netherlands, Austria and Luxembourg) and France. Belgium and Denmark could also be possible candidates, though they both present serious difficulties. Belgium has a very large debt and there are doubts on whether it will respect the key deficit criteria. Denmark, is a special case due to its opt-out clause which prevents it from joining without a public referendum which

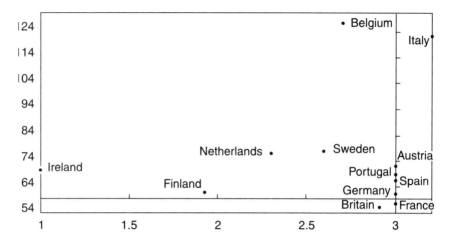

Figure 2.1 Public debt (y-axis) and public deficit (x-axis) forecasts for 1997
Source: European Commission forecasts for EU 15, April 1997, Brussels
Note: Here we exclude Denmark, Luxembourg and Greece. Their debt forecasts were: 67.2%, 6.5% and 108.3% respectively. For the deficit, their forecasts were: −0.3%, −1.1% and 4.9% respectively

would have a very uncertain result. The participation of France to this union is crucial to make it politically relevant. Chancellor Kohl (reported by Reuters, 8 November 1995) himself and, later Hans Tietmeyer, were quoted saying that an EMU without France would be 'unthinkable'.

A wider union seems to be becoming less unlikely given the substantial 1997 budgets in both Spain and Italy. Though in some areas Italy is lagging very far behind core countries e.g. with an over 120 per cent of GDP debt ratio, there is a chance that if the 3 per cent deficit criterion is met, as with Belgium, the debt criterion may be overlooked. The determination of countries such as Italy and Spain to be part of EMU from the start should not be underestimated. There will likely be pressure from core countries, in an attempt to enhance EMU stability, for Italy and Spain to join later on after some time spent within the ERM II mechanism.

Optimum currency areas

Very few would also argue that the EC is already an optimum currency area . . . That means that economic integration inside the EC has not yet reached the level where capital and especially labour mobility could act as near substitutes for changes in the exchange rate; or that wage and price movements in different countries correspond to changes in productivity rates so as to make exchange rate

14

realignments redundant; or even that the EC economy is sufficiently homogenous so that different countries and regions are not frequently subject to asymmetric external shocks.

(Tsoukalis 1993: 212)

Theory on optimal currency areas suggests that only countries with similar economic structures should share a currency, so as to avoid a shock to a particular sector hitting the countries unevenly, creating an imbalance which cannot be corrected by currency depreciation. Labour mobility and fiscal transfers are substitutes for economic homogeneity and justify why, for example, the US exists as a stable currency area despite having areas with very different economic characteristics. Europe shows a reasonable economic homogeneity, but – critics say – it shows a concerning low degree of fiscal solidarity and of labour mobility. The cultural and linguistic diversity of the region means that migration is low from one area to another. To balance this problem funds should be made available to support and encourage development in the less wealthy areas. Currently however, the EU has a total budget which is very small relative to the Union's GNP (1.15 per cent in 1992) and largely dedicated to the Common Agricultural Policy (the European Agricultural Guidance and Guarantee Fund (EAGGF), agricultural policy funds, took 56 per cent of the EC Budget in 1992). Moreover, development funds are only considered for structural imbalances and not for cyclical crisis. Our chapter on German unification deals with the problems of trying to impose a smaller currency union joining two very different areas. There are lessons to be learnt from that experience for EMU (see Chapter 4) for which much of its success was based on the availability of funds from the German government.

The disadvantages of being left out, in terms of possible reduced exports, foregone benefits of higher inflation credibility and lower interest rates means that non-core countries are making great strides to meet the EMU criteria and to be included in the 'first wave' of entrants. These countries, however, are also the most likely to suffer from the results of the lack of optimality of EMU, they are likely to experience more pockets of regional unemployment and their 'peripheral' position (see below) may mean that they lose out from investment opportunities. Though there has been some evidence of real convergence – OECD (1996) projections for 1996 show that all but three (Italy, Greece and Portugal) of the EU 15 show GDP deflators below 3 per cent – and attempts to reform institutional and structural inflexibilities, it is likely that a wider union could be more problematic. Therefore, though Europe cannot be regarded as an 'optimal currency area' in the sense described above, it does have more chance of working smoothly if there is a core-only union.

It is difficult to foresee the reaction of financial markets to a core-only monetary union, particularly its effects on those countries which are left out.

One possibility is that the impact will be moderated by expectations that those countries will be allowed in the union at a later stage. However, undeniably, there is a risk that:

1 Investors will be attracted to the newly created, stronger currency
2 The perception that failure to join in the first wave will lower non-core countries' incentives to pursue adjustment policies, implying increased fiscal laxity. In this sense, the events following the 1992 Danish referendum – which suddenly forced a reconsideration of the prospects for European integration – represent a worrying precedent
3 Higher interest rates in non-core countries will weaken their economic growth and pose questions of debt sustainability which could reinforce market pessimism in a self-fulfilling process

From the point of view of the countries included in EMU, the appreciation scenario could exacerbate the competitiveness problems already experienced to a certain degree in the last few years following weakness in the peripheral currencies. Concern has been voiced both in France and in Germany, and the German economy in particular has suffered from a strong DM (see Chapter 9). Interestingly, the European Commission has ruled out that any compensation or exception to the common market rules could be considered in case of large terms of trade imbalances, including those from a restricted EMU. 'Monetary fluctuations cannot be used to justify any violations of Community mechanisms or rules' (European Commission 1995a).

The question of how to react to this negative scenario is controversial. Policy options appear very limited (a discussion on possible options is in Chapter 10). A form of 'associate participation' to EMU for the non-participating currencies which took the form of a new ERM style peg would suffer from the same flaws. Ways to increase its credibility will not be agreed easily, even though, for countries such as Italy, they could be desirable. For example, a form of stronger Basle-Nyborg agreement (1987) – which established new procedures to improve access to European funds for countries willing to implement intra-marginal intervention in defence of their currencies – would clash against the opposition of the Bundesbank. In a speech in 1995, the President of the Bundesbank, Hans Tietmeyer, while saying that non-participating countries should continue convergence and avoid competitive devaluations, also argued that 'currency intervention should not impede or restrict the ECB in carrying out its monetary policy or in its ability to fight inflation. I do not put much weight on a currency system dependent on intervention' (Luxembourg, 25 October 1995). Yet, there is a recognition of the need to formalise arrangements between EMU and non-EMU members. For example, the Danish central banker Anderson has stated that 'Our preference is for some kind of ERM arrangement. It must involve mutual obligations . . .' (*Financial Times*, 27 November 1995).

ERM II

The ERM II system, proposed by the European Commission and ratified at the Dublin summit in 1996, is a system of arrangement for the 'outs' or 'pre-ins' of EMU designed to protect against 'competitive devaluation' and to prevent the single currency losing too much in terms of trade, in comparison to the non-core of countries left out at the first stage. At present the agreement is that the fluctuations between the euro and the currencies left out of EMU in the first wave will be limited to 15 per cent on each side of their central rate in the ERM II system. When the currency of a country that is left out of EMU knocks against the 15 per cent band, the ECB will be required to intervene in the forex market to push it back into the band. This support would not be unlimited however. It would be achieved without threatening the credibility of the ECB, i.e. without imposing on the ECB actions incompatible with its stated primary objective of price stability within the boundaries of the participating countries (as stated in article 105.1 of the Maastricht Treaty).

EU ministers have said that intervention would be dependent on attempts by the country in question to retain its macroeconomic stability. The Commission, in its proposal on ERM II, emphasises the connection between exchange rate stability and macroeconomic convergence. It states that a good performance as far as convergence was concerned would strengthen the case for support of an ERM II currency, if it came under attack. The ECB is likely to have the right to initiate realignment discussions, if it appeared that the central rate of a currency was out of line with fundamentals. ERM II could also allow a narrowing of fluctuation bands which could remain secret or be announced publicly. Known narrow bands would require 'automatic intervention' whereas secret bands would only be supported by 'co-ordinated' intervention, which is likely to be fairly limited.

The ERM crisis of 1992 occurred for two reasons. Firstly, a lack of sufficient credibility in the consistency and co-ordination of economic policies, and specifically low credibility in the ability of certain countries to control their fiscal policies. Secondly, a belief that central bank firing power of the countries with strong currencies would, rightly, be used only with discretion and, it is likely, in very limited amount. We think that a commitment to defend the currencies of the countries which do not participate in EMU is desirable and would create a system less burdened by lack of credibility than the ERM. The system would apply for those countries which are committed to continue pursuing economic convergence with the objective of joining EMU at a later stage. The ECB could be responsible for monitoring progress towards convergence. A strict adherence to a plan of fiscal adjustment could make the system credible to the markets, and this is what the European Commission's plan tries to emphasise, but the system is by no means immune to crisis.

Fiscal policy during EMU: the Stability Pact

1995–6 saw a shift in emphasis towards a stability system for EMU member countries, to monitor and punish excessive debt/deficits. This idea was already in the Maastricht Treaty, but in a more vague form than core countries thought suitable. Given the increasing possibility of a wide EMU, there was a great deal of concern about 'free-riding risk', i.e. the possible temptation for some countries to run large deficits in EMU, consequently having a detrimental effect on long term rates throughout the union. This explains German preoccupation about the selection of EMU participants being restricted to those who meet the criteria in full, and with progress on political integration and, particularly, with forms of fiscal control.

This German concern was expressed by the German Finance Minister Waigel's proposals for the procedures and punishments for excessive deficits and debts, as written in the Treaty. His version, the so-called Stability Pact, had its roots in the Maastricht Treaty article 104c(11), but was revamped in 1995. It retained the 3 per cent and 60 per cent deficit and debt levels as reference points, but made the sanctioning system *automatic* rather than relying on the discretion of the Council of Ministers (which would decide by qualified majority of two-thirds of the participating countries). The Waigel proposal suggested that a country should be fined 0.25 per cent of GDP for every percentage point of deficit in excess of the 3 per cent limit, with no upper limit on the amount that could be fined. The fine would be returned if the fiscal imbalance was to be corrected within two years. Punishments allowed for in the Maastricht Treaty included the restriction of European Investment Bank lending conditions and non interest bearing deposits and fines for countries which run excessive deficits. The Stability Pact rightly emphasises the need for greater attention to fiscal policy issues after EMU implementation, though convergence is needed for EMU to begin, it is even more important once the union is running. This pact addressed the fact that some countries may be allowed to participate in Europe without meeting the criteria in full, and calmed fears that those countries might continue to act without sufficient fiscal restraint.

The European Commission proposals on the Stability Pact (released in October 1996 and soon renamed the Stability and Growth Pact) trod a middle way between the more ambiguous Maastricht framework, and the automatic Waigel proposals. The Commission proposed a fixed and a sliding component to the sanction system. The size of punishment deposits was intended to be sufficiently high to act as a deterrent without being counterproductive. The fixed component would be 0.2 per cent of GDP, and the variable component would be 0.1 per cent of GDP for every 1 per cent of GDP the deficit overshoots the 3 per cent value. The ceiling for the whole deposit would be 0.5 per cent of GDP (i.e. a deficit of over 6 per cent of GDP would not imply a proportionally higher deposit). There would also be a fining system for debt to GDP ratios of over 60 per cent, with a flat fine of 0.2 per cent of GDP (though this was later scrapped). The upper limit of 0.5 per cent of GDP applied for the total annual amount of deposits regardless of what combination of excessive deficit/debts a country has. The deposit would be transformed into a fine if after two years sufficient action to correct the excessive deficit had not been taken. Deposits would be lodged with the Community and the interest on deposits and fines would be resources of the general budget of the European Communities.

This Stability Pact system however is subject to three weaknesses:

1   It imposes fines on countries already suffering from financial hardship – regardless of the reasons – potentially increasing their difficulties
2   It greatly reduces a country's independence in setting fiscal policy. All EU countries except Luxembourg have experienced budget deficits over 3 per cent at least once since 1990
3   It imposes a greater burden on countries with higher elasticity of deficit to GDP by allowing less room for cyclical stimuli

The main conclusion is that the recognised need for some form of fiscal co-ordination means that participants will require a long history of fiscal restraint and a high degree of political stability.

The European Commission Stability Pact proposals tried to address at least the first criticism, by making the 'exceptional circumstances' clause (by which a country could be exempt from a fine due to low growth) more amenable. In the Waigel Pact only a −2 per cent annual growth would justify exemption. This became a crucial sticking point in the negotiations between the EU Finance Ministers, in the run-up to the Dublin summit in December 1996, as many countries wanted some discretionary element in the decision on whether a particular country could be exempt from sanctions. The German contingent refused to shift ground, however, and in the end a last minute compromise was reached. It was finally decided that there would be automatic sanctions for countries which had an annual GDP growth of less than −2 per cent. For countries with GDP growth of between −0.75 and −2 per cent it would be possible to appeal for an exemption, for which supporting evidence would have to be shown, and a vote would be taken. (See the Appendix to Chapter 4 which contains full details on the Stability Pact procedures.) The agreement on the Pact was another affirmation that EMU would go ahead on time. It also affirmed that even if there was a wider EMU, including some countries without a historical culture of fiscal stability, then EMU would still have a sufficiently strong system to ensure the maintenance of fiscal austerity, and to guarantee the 'stability' of the union.

The election of the French Socialist government in spring 1997 increased the focus on the Stability Pact's weaknesses. The Socialist government complained that the Pact focused too much on monetary policy to the future detriment of EMU employment. It was agreed (after much last minute bargaining) that a two-point Protocol be added to the final version of the Pact. The first point would emphasise the co-ordination of economic policy between EMU partners and the second would address co-ordination of employment policy. French concern also led to an Employment Chapter. This would be based on articles 102a and 103 of the Maastricht Treaty, which recognise the need for co-ordination of economic policies. The main proposals were that guidelines for the employment policy of member states would be compiled, with each member required to provide an annual report on its employment measures. The implementation of these measures would be evaluated by the Council of Ministers. A joint report would then be made by the Council and the European Commission on employment in the EU. Employment policy will however remain the final responsibility of individual EU members. The German government prefer to emphasise this aspect, agreeing to back the Employment Chapter in the revised Maastricht Treaty, but saying they would not support expensive job creation programmes operated by the EU. They stress that the Chapter represents European co-ordination of *national* measures. Though the Employment Chapter seemed harmless enough, there were vast theoretical disagreements on how unemployment should be reduced. Harmonisation of these different methods will be almost impossible. Some countries think that more expansionary macroeconomic policies may be sufficient, others find this idea abhorrent. The French think additional/stricter regulation could help to cure unemployment, while other countries prefer to encourage labour market flexibility by keeping regulations to a minimum. The French have also suggested a shorter working week, though keeping wages constant, as a feasible way of tackling unemployment.

Regional adjustment and regional policies

Regional disparities: causes

We have emphasised already the importance of labour mobility and the necessity to have social support for EMU to be able to cope with the possibility of long-term and large transfers of wealth to disadvantaged regions (see Chapter 4). Increasing regional disparities are accepted as being one of the outcomes of EMU, but which areas will suffer most and why is important in determining how wide these disparities will be, and what outcome will result.

Regional differences within European nations are common, the north–south divide in the UK and the Italian Mezzogiorno are well-known cases. The causes of regional differences are easily understood: if a positive external shock occurs, this causes a rise in a particular region's exports. The result is a rise in wages and wealth in that region. Some of that new 'wealth' will end up outside the region, via an increase in imports, but the rest of that wealth goes to regional goods and services, causing an increase in employment or immigration. With wealth increasing in that region, but the positive benefits on surrounding regions small, regional disparity ensues.

Wage flexibility (emphasised in our German unemployment discussion in Chapter 8) can help to maintain employment in depressed regions, as with relatively lower wages, there may be some substitution of capital for labour, or an increase in investment due to the attraction of lower labour costs. This could increase the return to investment in the poorer region, but often this is not large enough to counteract regional differences. Wage inflexibilities prevent this equilibrating process. Wage inflexibility is a common and understandable issue; it is difficult to justify that workers in different areas doing the same/similar work should receive different wages. The reduction in real wages occurs therefore through the changes in relative prices in that region compared to other regions. The beneficial effect to the poorer region depends on price flexibility and the sensitivity of demand to changes in prices.

Theory of economic integration and evidence

The traditional view of economic integration is that the free movement of goods and services will, under strong assumptions, equalise living standards, productivity and returns to capital. The counter arguments suggest that in a customs union, with free movement of trade, capital and labour, certain areas will be more attractive than others and therefore business and industry will tend to accumulate in those areas. Thus in EMU regional disparities may increase rather than decrease. This may occur with highly industrialised areas, or areas with good communications, infrastructure and skilled labour forces (Myrdal 1957).

Unfortunately in this respect sheer geographical location is an important disadvantage for many of the less wealthy regions of the EU. These mainly lie in the geographical 'periphery' of the union and therefore they face extra costs in terms of transport and communication, and could also find it difficult to attract investment. There are also problems within countries whereby the more remote regions have to deal with worse infrastructure. Infrastructure is one direct way in which the disadvantageous positions of the periphery are to a great extent reduced, and counter-balanced. Factors such as the increasing of education standards and the expansion of the skills base could help to alleviate some of the more immediate disadvantages; in these areas there is substantial room for improvement e.g. latest data on adult literacy shows that Germany has a 1 per cent illiteracy rate, with Greece at over 6 per cent.

There are however benefits to different types of industry which rely on the lower wages and costs which may be prevalent in the less developed/poorer regions of a union (Balassa 1961). The growth of technology, and communications, and the reduction in importance of proximity to natural resources means that industries will become less bound to be in the 'right' location.

Krugman uses a model of specialisation between regions. Imperfect competition with economies of scale are assumed, and transport costs for the manufacturing sector, with an immobile agriculture sector. This study (Krugman 1989) shows that there are two key determinants as to how manufacturing becomes distributed between the two sectors:

1   The greater the economies of scale the more likely it is that the manufacturing sector concentrates itself in one region
2   The lower transportation costs become the more likely concentration becomes, due to companies taking advantage of economies of scale and easy access to markets

Factors which could reduce this concentration are:

1   Cheaper 'variable' costs (such as wages) on the periphery
2   A larger manufacturing sector, which tends to mean more divergence, as firms relocate out of central areas in order to serve peripheral markets better
3   Small centres or smaller countries could benefit from a reduction in trade barriers and transportation costs as they may be gaining more market by integration, and because they may be able to benefit from greater economies of scale

The sensitivity of weaker regions of an area is two-fold: they tend to consist of a higher proportion of diminishing, sensitive sectors and smaller marginally efficient firms. They are therefore much more susceptible to recessions and experience wider ranging and deeper problems arising from them. They are also more vulnerable on another front, in that they depend on a higher proportion of outside investment, either public or private, which tends to dry up quickly when growth turns down.

Regional policies

In the US, the reduction of regional disparities has been ascribed to a high degree of labour mobility and financial transfers through the central government budget. EMU however will not be able to rely on these factors (see above), and regional disparity remains a current issue. The regional disparity problem of European integration and of increased competition has been debated widely since the 1950s, but policy took a while to address these concerns. There were some specific regional policies in the EEC Treaty covering agriculture, transport and competition policies, but convergence was considered to be the main outcome of the growing links within the Community. There was generally a 'hands off' approach to regional problems leaving such matters to national governments. It was only the European Investment

Bank and some special policy protocols concerning southern Italy and East Germany, which were concerned with regional development. An enlarging Community and the first oil shock in 1973 brought more regional problems as unemployment increased dramatically and regional disparities worsened. These circumstances meant that there was more pressure on the Community to do something about these problems. This was justified as being a necessity both for closer economic and political integration, to bring about a level playing field for incomes and to enhance social cohesion.

For the success of monetary union, it was envisaged that EMU's suppression of national government policy instruments would be substituted at the EU level by greater structural policies. In 1971 the Community adopted a policy of more co-ordination of regional aid. 1975 saw the creation of the European Regional Development Fund. Greater enlargement of the Community increased the drive to include regional concerns to the most important Community policies. The reforming of the European Social Fund in 1972 and 1977 and the European Agricultural Guidance and Guarantee Fund are evidence of this.

The EC budget: an increasing regional policy role

The EC budget: 1988–92

An agreement by the European Council in February 1988 governed the creation of new budgetary resources, much tougher measures reducing Common Agricultural Policy expenditure and an improvement in redistributive policies. This agreement was followed in the same year by an inter-institutional agreement on the EC budget. An agreement was reached on its total size and the main items of expenditure for the period up to 1992.

The EC budget had only a limited size, relative to national budgets, with the legal requirement for balance between revenue and expenditure. Its re-allocation role can only be small therefore, but it has been growing steadily. In 1992 EC expenditure was about 1.15 per cent of Community GNP, more than double that in 1973. Other important financial operations, i.e. those outside the budget, include the borrowing and lending activities of EC institutions such as the EIB, and aid to the developing world through the European Development Fund. There is also a separate budget for the operations of the ECSC (European Coal and Steel Community).

The bulk of EC revenues comes from VAT receipts, and customs duties with the rest from agricultural levies and other sources. The proportion of custom duties has fallen due to General Agreement on Tariffs and Trade (GATT) negotiations and the resultant lowering of common external tariffs. A sharp rise in EC agricultural self-sufficiency explains most of the relative fall in agricultural levies, as well as the drop in price differentials between the EU and the rest of the world. This reduction in agricultural contributions has meant an increasing reliance on Value Added Tax (VAT) revenues. The upper limit of VAT contributions was set in 1970 at 1 per cent of a theoretical harmonised base, this level was raised to 1.4 per cent from 1986. Prior to 1986, any redistribution effect from the EC budget system, was based on chance.

> Before the introduction of the fourth resource, any redistributive impact of the EC system of revenue had been totally haphazard: the distribution of tax revenue among countries depending on their propensity to import from third countries (customs duties and agricultural levies), their propensity to consume (there is no VAT on investment), and the efficiency of their tax collection systems (southern countries in particular suffer from widespread tax evasion).
>
> (Tsoukalis 1993: 266)

1988 saw the introduction of the so-called 'fourth resource', i.e. national financial contributions weighted by GNP, a more equitable system, with more flexibility. There was also a ruling by the European Council in conjunction with this introduction, attempting to reduce the penalisation of EU members with relatively high consumption by reducing the VAT base by which VAT contributions are calculated, to a maximum of 55 per cent of GNP. The redistributive impact of the EU budget remains limited however, as more than half of it goes to agriculture expenditure. Structural Fund expenditure accounts for most of the rest, and it is this part that has the most redistributive element. Structural policies were improved a great deal with the Single European Act and the 1992 single market programme. Structural Funds were reformed in 1988 and they doubled in real terms from 1987 to 1993. The regional component of the EC budget expenditure rose from 4.5 per cent to 11.1 per cent between 1980 and 1990 (i.e. a rise from ECU722.7 million to ECU5209.7 million). Thus, there has been some effort in this direction, though this may have to increase substantially under EMU. Such efforts will be made more difficult by the fact that most countries are already struggling to keep their domestic budget deficits under control (see Chapter 4 on fiscal policy).

The EC budget 1993–9

The Delors II package was agreed in Edinburgh in December 1992. As the European Commission suggested, the European Council here gave top priority to structural operations in the Community's most underprivileged regions. The Edinburgh conclusions called for an increase in the resources provided for internal policies even though this increase was not as high as the Commission had hoped when it set the objective of establishing an environment favourable to the competitiveness of European industry.

There was little change in the Common Agricultural Policy, which is still governed by the guidelines set in 1988. This put the ceiling for agricultural expenditure at 74 per cent of the real rate of growth of the Community. Once again, the Community continues its commitment to regional and social development. Even more budgetary resources will be concentrated on the poorer regions of the EU where per capita GNP is less than 75 per cent of the Community average, these include southern Italy, Spain, Portugal, Ireland, East Germany and parts of Scotland. The Cohesion Fund will benefit countries with a per capita GNP of less than 90 per cent of the Community average – including Greece, Spain, Ireland, Portugal – to finance environmental or transport infrastructure projects to help those countries comply with Community legislation or guidelines, subject to the establishment/maintenance of an economic convergence programme by these countries. Delors II makes more substantial attempts to redistribute funds within the union. The Structural and Cohesion Funds together mean that together the four Member States (Greece, Spain, Portugal and Ireland) should get in 1999 twice what they received in 1992. See European Commission (1996a) for more information.

Other policies from Delors II include extra expenditure on internal policies which are predicted to increase by around 30 per cent (European Commission 1996a). The decision taken at the Edinburgh European Council on VAT was implemented on 31 October 1994. This decision raises the own resources ceiling to 1.21 per cent of GNP in 1995, and in stages up to 1.27 per cent of GNP in 1999. The uniform VAT rate will be reduced from 1.4 per cent to 1 per cent in 1999 and the VAT base taken into account will be restricted, being cut in stages to 50 per cent of GNP instead of the current 55 per cent. The Member States eligible for assistance under the Cohesion Fund will have their VAT base restricted to 50 per cent of GNP in 1995.

Conclusions

After much discussion, dating back to the post-war period, and considerable preparation, monetary union should take place as scheduled in 1999. This union will be justified by a number of economic factors, although, we think, political motivations will be dominant in making the final step forward. There are two main scenarios: a core union, with a limited number of initial participants, or a wider union. In any case, we expect most peripheral countries to be part of EMU by 2002, when euro coins and notes will also be introduced. This expectation is enhanced by the vigorous efforts by Spanish and Italian governments to reach the deficit criterion 3 per cent level in 1997.

The possibility of a restricted monetary union poses the consequent problem of what happens to those countries left out from the first wave of entrants. We believe that there are serious risks of speculative attacks on non-participating countries, particularly on those who do not participate due to non-compliance with criteria rather than political choice. This is a result of fears that non-participation will result in divergence in economic indicators. The consequence of this possible crisis should be one of the issues at the top of the agenda for policy makers. A form of associate participation to EMU – with a commitment from the European Central Bank to actively support non-participating currencies – would be highly desirable. This, clearly, would have to be associated with a binding commitment from the countries involved to continue the convergence programme, with compliance monitored closely by European bodies. For further analysis on ERM II see Chapter 10.

A wide EMU, whether at the first wave or later on, could have problems in terms of wide regional disparities. These will have to be combated with proactive EMU budget policies to redistribute funds from more wealthy areas to those which are disadvantaged. Peripheral areas could also see some disadvantages from lack of private investment flows and these will have to be encouraged, if large unemployment disparities are to be avoided. Structural changes, such as increasing regional wage flexibility, could help to alleviate regional unemployment. Unemployment issues are discussed further in Chapters 7 and 8.

APPENDIX: BENCHMARK DATES FOR INTRODUCTION OF THE EURO

(EMI 1995) as adopted by the Madrid EU Summit December 1995.

Overview of changeover actions undertaken by the authorities

Action by the European System of Central Banks (ESCB)

Between the date of the decision on the move to Stage Three and its actual start:

- Prepare for the changeover to the European currency in the execution of monetary and exchange rate policy as from the start of Stage Three, at the level of both the ECB and national central banks
- Make the ECB operational and prepare it to employ all necessary instruments
- Decide on, and undertake final testing of, the framework for the ESCB to operate entirely in the European currency from day one of Stage Three
- Start production of the European banknotes and announce their date of introduction as well as the date at which national banknotes will cease to be legal tender
- Assist in the preparation of the necessary legislation to be adopted with respect to the introduction of the European Currency

From the start of the European currency area onwards

- Conduct the single monetary and foreign exchange rate policy in the European currency
- Start the operation of the TARGET payment system in the European currency
- Provide conversion facilities to counterparties who are unable to translate between the national and the European monetary units
- Support the co-ordination of market participants' actions so as to ensure the smooth functioning of an EMU-wide money market in the European currency
- Encourage and support efforts to bring about the rapid development of a foreign (continued) exchange market in the European currency and, where appropriate, quote third countries' currencies against the European currency only
- Exchange national banknotes at par value
- Monitor changeover developments in the banking and finance industry
- Co-operate with the public authorities as well as with the financial institutions in order to assist in an orderly changeover of both the public and the private sector

The six-month period for changing over all cash and non-cash

- Put into circulation the European banknotes (and coins) transactions
- Withdraw from circulation the national banknotes (and coins)
- Monitor changeover developments in the public and private sector insofar as they have a bearing on the financial system

The completion date of the changeover

- Continue, as a service to the public, to exchange the old national banknotes and coins for European ones

Suggested action by the public authorities

Between the date of the decision on the move to Stage Three and its actual start

- Appoint the ECB's Executive Board
- Adopt various acts of complementary Community legislation for the establishment of the ESCB and the application of all instruments of monetary policy
- Adopt European and national legislation to provide for the introduction of the European currency

- Start the production of European coins and announce their date of introduction as well as the date at which national coins will cease to be legal tender
- Launch a wide-ranging public information campaign on the introduction of the European currency

From the start of the European currency area onwards:

- New public debt expected to be issued in the European currency
- Announce the specific organisation of the changeover of public administrations
- Install oversight mechanisms at the European and national levels to monitor the progress in the private sector's changeover and give guidance where appropriate

The six-month period for changing over all cash and non-cash

- Implement the complete changeover of the entire public administration, while continuing transactions to accept payments expressed in national monetary units as long as national banknotes and coins remain legal tender
- Put into circulation European coins
- Monitor the changeover in the private sector

The completion date of the changeover

- Establish the European banknotes and coins as the only legal tender by cancelling the legal tender status of national banknotes and coins
- Continue for some time to assist the public in the new single currency environment

3

GERMAN UNIFICATION AND EMU

A lesson for the future?

Introduction

The German unification experience is useful to study in regard to EMU for many reasons. Firstly, it is an example of a currency union which was able to take place in almost ideal circumstances. Though there was little in the way of economic convergence, the process had wide popular support, and labour mobility was expected to be high. Large amounts of government investment and flows of funds were also made available for East Germany, with little opposition from the West German population. Even given this beneficial environment, large regional disparities still exist between East and West, in some cases exacerbated by inappropriate policies.

Secondly, with the German government and central bank clearly central to the EMU process, their experience with unification will be a large determinant of their attitude towards the make-up of EMU, the transitional process between 1999–2002, and the strictness with which they wish to see the Stability and Growth Pact (the system for monitoring and punishing governments for fiscal laxity after the start of EMU) implemented. The Bundesbank does not want to see a repeat of the negative consequences of the German Monetary Union (GEMU). The Bundesbank is therefore primarily concerned with the maintenance of stability after the birth of EMU in 1999 and in the transition period. The Bundesbank's worries about EMU prospects, and strictness in terms of convergence before EMU and continuing within it can be understood more clearly in light of the German experience.

The optimum currency area approach

Economic theory on what denotes an 'optimal currency area' emphasises the size of a currency area as well as social cohesion and labour mobility within the union (see Chapter 2).

Size of currency area matters due to the extent of diversification of a region's resources. The less diversified a region's products are, the more difficult it is for it to adjust to external shocks, especially without means of its own exchange rate; and therefore, the more difficult it is for a poorly diversified region to prosper in a monetary union. In a large currency area a region which is reliant on a few industry sectors or products tends to find it difficult to average out external shocks. Given this line of argument some less diversified regions may suffer from EMU and these are likely to be concentrated in non-core countries.

Social cohesion within the currency union is also very important. If, as in Germany, there have to be quite large transfers between regions there has to be the democratic will to accept this. Even given German preoccupation with solidarity, unification has caused a certain amount of social disunity and resentment between Easterners and Westerners. In EMU, the members of the more wealthy regions may have to accept a large flow of funds to those which are poorer, perhaps for the entire life of the union.

Labour mobility is often regarded as an essential tool for regional adjustment but has been hindered in Germany by fairly high wages in the East. In the EC as a whole, mobility seems to be low, the number of foreign residents from other EC countries was only 4.5 million out of the 342 million total EC population (just over 1 per cent). Labour mobility is lacking even *within* countries, e.g. between northern and southern Italy and northern and southern England. It may be dangerous therefore to rely on the presence of a large degree of mobility in EMU.

Given that labour mobility is lacking, an effective means of transferring EC funds will be required, but this is also not evident. The Community budget is small and national budgets would be autonomous, therefore the fiscal policy of the EMU as a whole could be somewhat ineffective at distributing funds to the areas in most need (see Chapter 2).

With little fiscal co-ordination there needs to be a strict punishment system to keep countries on the fiscal 'straight and narrow'. The 3 per cent ceiling for public deficits and the 60 per cent of GDP for public debt will be used as reference values after the birth of EMU, but the system of fines and reprimands designed to keep union countries in line depends on a strict degree of implementation. The Stability Pact is designed to do this but there is a risk that if the implementation of the Pact is not strict, destabilizing forces may quickly gain hold (see the Appendix to Chapter 4).

With no reliable, large EC transfer system, and insufficient labour mobility, EMU may result in large regional disparities of wealth. This will have serious consequences both on the political stability of the union and on the economy. The inflation risk of EMU to Germany will be large – as with German unification the inflationary pressures and resulting high interest rates instigated much economic hardship – but these will be minimised if the convergence criteria are respected and continue to be observed after EMU's hatching.

German unification: shocks and ripples

The unification of Germany has resulted in large fluctuations of activity in West Germany as well as East. Transfers to East Germany, financed by borrowing, gave big fiscal boosts to demand at a time when the West German economy was already close to overheating. Consequently pan-German economic growth accelerated from an average of 3.5 per cent in 1988–9 to nearly 6 per cent in 1990. This resulted in increasing inflation. Excessive pressure on domestic resources led to a public finance deterioration accompanied by a balance of payments deficit. The latter began due to an increase in imports (as demand for resources outgrew domestic capacity) and a switching of 'exports' from West Germany to Eastern Germany instead of to other countries. The deficit was sustained by an appreciating DM and high prices. This loss of competitiveness resulted in inflation for the rest of Europe (European Commission 1990, 1994, Corker *et al.* 1995).

German adjustment thus had widespread ripple effects in its European neighbours. The response to this huge fiscal stimulus to Eastern Germany, and to German inflation was tight monetary policy. The German discount rate rose from 6 per cent in November 1991, to a peak of 8.75 per cent in July 1992. Higher interest rates followed in the rest of Europe – to counter currency depreciation against the DM – with the resulting economic consequences on demand.

The combined effects of a stronger DM, tighter monetary policy and budget deficit reduction led to a weakening of foreign and domestic demand, and recession. The German recession reached a bottom in the first quarter of 1993, and was also accompanied by a large fall in employment due to extensive restructuring. The recession hit East Germany more severely than the West, real GDP fell by at least one-quarter in the eighteen months to the end of 1991. The collapse of traditional export markets in the former socialist bloc and a shift in consumer preferences towards higher quality goods imported from the West worsened the fall in manufacturing output in East Germany. Enterprises and co-operatives saw all their markets fade away. Markets in the CMEA (Council for Mutual Economic Assistance) collapsed and even within East Germany, producers left their previous suppliers, switching to West German equivalents. The contraction in the production base of Eastern Germany led to a rise in unemployment, reaching 15 per cent of the dependent work force. This was despite substantial emigration from East to West, large scale retraining and early retirement schemes.

Expansion followed in 1993, with manufacturing output growing by 6 per cent and then by 9 per cent in 1994. In 1993–4 Germany also experienced an important recovery in its competitive position, with domestic unit labour costs falling due to both large productivity gains and small real wage increases (unit wage growth fell from a peak of 6.7 per cent over the previous year in March 1993 to −1.6 per cent in June 1994). Competitiveness

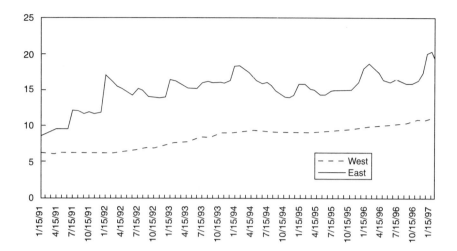

Figure 3.1 West and East German unemployment rates 1991–7
Source: German Labour Office

increased due to some DM weakening (from mid 1993), and a rebound in foreign demand, resulting in an improved trade balance. Despite this, East German unemployment remains relatively high at about a 15.6 per cent average for 1996 against about 9 per cent in West Germany for 1996. Prices in East Germany however, have come down more or less to West German levels from 1995, the latest 1996 inflation figures show an average for East Germany of 2.3 per cent over the previous year, with West German inflation at a 1.5 per cent average.

The prospects for East Germany look somewhat shaky however in the run-up to 1999, with construction in the East (the main engine of growth for most of Germany) taking a strong plunge due to a combination of an ending of unification construction projects and a reduction in public works funding, due to expenditure cuts to reach the 3 per cent deficit EMU target. Most notably unemployment rates in the East and West are still very different. East German unemployment is now at 18.1 per cent (March 1997), compared to a 10.2 per cent figure for the West. East German unemployment has risen substantially since unification. There are also many fears that this differential could widen further in the next few years, now that the main construction efforts have finished, and that public investment has dried up given the German government's attempts to meet the 3 per cent target.

Fiscal transfers – the solidarity pact

The accelerating government deficit ensuing from unification forced some fiscal tightening in the form of measures agreed in early 1993, the so-called

'Solidarity Pact' that included a package to be implemented over the medium term with the intention of restoring a better fiscal position. These included: the re-imposition of a 7.5 per cent solidarity surcharge on income tax obligations effective in 1995, a reduction in unemployment benefits as of 1994, and an increase in the fuel tax in 1994, with the proceeds to be used to finance a reform of the railways. In addition, several steps were taken to streamline family assistance programmes, to cut other discretionary spending and to reduce tax shelters and tax loopholes. These measures assisted the deficit to fall from its upward trend from 1992, but it still has some way to go to reach the levels of the 1980s. The central, regional and local authorities are estimated by the Bundesbank as running a deficit in 1995 of DM95 billion (compared with 106 billion in 1994). This represents a fall of about 50 billion, given that the Treuhand (a government agency established as part of the transitional arrangements for German unification to oversee the disposal of East German State assets) still showed a deficit of 37 billion for 1994, when it terminated its activities. This fall between 1994–5 does represent a substantial fiscal improvement, but less so given that DM30 billion of this was due to the tax increases at the beginning of 1995, e.g. the solidarity surcharge and increases in insurance and property taxes.

East Germany – still problems

Investment is essential for growth but it is doubtful whether East Germany will yet have the base needed to encourage investment. Although public investment has been strong, private investment has been slow to follow. There has been a considerable effort to rebuild East Germany's public infrastructure especially in transportation and telecommunications. Generous assistance has been offered to potential investors in the area including tax allowances, accelerated depreciation and subsidised credit. Also, buyers of enterprises are required by the Treuhand agency to make contractual commitments to a specified volume of investment linked to pledges to maintain a specified level of employment. In the run-up to EMU however, the fiscal squeeze required to reach the 3 per cent deficit target has meant that many public works projects and construction investment in Eastern Germany have had to be curtailed. The resultant business pessimism in 1995–6 is evident in Figure 3.2.

The initial increase in gross fixed investment from less than 20 per cent of GDP in 1990 to around 50 per cent of GDP in 1993 seems to have diminished even further. Eastern Germany still falls far behind the West, in terms of capital stock; it is generally estimated to have only about 10 per cent of the total German capital stock, whereas its size should suggest 20 per cent. Early surveys laid the responsibility for the lack of private sector investment at the fault of bottle-necks in public administration. In more recent surveys

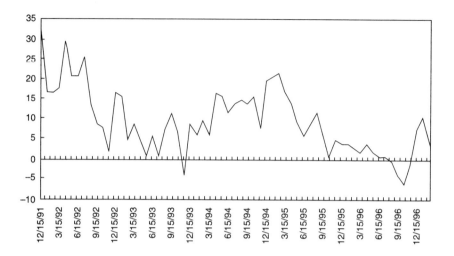

Figure 3.2 East German business development expectations (six month horizon)
Source: IFO Institute, Frankfurt

however it is the high wage costs that have become the predominant concern. The fundamental East German problem being the disincentive of high wages on investment.

Unemployment stays high

Productivity growth in East Germany has lagged behind the growth of wages, with East German unit labour costs about 37 per cent higher than in the West in 1995. Wage rates in East Germany have been far out of line with productivity due to the initial near-elimination of the wage differentials between East and West German wages due to reasons of equity and to prevent migration. Not only is the average wage rate substantially higher than the marginal product of labour, but the share of labour in national income exceeds 100 per cent, implying a business sector currently with negative profitability.

Excessively high wages affect both the level of output and the propensity to invest. The effect on the former results from the reduction in the demand for labour. Labour has continued to fall despite production bottoming out in 1991. Direct and indirect labour subsidies are widespread in East Germany helping to stall the adverse effect of high wages on investment and growth, but they are insufficient. High wages look set to continue as in most sectors of the East German economy, management and labour have agreed clauses to adjust negotiated wages and salaries to the level in West Germany. Therefore the higher wage round settlements of 1995 have become more or less automatically effective in the new Länder too. Indeed, in some instances the agreed basic remuneration has been increased to a higher proportion of the corresponding West German wage level, e.g. in 1995, in the metal-working and electrical engineering industries remuneration was raised from 87 per cent to 94 per cent of the West German level. On the whole negotiated wages and salaries rose by about 15.5 per cent by 1996 compared to the end of 1994. This eroded profit margins, preventing expansion (Corker *et al.*).

In May 1995 the number of unemployed fell below the million mark for the first time since the autumn of 1994, unemployment started to fall markedly in 1995 but then rose again in 1996 to reach 17.5 per cent in February 1996. February 1997 saw unemployment in the East rising again to 18.9 per cent. With unemployment high and wages more or less fixed to West German levels, the mechanism of wage flexibility bidding down the wages rates and thus bringing the unemployment rate down is not accessible. Keeping East German wages artificially high – although meant to reduce migration – results in higher unemployment that could lead to higher migration anyway, though on a longer term basis. This lack of improvement in unemployment has been despite fiscal transfers to East Germany which have been far greater than expected averaging well over 4 per cent of total German GDP in the 4 years to 1994 (Corker *et al.* 1995). Transfers to the east have been very large at about DM207.6 billion for 1995 (about 7 per cent of GDP) and DM196.5 billion in 1996 (about 6.5 per cent of GDP).

Conclusion: implications for EMU

The German unification had recourse to large flows of funds into Eastern Germany, as well as having a strong political and social impetus towards unity. It also had another safety valve, labour mobility, although this did not work tremendously efficiently due to high wages in East Germany. With the initial period of German unification so problematic, the outlook for the initial transition period of EMU could also be difficult. Unlike the German experience, transfers between EMU areas will be limited, as EU budgetary policy still remains fairly small (see Chapter 2). Therefore, regional disparities (also dealt with extensively in Chapter 2) could be larger and longer lasting than seen with German unification. Unemployment is likely to increase sharply in some regions, and it may take some time to reduce these disparities. The lack of wage flexibility in Europe may prevent regional disparities from being equilibrated.

Though there will be some fiscal transfers, it may be difficult to attract private investment to the disadvantaged areas of EMU, to provide jobs in these areas. The ECB may be very reluctant to cut interest rates to deal with these 'peripheral' area problems, as the risk of high 'core' inflation could be considerable. Though convergence will be higher between EMU member states than between East and West Germany, transfers and labour mobility are likely to be lower. Given these factors one can surmise that without sufficient labour mobility, the emphasis on fiscal austerity, and the 'Stability Pact' will be great.

4

SOLVING THE DEFICIT PUZZLE
Why reducing government deficits is a priority

Introduction

Reducing budget deficits has become every politician's obligation. Talk of balanced budgets, lower deficits and rehauling social services is at the centre of electoral debate in most countries. Strict deficit targets are the norm, from those in the Maastricht Treaty to the balanced budget target in the US. A change in the political climate justifies part of this emphasis, together with the rapid increase in the size of budget deficits and debts. Trends in the debt to GDP ratio have been striking: in 1980–95, the average gross public debt in industrial countries swelled from about 40 per cent to about 70 per cent of GDP. Most countries, including France, Germany, Italy, Japan, the Netherlands, Sweden and the United States, experienced roughly a doubling of their debt over this period. Among the highest debt countries, Belgium and Canada, with Greece and Italy, have debts near or over 100 per cent of GDP (OECD 1996 and IMF 1996). This raises questions of sustainability over the long term and the resultant economic effects on growth, employment and inflation. The success, or otherwise, of budget efforts, both globally and domestically, is fast becoming the crucial issue for bond market investors.

Growth in public deficits: a bad thing?

Governments can be seen as performing a double role of stabilisation and promotion of growth, and of income redistribution in favour of lower earning households. In the 1970s the political climate became more favourable to government intervention in the economy. This has contributed in part to the impressive growth in public deficits and debts seen in the last two decades. The underlying 'ideology' was that centralised intervention, assisted by economic expertise and political vision, could increase people's welfare. The emphasis changed in the 1980s when the idea of free market forces came back into favour as the best way of promoting efficient resource allocation, supposedly without the need for public intervention. This represented an ideological reaction to the very high growth in spending and taxation and the high levels of inflation in the 1970s (see the interesting account in Skidelsky 1995).

Incentives: do deficits make you lazy?

The traditional Keynesian view, favouring greater government intervention, was borne out of the concept of deficient aggregate demand causing resources to be unused. The priority was to get these unused resources, particularly labour, back to work. Subsequently, for economies working closer to their full potential, the focus then shifted on to how to promote quicker, smoother and more efficient growth. Policies based on high taxation, and in particular high marginal taxes on top incomes, have been viewed as negative due to their adverse effect on incentives to work/invest, thereby depressing economic growth.

Similar conclusions were reached in industry, with more emphasis on capital formation and on efficiency in the use of resources. The decline in unemployment in the 1960s, and a subsequent decrease in real GDP growth, shifted attention from the need to bring a larger number of people into work to the need to increase output per worker. The accumulation of fixed capital and its positive impact on productivity and on long-term economic growth also received greater attention. In order to promote investment, people began to look at ways of increasing the supply of savings, often by removing what were perceived as negative incentives (e.g. state sponsored pension schemes) and to increase capital accumulation (e.g. by lowering corporate taxes or removing capital gains taxes). Initially, the focus was on replacing public incentive destroying schemes by private market-led solutions. These were aimed at reducing distortions brought about by high taxes and regulation (see Feldstein 1994 for a comprehensive discussion of these issues). Interestingly, at a later stage, it was recognised that public investment in areas such as education and infrastructure (roads, bridges, research etc.) might have a beneficial role.

Macroeconomic effects

Following the same line of thought, people increasingly perceived budget deficits as harmful to economic performance. A high deficit may be harmful in two main ways:

Spend more, save less

A high deficit may reduce the amount of domestic national savings available for investment. This implies that countries with high budget deficits either experience large current account imbalances (as the country needs to absorb resources from abroad in order to finance the excess domestic demand) or falls in private investment. In the first case, it is arguable whether current account imbalances can be sustained in the long term. In any case, borrowing from abroad drains a country's net wealth. Increased borrowing from abroad also implies that a country imposes on itself the obligation of servicing foreign debt. In the second case, if private investment has to compete for scarcer domestic savings, a country would pay the price of higher real interest rates. This 'crowding out' effect reduces private investment, damaging long-term growth prospects. Note also that high deficits cause debt servicing costs which have to be financed by higher taxes.

In practice, the actual impact of large deficits on growth is a sticky issue. It is hard to measure, because a multitude of factors impact long-term growth. Attempts to quantify this effect have produced quite different results. Ball and Mankiw estimated that a doubling of the debt/GDP ratio from the current level would lead to a loss of output in the area of 6–12 per cent in the US. They argue that current output in the US is 3–6 per cent lower than it would have been without the fiscal imbalances of the last few years. On the other hand, R. Johnson argues that these figures are largely overstated; they rely on a link from debt to interest rates and from the latter to investment, which is empirically questionable (these papers are from the Federal Reserve Bank of Kansas City Symposium 1995). Overall, it is widely recognised that budget deficits cause distortions to the economy, but the actual negative impact on growth is very much uncertain.

Sustainability

The sustainability of public debt depends on a combination of domestic interest rates, the growth rate of GDP and on the primary budget balance (i.e. the budget deficit excluding debt servicing costs). If a country's primary balance is zero, the debt/GDP ratio will tend to rise as long as the interest rate on the debt is higher than GDP growth. In this case, the capacity to redress the situation depends critically on a country's ability to run large primary surpluses, a condition which often implies hard social choices, and which puts political stability under test. Failure to do this would put a country in a situation of ever growing, possibly exploding, increases in public debt. The steep rise in debt ratios in many countries has indeed increased concern over a possible hard-landing scenario: a country unable to address its fiscal imbalances could lose the confidence of investors, and the increasing perception of a default risk could also cause investors to liquidate their debt holdings. The potential result would be a dramatic drop in bond and share prices, a rise in real interest rates which would depress output and cause a likely collapse in household spending. The exchange rate would also suffer heavy losses. Free capital mobility and deregulated financial markets have increasingly assumed the role of wardens of stability, several cases of fiscal adjustments in recent years have been started or encouraged by the outflow of funds triggered by market uncertainty.

A seemingly upstoppable fiscal trend

Here we discuss the other reasons why budget deficits were allowed to rise at such a fast pace. These are associated with the political process and long-term economic trends which have contributed to changing the political climate towards public debt.

Long-term gain, short-term loss

Theory The political process makes fiscal decisions difficult to revert. The effects of large budget deficits, especially in the presence of efficient capital markets, are largely long term and not immediately visible to the general public, at least compared to other economic variables such as unemployment and inflation. This makes it more difficult for politicians to take the decisions necessary for a reduction of the deficit that is likely to lead to short-term unpopularity. Interestingly, Gallup opinion polls throughout the 1980s showed that more than half of those polled supported a balanced budget, however less than 10 per cent were in favour of cuts in entitlements, and only around 20 per cent would support tax rises. One of the problems with social security and entitlements generally is that during recent years they have increasingly become universal, i.e. they benefit the needy, but also the middle classes. Attempted reforms which preserve the role of entitlements as a safety net but substantially reduce benefits elsewhere are often unpopular with the middle classes, a weighty constituency. The feeling that those benefits represented acquired rights, often ingrained in people's expectations and culture, makes profound reforms very difficult.

Practice In the case of the US during the 1980s, politics led to a paradoxical result: the largest budget deficits were created by the Reagan administration, apparently committed to lowering government intervention in the economy and giving greater emphasis to market forces. Such a platform led to the quick implementation of the easy part – tax reforms – but attempts to reduce spending were made difficult due to political wrangling. The results were obvious. The 1981 reforms led to a fall in revenues of 1.3 per cent of GNP between 1980 and 1983 (the reform included a first year 5 per cent cut in all tax rates and a reduction in the top tax rate on unearned income from 70 per cent to 50 per cent). In fact, higher military and interest spending actually caused an increase in overall outlays, so that the deficit rose as a percentage of GNP, from 2.8 per cent in 1980 to 6.3 per cent in 1983. Several attempts were made throughout the 1980s (including tax increases) in an attempt to reduce the deficit, though these only partially offset the effects of the 1981 tax reforms. As Poterba (1991) notes: 'the most important budgetary lesson of the first two years of the Reagan presidency is that it is easier to cut taxes than to cut spending.' The claim from radical supply-siders that cutting taxes would eventually raise revenue turned out to be a misjudgement.

Demographics

Demographics have also worked against governments and are expected to continue to do so in the future. The expected ageing of the population in many industrial countries means that in the future there will be a larger number of elderly people in need of support, but relatively fewer people working and paying taxes on labour income. Demographic developments had been quite favourable to the budget position between 1950 and 1980, largely due to the post-war baby boom entrants into the labour force. That generation had to support a relatively low number of retirees. IMF (1996) data on the demographic 'dependency ratio' (i.e. over 65s relative to the population of working age) notes that it has drifted only slightly higher over the last four decades. It is, however, expected to increase sharply over the next fifty years. Germany, Italy and Japan will be among the worst hit, with the ratio suggesting that there will only be two people working for each retiree, compared to about five now.

Other related factors have led to miscalculations which have exacerbated the deficit in areas such as pensions and health care. Increases in health care costs and in structural unemployment (particularly in Europe) are two elements adding to the larger than expected increase in life span. The issue of hidden liabilities is discussed further below. Hidden liabilities can, for example, take the form of loan guarantees which do not cause initial outlays, but can impact the deficit in subsequent periods.

Slower growth and higher interest rates

Slower growth and higher interest rates have also impacted deficits negatively. In industrial countries, productivity growth has led to a slowdown in earnings and economic growth rates generally. In the US, productivity grew by 2.8 per cent in the 1950s and 1960s. Between 1970 and 1990, the annual growth rate of productivity fell to 1.2 per cent. A similar trend was observed in most other industrial countries. Moreover, monetary policy geared to the control of inflation also exacerbated the deficit problem. As inflation was lower than expected, real rates were high and so, therefore, were the rates paid on government debt. As a result, debt servicing costs have also contributed to the rise in the debt/GDP ratio. Indeed, debt servicing costs have increasingly become a sizeable part of most countries annual deficits; in Italy they represent over 10 per cent of GDP and are larger than the deficit itself.

Other issues

Enjoy now, pay later

The budget outlook goes from concern to panic if one uses generational accounting procedures to analyse future deficit prospects. The procedures (proposed by Auerbach, Gokhale and Kotlikoff 1994) start from the consideration that an increase in the current deficit (to the extent that it will have to be paid back by higher future taxes) causes a redistribution of resources between generations (future generations will face higher taxes to pay for current deficit-financed spending). Using a large amount of data, generational accountants calculate the lifetime net tax rates which face different generations under current policies (as a share of the present value of its per capita lifetime labour income). The procedure can be used to assess the implications in distribution terms of any fiscal policy decision across generations.

In the US case, Auerbach, Gokhale and Kotlikoff show that current fiscal policy has significant imbalances, suggesting that future generations would have to bear a tax burden of 84 per cent of their income. They conclude that current US fiscal policy can be regarded as unsustainable. Generational accounting puts the emphasis on the intergenerational effects of current fiscal choices which, as we mentioned above, in the case of social spending, particularly health and pensions, are a very relevant topic. The case of US social security is of particular interest. Up to the 1980s, the system was largely 'pay as you go', i.e. contributions from workers were paid directly to current beneficiaries. In 1983, following reports from the Greenspan Commission, Congress started to address the long-term solvency issue. This resulted in increases in tax rates and other changes which virtually ended the 'pay as you go' system and led to the accumulation of a large trust fund (which, by 2020, could be 30 per cent of GDP). Many European pension systems are still based on a 'pay as you go' system. Recent reforms in Italy, for example, have attempted to restore generational balance by adjusting pension parameters – such as rate of returns, contribution levels, number of working years – but still within a 'pay as you go' framework.

In practical terms, generational accounting, while highlighting many of the solvency risks outlined above, contains significant flaws. The conclusions are very sensitive to the starting assumptions so that, even for the IMF, it appears of little use for policy purposes. The results are sensitive to the date by which the budget must be balanced, which is arbitrary. Also, changes in assumptions on parameters such as productivity growth, the behaviour of private consumption, the discount rate for the generations and future demographic trends change the results very significantly.

Tax and spend

Another popular area of debate is the causation of spending and taxation. A common, more 'conservative' argument is that high taxes tend to cause higher spending. According to this argument, one of the reasons for the increase in public spending during the 1970s in the US was the lack of indexation of tax brackets, coupled with a period of high inflation. This progressively shifted each income group into higher tax brackets. The higher level of taxation has thus resulted in ever increasing levels of spending. This interpretation justifies why conservatives tend to associate spending cut measures with attempts to reduce the tax burden. Note, however, that significant consolidation efforts have frequently been associated with initial increases in revenue. The OECD reports that, out of all cases of significant fiscal consolidation considered in their recent study, only one was achieved without tax increases (OECD 1996).

Constitutional reforms

Constraints and punishments

Numerous attempts have been made to regulate deficits by imposing constraints on politicians. The reasoning behind this is that politicians have short-term horizons (due to the need to get re-elected) and therefore as government deficits cause long-term damage, the imposition of long-term constraints would be for the general good. Constraints could take the form of constitutional limits on the amount the government can borrow, and on the size of the annual deficit, or external limits on the deficit, or multi-year public targets. Punishment goes from the simple loss of popularity of missing the targets, to automatic cuts in spending outside government control, to being left out of monetary union in the European case. From the politicians point of view, external constraints can be a way of minimising the loss of popularity of certain decisions, but the problem is that external constraints cause a significant loss of flexibility in handling unforeseen events, e.g. tough deficit targets might be counterproductive in the case of very weak economic growth.

Designing rules

Given the multiplicity of factors which affect fiscal policy, the design of strict rules is of great difficulty. Generally, a better measure of fiscal stance would be the so-called 'standardised employment deficit' which shows the level of the deficit that would occur under current law if the economy was growing at potential GDP, thus excluding the cyclical component. The US Congressional Budget Office presents a rule of thumb on the growth impact of the deficit. In 1995, a 1 per cent fall in growth would have increased the deficit by US$10 billion. Generally, it would be unwise to try to reduce the part of the deficit simply due to slower than average growth. However, measures of the deficit vary significantly so that it is difficult to use them for legal purposes.

The US case: the Gramm Rudman Hollings Act

In the US, the idea of setting rules for budget formation and imposing constraints on policy makers has been popular for some time. For example, a Balanced Budget Amendment (BBA) was proposed as early as 1982. The complex procedures needed for a Constitutional Amendment (which requires qualified majorities in Congress and approval by a number of states) led to its dismissal after various attempts. Following a continuing debate, in 1986, Congress approved the Gramm Rudman Hollings (GRH) Act: this imposed so-called sequestration rules to discretionary spending, i.e. an automatic cap on spending when limits were exceeded (and incidentally set 1991 as the date in which the budget would be in balance). In the case of entitlement/mandatory spending (except social security and interest payments which were exempt from the GRH) the act imposed a 'pay as you go' system, for which any increase in spending would have to be matched by increases in taxes.

The GRH Act in practice

Looking back, the law did impose some constraints on the budget, but these resulted more from the fact that specific targets increased public awareness on the deficit issue, than for the provisions themselves. The main problems experienced with the act were:

1 It was a law, not a constitutional amendment, therefore its credibility was flawed by the fact that it could be easily changed if its provisions turned out to be too tough
2 Since the need to account for different rates of economic growth was recognised, the act contained special provisions in the case of lower/higher than expected growth. These valves were subject to abuse, e.g. in terms of very optimistic/pessimistic forecasts. This could be used, e.g. to allow for a President-friendly budget near election time. A major difficulty was in formulating a rule with provisions for emergency situations, the act needed to allow for more flexibility, without being subject to abuse
3 One of the early problems experienced by the act was that it gave a lot of power to those in charge of enforcing the rules. Specifically, because of the power the act gave to the State Accountant (who was nominated by Congress), it was declared unconstitutional in its original form

The GRH was abandoned in 1990 following weak economic growth and a round of tough Congress negotiation which resulted in a new 'Budget Enforcement Act', based on multi-year targets. The act still contained some of the provisions in the GRH (see Sheffrin 1991 for a detailed critical account of the GRH). A further attempt to impose a Constitutional rule for a balanced budget, proposed by the Republican majority after the 1994 mid-term elections, also failed. The FY 1995 budget, nevertheless, saw a cross-party agreement in principle to balance the budget by 2002, but the parties failed to agree on the details and the whole process was postponed.

European targets: the Maastricht criteria

In Europe, the Maastricht Treaty is the biggest pan-European attempt to limit budget deficits by imposing legal constraints. In fact, the two most important of the five criteria for the participation into monetary union directly refer to public deficits and debts. They state that countries must have deficits below 3 per cent of GDP and debts below 60 per cent in the year before monetary union takes place. Article 104c of the Maastricht Treaty says that 'Member States shall avoid excessive deficits', with Article 1 of the following protocol specifying the 3 per cent and 60 per cent reference values. Note that Article 104c(2) allows some flexibility as the criteria may be interpreted more loosely when significant progress has been made toward reaching the specified ratios or when the situation is considered 'exceptional or temporary'. Ultimately, the decision on whether an excessive deficit exists is taken in the European Council by qualified majority. The criteria were initially meant more to harmonise the economic positions of the participating countries. Increasingly, they have become strong constraints for domestic policy makers even beyond the significance of monetary union. Domestically, the Maastricht criteria have become the benchmark against which the performance of politicians in controlling budget deficits is measured. On the other hand, it provided them with an external incentive to propose tough fiscal measures.

Meeting or missing Maastricht?

The criteria have become particularly relevant as slow economic growth has made it possible that even core European countries, such as Germany, might miss the 3 per cent deficit level. The deficit criterion also provided an incentive to continue the fiscal consolidation effort even in the presence of weak economic growth, in fact this has exacerbated the weak growth scenario. At the European level, country concern for the fiscal rectitude of their partners in monetary union is also justified in light of the analysis above. High deficits within the currency area potentially cause high interest rates and market volatility, with an adverse effect on all participating countries. This justifies the attempts to impose constraints on the budget deficit after monetary union takes place. The Maastricht Treaty itself (Article 104c(11) European Commission 1992) states that, if a country fails to take appropriate measures to reduce 'excessive deficits', the Council might take appropriate measures. Those include fines, non-interest bearing deposits etc. A step further is the 'Stability Pact', highlighting a particular German concern over the risk of fiscal profligacy from partner countries. The Stability Pact is discussed in Chapter 2. Many of the problems highlighted above for the US case, such as the lack of flexibility, also apply to Europe. In the case of Europe, these problems might be exacerbated by doubts on whether Europe represents an optimal currency area (see Chapter 3 and *The Economist* 1996). Regional differences within the EU mean that asymmetric shocks could hit regions in different ways. Resulting imbalances could be corrected in three ways: with lower real wages, with labour mobility – workers moving from the depressed region to another – or by a fiscal expansion to spur demand. Fixed exchange rates make an adjustment in real wages more difficult while the EU has a low level of labour mobility, so that fiscal policy might gain greater relevance at the national level as a shock absorber. The Stability Pact allows for a deficit of up to 3 per cent and contains provisions for exceptional circumstances (see the appendix to this chapter). Moreover, it is likely that the EU budget will in the future play a greater role to correct regional imbalances. Nevertheless, the issue of whether the Stability Pact leaves enough room to correct asymmetric shocks might be critical for the success of EMU. The risk that a deficit rule might be perverse has been highlighted by some commentators who have called for greater national fiscal discretion.

Three European cases

Sweden: big spender makes big effort

Sweden has been known as one of the most high public spending economies. It had the fastest growing state debt sector in the industrialised world but, since 1991, has made substantial efforts with the aim of bringing the budget deficit into balance in 1996. This will not be achieved, and the targets have been revised to bring the 1996 budget deficit to 3 per cent of GDP in line with the EMU criteria. Sweden's overall public finances deteriorated sharply from a large surplus in 1990, to a deficit of 10.8 per cent of GDP in 1994. But measures adopted by Parliament under the Bildt government were able to reduce the fiscal deficit sharply from −10.8 per cent to −8.1 per cent of GDP in 1994.

The early 1990s: reasons for budget deterioration

The deterioration in Sweden's financial balance was mostly the result of central government financial problems. The general government financial deficit reached a peak in 1993 at 13.5 per cent of GDP; from then the primary deficit improved from 7.5 per cent of GDP in 1993 to 4 per cent of GDP in 1994. This was largely due to the end of public support to the banking system, which amounted to about 3 per cent of GDP in 1993. The deterioration in the general government financial position over the four years to 1994 reflected both a decline in the aggregate revenue ratio and a rise in overall spending. Public spending increased from 61 per cent in 1990 to an estimated 70.5 per cent in 1994. The main factors which led to this were a large increase in household transfer payments and in growth related entitlement programmes. Debt interest payments also contributed largely to the spending ratio. Transfers to households increased by about 5 per cent of GDP, to 25 per cent of GDP in 1994. About half of this was unemployment related expenditure, and the other half was pension costs (due to demographics and the impact of indexation in a falling inflation scenario). These higher costs more than offset reductions in health and work injury insurance (cut as part of the 1992–4 fiscal adjustment programmes) with an effect of about 1 per cent of GDP.

On the revenue side, the revenue ratio fell from 65 per cent of GDP in 1990 to 60 per cent in 1994. This was mainly due to a drop in tax collections. Much of the fall was due to reforms in 1990–1, designed to be revenue neutral but leading to a shortfall of about 1 per cent of GDP, most of which hit central government finances. Reductions in direct taxes were also seen over the longer period up to 1994, due to the switching of the composition of GDP towards exports rather than domestically produced goods, thereby contracting the VAT base. Other contributing factors were the introduction of the 1992 emergency package, which lowered income taxes by more than 4 per cent points.

1992–4: running to stand still

In the early 1990s, Sweden experienced its deepest recession since the 1930s. In three years public debt doubled, unemployment tripled, and public deficit increased tenfold. In 1994, the general government budget deficit was the largest in the OECD area, at 10 per cent of GDP. The early 1990s did see some positive moves taken to reduce government spending and to increase revenues, but the plunge in domestic demand made any real progress impossible. In the first emergency package in 1992, an additional fee for health care and higher excise taxes on gasoline and tobacco were important measures, with the second 1992 emergency package reducing the employers' payroll tax by 4 per cent. The proposed reduction in VAT had to be abandoned, and a special VAT was brought in on food. In 1993, the payroll tax for unemployment payments was increased. Ministry of Finance estimates show that the total budget savings between 1992 and 1994 were of SK90 billion (about 7 per cent of GDP). Lower spending contributed about two-thirds of this. Most of these savings resulted from reductions in transfers to house-holds, and reductions in local government taxation. Housing grants and sub-sidies were also reduced. Tax and revenue increases between 1992–4 were important and have been estimated at SK25 billion (just below 2 per cent of GDP).

Budget policies 1994–5: the big push

The savings packages from November 1994–April 1995 came on top of the structural SK18 billion in savings that came from plans approved earlier. Thus, the Finance Ministry has estimated that budget savings of about SK95 billion (more than 6 per cent of GDP) can be expected in 1994–8, with about two-thirds of that effect talking place in 1995–6. These measures are offi-cially estimated to stabilise the ratio of public debt to GDP by 1996. Sweden's Social Democratic government (which took power in late 1994) instituted an unprecedented series of spending cuts and tax increases due to save 7.5 per cent of GDP over three years. The Social Democratic govern-ment, elected in September 1994, announced a series of measures to reduce the deficit. In November 1994, a savings package was introduced to cut the deficit by SK56 billion by 1998 (4 per cent of GDP). This included SK 36 billion in tax increases, and SK20 billion lower spending. The tax increases in the November 1994 savings package included the increase of the marginal rate of income tax for the upper income tax bracket, from 50 per cent to 55 per cent, an increase in social security fees by 3 per cent, the elimination of the tax exemption on dividend payments, and the reduction of the indexation provisions on tax brackets. The main elements of the spending measures announced in November 1994 consisted of a reduction in family allowances and a move to only partial indexation of social security benefits.

Spending reductions of SK19 billion announced in January 1995 covered all ministries, with the largest reductions coming from changes in pension and other transfers. On the expenditure side, savings came from a fall in the replacement ratio for unemployment, health and parental insurance to 75 per cent. The projected savings made room for a cut in VAT on food from 21 per cent to 12 per cent.

The future: targets and setbacks

The Swedish targets for the public deficit are to bring the ratio below 3 per cent in 1997, and to balance the budget by 1998. Permanent budget improve-ments will total SK8 billion. The coming two years should also see SK3.5 billion from privatisations. The spring budget, seen in early 1996, was wel-comed by the markets. It included a three year ceiling on public expenditure targeting twenty-seven areas for each year (this is expected to be easier to monitor on a continuous basis than a deficit target) and budget improvements worth SK10 billion in 1997. Since 1994, fiscal adjustment measures have been aimed at stabilising the public debt ratio. Great progress has been made by the government since 1994, but this progress was put at risk by the lower than expected growth rates seen in 1996. Total budget savings are estimated at SK95 billion from measures with effect between 1995–8. The outlook for Swedish finances seems fairly positive, large manoeuvres have been made, even from 1992. Though low growth and high unemployment provide obstacles, there is a strong political will to reduce the deficit further.

Germany: the unification stumbling block

Unification has had a substantial effect on German public finances, causing the deficit to widen from a small surplus in 1989, to a 2.6 per cent deficit in 1992. Large transfers to Eastern Germany (about 4–5 per cent of Western GDP each year) caused increases in public spending which undid the fiscal gains achieved between 1982 and 1989, when the general government budget was brought back into balance. The source of the problems was not unification per se, but the severity of adjustment problems in the East, and the added burden of recession in the West. In 1993 the deficit increased to 3.3 per cent. The public sector borrowing requirement (PSBR) increased to 5.2 per cent of GDP.

The 1980s: fiscal consolidation

Pre-unification, progress was made in fiscal consolidation. The CDU-CSU/FDP coalition government under Chancellor Kohl came to power in September 1982. With the economy moving into recession, fiscal policy was top of the agenda. Kohl's 1980s programme consisted of a medium term framework for budgetary consolidation and tax reform, and on structural policy measures to reduce inflexibilities and distortions especially in the labour market and the tax system. The budget laws of 1983 and 1984 were central to this programme. Other important items were the tax reforms of the late 1980s, the privatisation schedule announced in 1983, the Employment Promotion Law of 1985, and the 1989 health and pension reforms.

The tax system reforms emphasised increasing work incentives. Tax reforms were implemented in the late 1980s, in three stages, with net tax relief of DM11 billion in 1986, DM14 billion in 1988, and DM24 billion in 1990. The tax reform of 1986–90 offered net tax relief mounting to DM48.5 billion. The very high marginal rate of taxation for middle income earners was reduced as well as some distortions in the tax system. The entry rate of taxation fell from 22 per cent to 19 per cent and child allowances were raised. These reforms substantially reduced state revenues. The 1980s saw a reversal of the rapid growth of social transfers and government consumption previously seen. Public investment was cut sharply and social expenditure was also reduced. The pension reform of 1989 included changes such as the linking of benefits to the path of wages and raising the retirement age to 65 years for both men and women. The 1989 law on the structural reform of the public health system sought cost savings by cutting some benefits and increasing cost sharing on the part of consumers, though balancing this with cuts in contribution rates.

Criticisms of this period of fiscal reform, however, are manifold. The lack of cuts in subsidies has been criticised for weighing heavily on public investment depressing growth prospects. Private business investment failed to 'crowd in' as strongly as was expected, due to few signs of lower long-term interest rates. In fact, the growth experienced in the 1980s was, to a certain extent, deceptive. The strength of the economy was due not only to increases in domestic private and public investment, but was in 1984–5 particularly dominated by export growth from increased US demand.

1993: the impact of unification

In 1993 the German federal deficit was DM66.9 billion, compared to the initial estimate of DM43 billion. Unification caused higher transfers to the Federal Labour Office (DM24.4 billion compared to DM8.9 billion in 1992), accounting for about half of the total spending increase. Spending by the federal states grew by 5.4 per cent, due predominantly to public sector wage increases. A general pay increase of 3 per cent was exacerbated by the rise of wages in Eastern Germany to 80 per cent (from 74 per cent) of Western levels, an increase designed to reduce East to West migration. Local authority spending was pushed up by the sharp rise in social assistance payments associated both with shedding labour and the influx of people seeking political asylum.

Revenues also undershot initial estimates, so that the combined deficit of states and municipalities widened from DM48.9 to 55.8 billion in 1993. This was partly offset at the general government level, by a higher social security surplus (up from DM4.4 billion to DM12.2 billion, due to lower health spending, and higher contributions by the old/previous states). Overall, if the deficits of the Treuhand agency are included, along with the Federal Railways and the Post Office, the aggregate borrowing requirement of the public sector rose to DM160 billion, or 5.2 per cent of GDP in 1993.

1994–5: falling tax revenues start to bite

The Federal Consolidation Programmeme adopted in 1993 was part of the government's commitment to the Solidarity Pact. The aim of the programme was to halt further deterioration of government finances due to unification. In the 1994 budget, the government introduced a second package of corrective measures (the Savings Consolidation and Growth Programme). The savings amounted to DM21 billion (or 0.6 per cent of GDP), consisting

Table 4.1 Public sector transfers to Eastern Germany (DM billion)

	1991	1992	1993	1994
Gross Transfers	140	152	169	178
Receipts	33	37	39	42
Net Transfers	107	115	130	136

Source: Federal Statistics Office, Germany

Table 4.2 Public sector finances, Germany

DM billion	1993	1994	1995	1996
Expenditures	1599.0	1662.0	1757.5	1792.0
Receipts	1489.0	1582.0	1634.0	1654.0
of which tax revenue	772.9	811.2	838.6	824.3
Deficit	−109.7	−80.6	−122.6	−137.9

Source: Deutsche Bundesbank Monthly Reports, 1997, Frankfurt

mainly of social spending reductions (DM15 billion) particularly in unemployment benefit/assistance, with a pay freeze for civil servants and a 1 per cent cut in jobs. The Solidarity Tax surcharge and successful attempts to control public spending have been offset by falling tax revenues. This has meant a deficit increase of 16 billion, i.e. 0.5 per cent of GDP, to 3.5 per cent of GDP in 1995.

The 1996 deficit and the 1997 budget

Finance Minister Waigel has said that the 1996 tax revenue is coming in at about DM11.8 billion short of plan. This will have to be balanced with spending cuts this year. The risk to the economy is that these cuts (made necessary due to lower than forecast growth pulling tax revenues down) may push growth even further down, making it more difficult to reach the targets in 1997.

The push to bring the German deficit down to the EMU criteria level (3 per cent of GDP for 1997 data) is obviously at the forefront of these cuts, but another main idea of the reforms is to lower the share of social payments in gross wages to less than 40 per cent, and the government's share of the economy to 46 per cent from 51 per cent by the year 2000. The government is obliged to make certain reductions in taxes, as part of its moves to reduce the tax burden on individuals. It had hoped to reduce the solidarity surcharge on income tax to 6.5 per cent on 1 January 1997, and to 5.5 per cent from 1 January 1998 (from 7.5 per cent) with an estimated giveback of DM8 billion, but due to political pressure to find compensation in other areas, this has been postponed by one year. Other reforms which will influence the 1997 deficit are: (a) the wealth tax abolition at the end of 1996, (b) inheritance tax revisions, and (c) the abolition of inheritance tax on the family home. The

51

government will also lose revenue due to (d) abolishing the trading capital tax from January 1997 (with an estimated revenue loss of DM44.1 billion). The abolition of tax exemptions and loopholes should see around DM32 billion in extra revenues (such as tax evasion measures, limiting tax write-offs, and scrapping some tax breaks on aircraft and ships).

Widespread taxation reform   The simplification of Germany's tax system is still being discussed, with two models being mooted: tax bands of 15 per cent, 25 per cent and 35 per cent (FDP proposal) or tax bands of 8 per cent, 18 per cent and 28 per cent (CDU proposal) each for income of DM12,000 p.a., 20,000 and 60,000. The tax reforms of the government generally have been criticised due to the fact that they seem to benefit the wealthy.

Corporate reforms   The corporate reforms in the 1997 budget are aimed at reducing labour costs, including the costs of hiring and firing, and sick pay. They include raising the number of employees required before legal protection from firing is needed, from five to ten. Plans to cut sick pay to 80 per cent of the normal wage have not been implemented at the firm level due to widespread labour protests. The government is making some attempt with these measures to encourage business and measures to support new companies, improving access to venture capital, as well as importantly, reducing business taxes such as abolishing the local capital trading tax (to be included in the 1997 tax bill) which was charged irrespective of whether the business had made a profit or not.

Welfare reforms   Pension reforms with health insurance cuts and a delay in child benefit increases should add up to a cut of DM28 billion of government spending. This should have a large effect on consumption, and savings, as disposable income falls by this amount in 1997. This will help to keep GDP under 2 per cent for 1997.

The future

After the set back of unification for public finances, Germany has made a substantial effort to bring the deficit back in line. The government has made some effort to reduce inflexibilities in the labour market, and plans to reduce the tax burden considerably in the future. Low growth has put at risk the attainment of the Maastricht 3 per cent criterion, given mounting political pressures to increase public spending to alleviate growth problems.

Italy: late starter, but good sprinter?

In the last few years, Italy has made considerable progress in correcting fiscal imbalances, achieving four consecutive years of primary surpluses (public balance excluding interest costs). Successive governments, many of which were composed by technocrats, were forced by a deteriorating situation and by financial market turmoil to act to start bringing public finances under control.

Progress from 1993

A combination of disregard for the growing budget deficits and of increasing real rates (due partly to the higher stock of debt and partly to Italy's financial liberalisation) resulted in budget deficits systematically over 10 per cent in previous years and in a public debt which had reached over 120 per cent of GDP. As a result of government action (as Figure 4.1 shows) the debt to GDP ratio fell in 1995 for the first time in many years. This progress has been the result of a number of budgets, starting with the large 1993 budget by Amato (worth over IL90 trillion). These represented largely a structural break from the past, even though some of the measures have represented temporary belt-tightening efforts, unlikely to be sustained in the future. Although considerable progress has been made, Italy will need to grab a reward in terms of lower yields in order to consolidate this progress. Interest payments still represent over 10 per cent of GDP. Italy is well positioned to reap this reward, but more is needed both in terms of further fiscal effort, lowering inflation expectations and ensuring a stable political landscape. Participation in EMU, with the consequent lower interest rates, would obviously be very beneficial.

Revenues

Considerable effort was made to increase taxation, especially at the beginning of the adjustment process, with tax pressure (i.e. total tax revenue as a

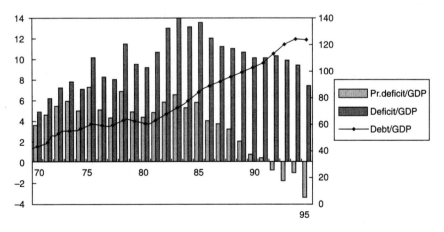

Figure 4.1 Debt, deficit and primary surplus
Source: Minestero del Tesoro, DPEF 1995 (1995 is the official forecast), Rome

percentage of GDP) growing from 39.8 per cent in 1990 to 44 per cent in 1993. This effort was partly unwound in the following years, due to political difficulties and cyclical weakness (the ratio fell back to 41.8 per cent in 1994). The 1993 budget of Mr Amato brought tax pressure to a very high level, although partly through temporary measures (such as a tax pardon). The permanent measures utilised included increases in income tax, both on individuals and companies. Tax revenue grew sharply both in 1992 and 1993, despite (and partly responsible for) the recession, and subsequently fell in 1994. In 1995, tax pressure was increased again as a result of both the 1995 budget, with largely a one off impact, and of Dini's mid-year mini budget, which increased both VAT and petrol taxes (with those measures having a permanent impact). The new government of Prodi, elected in 1996, has pledged to keep tax pressure unchanged over GDP. However, the government has later decided to accelerate the fiscal adjustment in an attempt to reach the 3 per cent deficit/GDP Maastricht fiscal criterion in 1997. As a result, it has passed a IL12.5 trillion exceptional tax – the euro-tax – to make the 3 per cent level feasible. Note that, even with the euro-tax, the level of taxation in Italy compares favourably with other European countries and it is similar to countries with a similar size of public spending, although the increases in the last few years have created considerable political tension. Two main reforms are often discussed:

1   The Prodi government presented the outline of a wide-ranging tax reform, aimed at reducing the number of taxes by widening the tax base. Also, there are plans to shift part of the tax burden from central government towards local authorities
2   Fighting tax evasion: the amount of evaded taxes was once estimated by the government at IL100 trillion (Ministero del Tesoro, DPEF, 1995)

Spending

On the spending side, as a percentage of GDP, total government spending (excluding interest payments) has stopped growing and has fallen, although the fall has not been enormous. However, much of the success must probably be measured in terms of stopping the excessive growth of certain spending items, particularly social security, which is almost three-quarters of all non-interest spending. More progress needs to be obtained in spending reductions. The Prodi government was elected on a platform of deficit cutting, but with an eye to maintaining welfare state provisions.

In social security, where pensions and health are the two main items, spending as a percentage of GDP grew by around 12 per cent from 1985 to 1992, and has stabilised since then, largely as a result of the reforms of Amato, though these failed to have a sufficiently lasting impact. The subsequent reforms by Dini are designed to ensure stability over GDP in the long term. The generosity of the pension system in Italy depended on a number of factors: low retirement age, access to retirement after a relatively short period of work, and excess of indexation. There were also other peculiar problems such as liberal access to invalids pensions, different treatments for sectors etc. Amato and Dini profoundly reformed the system, the Dini reforms in particular introduced a new system, though still within a 'pay as you go' framework. The four main changes are:

1   Measuring pensions to actual contributions paid (not on wages)
2   Introducing a flexible pension age with incentives for those who work longer
3   Pension contributions are accrued based on growth of nominal GDP
4   Pensions have been made more homogeneous across sectors

The new system has been criticised because:

• It is slow to become effective (it will only be fully running in eighteen years, up to 2013)
• The coefficients are too generous, especially if nominal growth is strong

However, the new structure represents a very significant improvement, putting in place a new system which can be more easily adjusted in the future. The health service has seen various spending reduction measures, but in a less comprehensive reform.

Public employment represented another important item as job creation was strong in the 1980s and public wages, largely for political reasons, tended to grow faster than private sector wages. In subsequent budgets, limits on turnover led to the number of public sector employees dropping from 1993, albeit by a limited amount. Also, wage agreements in 1993 led to a sharp drop in real wages. More recently, wage settlements have tended to be higher than inflation, and a significant reduction in the number of employees is hard to foresee. Government action in this area is critical. Investment spending has fallen significantly, partly as a result of previous budgets, partly due to fears following the 'clean hands' wave of judicial enquiries on corruption. Debt servicing costs attract immediate attention representing a staggering 19 per cent of total spending. Clearly this is largely outside direct government control, but it is still worth noticing that a 2 per cent fall in interest rates could save the government IL18 trillion in one year (almost 1 per cent of GDP) or two-thirds of the 1997 budget.

Staying on track

Italy has reached a position where fiscal policy should guarantee substantial primary surpluses. With additional measures, some of which are exceptional

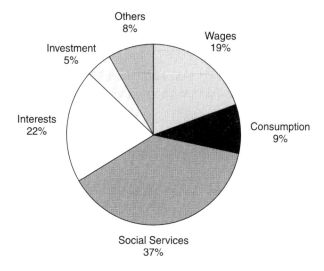

Figure 4.2 Composition of spending for public administrations in 1995
Source: Bank of Italy, Relazione Annuale Appendice Statistica 1995, Rome

in character, the government aims to bring the total deficit to 3 per cent in 1997 in line with the Maastricht Treaty. This is a pretty remarkable achievement. Following the government line, achieving those high levels of surpluses will bring the debt/GDP ratio down from 126.5 per cent in 1996, to 121.2 per cent in 1998. Large primary surpluses are hard to maintain and already the high tax burden and the spending cuts have caused political difficulties. Interestingly, the current government of Prodi intends to combine deficit reductions with concertation i.e. taking decisions in conjunction with all social partners such as industrialists and Unions. In this sense, Italy will provide an interesting political experiment. Progress has undoubtedly been made, but Italy is not yet out of the woods. A combination of lower interest rates and some political stability could give Italy a sprinting finish.

Conclusions

The rapid growth of budget deficits and debts means that redressing fiscal balances has become a top political priority. Large deficits pose problems both in terms of long-term economic performance and in terms of financial stability. The issue is made particularly urgent by the growing burden represented by a number of schemes, particularly in social security, which raise questions of long-term solvency. Also, a change in political climate seems to have made people less tolerant of high tax rates and less keen on widespread state intervention, shifting preferences towards targeted public schemes of more limited size and scope.

Various attempts have been made to impose mechanical budget targets. These can provide a useful focus for the political debate and can create a public commitment to a deficit reduction programme. Alone, however, they are unlikely to replace intense political negotiations on spending and tax policy. Goran Persson, Swedish Finance Minister, presents the following interesting guidelines: fiscal programmes 'must be designed so that the burdens of consolidation are shared fairly', they 'have to be designed as a comprehensive programme. ... By presenting the measures together, it becomes clear to all interest groups that they are not the only one to make sacrifices'. Finally, programmes must be transparent and 'never say it won't hurt' (statements in Jackson Hole, USA, 1995). Persson's statements show that, while deficits are essentially a long-term economic issue, they must be addressed via a complex political process and based on widespread consensus. The long-term effects of the mix of policy should also be assessed, e.g. a tax on capital or cuts in education and research have presumably an adverse effect on future growth. The choice of where cuts should be concentrated, the mix of spending cuts and tax increases and the overall size of the government leave ample scope for different political solutions.

Fiscal consolidation efforts can be made difficult by the short-term negative impact that they have on economic growth. A favourable policy mix, and in particular an accommodating monetary policy, can create a more favourable environment for fiscal consolidation. In the long term, also, rules to control deficits might decrease the role of cyclical deficits as automatic stabilisers and call for a more proactive monetary policy in stabilising output fluctuations. Financial markets also play an important role. Pressures from financial markets have increasingly been instrumental in forcing reluctant countries to proceed towards fiscal consolidation. Global markets have made it more difficult for countries to adopt unsustainable policies as investors quickly react to impose risk premia on the country's assets. Financial markets can also play a role in facilitating the adjustment process. As the US Economic Report of the President (1996: 69) notes 'a forward-looking response of financial markets to deficit reduction can accelerate the decline in real long-term interest rates, bringing forward the investment dividend associated with balancing the budget'. This effect has not always materialised: the OECD notes that long-term rate declines took place in only a limited number of cases of fiscal consolidation (OECD 1996). Moreover, financial volatility has made the stance of policy more difficult to assess and to control. Currency appreciation associated with fiscal consolidation can exacerbate the restrictive impact of fiscal policy. A high level of co-ordination between government and central banks is required to minimise the output losses associated with deficit reductions.

APPENDIX: THE EUROPEAN COMMISSION
PROPOSALS FOR THE STABILITY PACT (1996)

October 1996 saw the release of proposals by the European Commission on the Stability Pact, and the monetary regulation of EMU. These proposals are crucial in ironing out many of the uncertainties surrounding the implementation of EMU, and especially the changeover to the use of the euro from national currency units. These proposals were ratified in the Dublin summit (13–14 December 1996), though only after long and intensive negotiations on the Stability Pact. We highlight the important aspects of each regulation and explain the consequences and intentions of the Commission proposals.

The proposals by the European Commission for the Stability Pact were presented on 16 October 1996. With much speculation that the deficit and debt criteria may be interpreted with some flexibility, when the decision on Member States is taken, the Stability Pact has taken on the role of guardian of EMU, particularly to those concerned about problems of maintaining convergence and stability. The Stability Pact has its roots in the Maastricht Treaty itself, with a system of surveillance, deposits and fines detailed there for both excessive debt and government deficits. The Commission's proposals are very much along these lines, but suffer by comparison (in terms of strictness) with the Stability Pact proposal made by German Finance Minister Theo Waigel in 1995.

A twin-track strategy

The Commission proposed a 'twin-track strategy' combining a preventive early warning system, and a deterrent. The former part would require close monitoring of individual country budgets, with governments submitting 'stability programmes' with medium term budgetary targets (close to balance or in surplus). These targets should abide by the 3 per cent ceiling for deficits, 'apart from unusually severe economic downturns or other exceptional conditions', and should be made public. These budgetary targets will be examined by the Commission, which may decide to endorse them, or recommend that they should be strengthened. Updated programmes would also go through the same process. The targets required for the medium-term plans are detailed in the accompanying box.

Proposals for annual submission of a 'stability programme' by Member States

A stability programme shall contain:

(a) medium term objective and adjustment path for the government surplus/deficit as a ratio to GDP; expected path for the government debt ratio

    (b) main assumptions about expected economic developments such as real GDP growth, employment/unemployment, inflation and other important economic variables
    (c) description of budgetary measures being taken to achieve the objectives of the programme
    (d) commitment to take additional measures when necessary to prevent slippage from targets

(European Commission 1996a)

Constant monitoring

These targets would be monitored constantly by the European Commission. Departures from the targets would prompt a warning from the Commission, in the form of a recommendation to take 'budgetary adjustment measures'. If the divergence is seen to persist or worsen, the Council would then make a recommendation to the Member State to take 'specific corrective action', and may make its recommendation public.

Unanimous voting

The Commission uses Article 104c(14), subparagraph 2, as the legal basis for all aspects of the excessive deficit procedures, under this European Council should act unanimously on these matters, 'the Commission believes that the credibility of the stability pact . . . will benefit from a unanimous vote of the Member States'.

Speeding up the excessive deficit procedures

The Commission proposals also include a regulation (European Commission 1996a) on speeding up the excessive deficit procedure and sanctions, as compared to the timetable in the Maastricht Treaty. The timing of the assessment and punishment procedure has been reduced to ten months, the schedule is shown in the following section.

The timetable of the excessive deficit procedure

1   The issuing of recommendations should be finished by the May after the year in which the excessive deficit occurred
2   It is intended that there should be a relatively short period for the government to have adopted corrective measures (at most four months after the issuing of the Council recommendation)
3   Once the Council has decided that insufficient effective action has been taken by the Member State to correct the deficit for the new year, the imposition of sanctions should take place by December.

4   the maximum length of the whole procedure should not be longer than 10 months

Speeding up the later steps of the procedure will rely on how 'effective action' is to be assessed. The Commission proposes to consider publicly announced government decisions as the basis for assessing the corrective measures taken, but there is still some ambiguity here.

Exceptional and temporary circumstances

The original European Commission recommendation was that the interpretation of the 'exceptional and temporary' circumstances was clarified further. This clause gives leeway to countries whose deficits may be due to particularly harsh economic conditions. The Commission proposal was as follows:

> The excess of a government deficit over the reference value shall be considered exceptional and temporary . . . when resulting from an unusual event outside the control of the relevant Member State and which has a major impact on the financial position of the general government, or when resulting from a severe economic downturn, in particular in the case of significantly negative annual real growth.
>
> (European Commission 1996a)

This was still fairly ambiguous, and caused some concern especially amongst German officials. Unlike the original Waigel proposal it did not stipulate a particular level of low growth which would constitute a 'severe economic downturn'. In the Waigel Pact proposal a fixed −2 per cent GDP growth level was regarded as triggering off the 'exceptional circumstances' considerations, though this was a very low level to set the trigger, a definite figure has the advantage of giving little room for political negotiation. After much intense debate in the run-up to the Dublin Summit (December 1996) it was finally decided that there would be automatic sanctions for countries which had an annual GDP growth of more than −2 per cent. There would also be a 'grey zone' however, for countries with GDP growth of between −0.75 and −2 per cent. These countries would be able to appeal for an exemption, for which supporting evidence would have to be shown and a vote would then be taken by the EMU Member States as to whether an exemption would apply. The final agreement suggests a stricter approach to countries with excessive deficits than the initial Commission proposal, more in line with the initial Waigel Pact. This Stability Pact does seem to be a good mechanism to maintain a stable union, but much obviously depends on the nature of its implementation.

The Commission also recommends that one-off excessive deficits are allowable:

In addition, if the unusual event of the severe economic downturn has come to an end or if it is forecast that it will come to an end in the calendar year following the year in which the deficit exceeds the reference value, budgetary forecasts provided by the Commission must indicate that the deficit would fall below the reference value in this same following year.

(European Commission 1996a, Section 1, Article 2)

If this clause goes through into the final Stability Pact agreement then it does give additional leeway to countries who miss the deficit criterion in any one year. Again much depends on how this rule is implemented in practice.

The punishment system

The size of punishment deposits is intended to be sufficiently high to act as a deterrent without being counterproductive. The Commission proposed a fixed and a sliding component to the deposit system. The fixed component would be 0.2 per cent of GDP, and the variable component would be 0.1 per cent of GDP for every 1 per cent of GDP the deficit overshoots the 3 per cent value. The ceiling for the whole deposit would be 0.5 per cent of GDP (i.e. a deficit of over 6 per cent of GDP would not imply a proportionally higher deposit). The original Waigel proposals were that violators of the 3 per cent deficit limit within the union, should be fined by 0.25 per cent of GDP for each percentage point of excessive deficit over the 3 per cent limit. This would be an automatic fine, with a fairly stringent 'exceptional cases' clause (see above).

Non-compliance with only the criterion relating to the government debt ratio in Article 104c(2b), would induce a fixed deposit of 0.2 per cent of GDP. The upper limit of 0.5 per cent of GDP applies for the total annual amount of deposits regardless of what combination of excessive deficit/debts a country has (the debt overshoot fine was subsequently abandoned). The deposit would be transformed into a fine if after two years sufficient action to correct the excessive deficit had not been taken. Deposits would be lodged with the Community and the interest on deposits and fines would be resources of the general budget of the European Communities.

5

IN BUNDESBANK CLOTHES

Issues on central bank independence

Central bankers are only human.
(Blinder 1995)

Introduction

Inflation in the industrialised world has been described as moribund, or even 'already dead and buried', at the very least a profound change has taken place. While in the late 1970s, inflation was double digit in almost all industrial countries, currently inflation rates above 3 per cent are the exception. The IMF (1996) reports that so far in the 1990s, inflation in industrial countries has averaged 3.5 per cent as opposed to 6 per cent in the 1980s. Only few remember that in the 1970s even the free-market oriented Federal Reserve was fighting inflation using means such as formal credit controls (in 1980, under President Carter). Currently, much of the debate on inflation focuses on the rather luxurious choice of whether central banks should be happy with a 2–3 per cent inflation rate or whether they should go all the way towards achieving price stability (zero inflation) at the cost of lower growth. In that sense, the fight against inflation can be said to have been largely successful.

Part of this success has been ascribed to the working of independent central banks. Economic theory produced a large body of work to describe the link between the independence of central banks and the inflation performance of a country. The common results are based on the ideas that inflation is essentially a monetary phenomenon and independence in itself – i.e. the belief that monetary policy will be outside the control of elected politicians – should lead to an improvement in inflation, in some cases before any action is taken. In other cases, the central bank has to gain a reputation for having a low tolerance for inflation (the so-called credibility bonus).

In practice, the link between independence and low inflation is rather fuzzy. First, the legal constitution of a central bank as independent is by no means a guarantee of price stability. At the same time, price stability can be achieved by central banks which are considered 'dependent'. Still, on average, there is some empirical regularity supporting the view that, where central banks operate independently of the government, they tend to have a better inflationary record. However, empirical conclusions are made hard to interpret by the fact that many other elements can influence a particular result. Other factors – some of which are discussed below – might be responsible for the apparent correlation between independent central banks and low inflation. Political judgement and practical experience, therefore, both contribute to one's view of whether independent central banks are effective and desirable. To emphasise the importance of the debate one could go as far as to say that after the Greek notion of democracy and the French 'distinction of powers', the independence of central banks reshapes the 'distribution of competencies' in democratic societies.

Central bank independence in theory

Credibility and time consistency

The main body of work on central bank independence stems from applications of 'game theory' to macroeconomics. The most relevant concept is the idea of time inconsistency. In simple words, the concept is as follows: suppose that the government wants to maximise a nation's well being by creating an environment of low inflation and low unemployment. The government's best policy would be to announce that inflation will be kept low so that price and wages will be set according to expectations of a low inflation rate. However, once wages and prices have been set, the government will find it convenient to deviate from the announced policy. The government has an incentive to cheat by using pro-growth policies to lower unemployment at the cost of a slightly higher inflation rate. Wage and price setters, which are assumed to be forward looking, know that the government will have an incentive to deviate from its announced, low-inflation policy. They will, therefore, take this into account when taking their decisions. In particular, they will set wages and prices at a higher level. In so doing, they will lead to higher than optimal inflation and they will put the government in a position of being unable to affect unemployment. The end result is that the economy will find itself with an unemployment rate unaffected by government policy, but with a higher level of inflation than that preferred by society (inflationary bias).

To better clarify the concept of time inconsistency consider another, unrelated case: suppose the government thinks that it is a good idea to promote fixed investment. The best policy would be to impose low investment taxes. This should provide an incentive for the private sector to increase spending in machinery. However, once the private sector has invested, and the machines are in operation, the government could be tempted to reverse its policy and increase taxes. Its previous 'optimal policy' – low taxes – is no longer optimal once the machinery has been bought. Now the government's best policy is to increase taxes to boost revenue. The problem is that the private sector – aware of the government preferences – would be likely to take the higher taxes into account when formulating its decision. The result, in this set up, would be that the private sector would not trust the government's low tax promise. The effect of the low tax policy on investment would be lower than if the government had been able to convince the private sector that its pledge would not be broken.

When discussing time inconsistency in the case of inflation one should be aware that the reasoning works within a specific framework, based on a short-term Philips Curve (introduced by Lucas 1973). The model is based on the following ideas: a) That monetary policy cannot affect the rate of growth of a country in the long term. Therefore, monetary expansions ultimately lead to inflation with no sustained impact on economic growth. b) That the only way in which monetary policy can affect growth in the short term is via inflation surprises, i.e. when monetary growth is greater than people expect. This leads to faster short-term growth – a purely temporary phenomenon – but also to permanently higher inflation. In order to return to lower inflation a reverse surprise is necessary, with a consequent period of weaker economic growth. Lucas' model is complex and has numerous consequences and versions. The main points are shown above. Note that Lucas' view hinges on the idea that economic agents have rational expectations, they know and understand the working of the economy.

The combination of the Lucas view of economic policy and the idea of time inconsistency explains why – according to models discussing central bank independence – the economy can end up in a situation of high inflation and unchanged unemployment. Other models highlight different reasons why an inflation bias might occur. Seigniorage is another example. Seigniorage refers to the ability of a government to finance its spending by printing money (causing what is commonly referred to as an inflation tax). A government might maximise the amount of seigniorage for a given rate of inflation if it can convince people that inflation will be kept low and seigniorage not abused. In developed countries with well functioning capital markets, the employment motive seems to dominate monetary policy. In countries with thin capital markets and relatively inefficient tax systems, the need to resort to the inflationary finance of budgetary deficits is a prime motive for inflation (see Cuckierman 1992). Finally, another reason for which government might be tempted to expand monetary supply is the attempt to push down interest rates in a bid to lower the fiscal burden of servicing a large public debt.

A final point concerns the political nature of the inflationary bias. Some work has been made on reading economic outcomes as the result of how political decisions are formulated: for example, the attempt to lower unemployment at the cost of future higher inflation might be caused by an incumbent government's attempt to be re-elected as elections approach (office motivation). Alternatively, a government might have an ideological preference for low unemployment, even at the cost of higher inflation (e.g. partisan politicians). These ideas have often been used as major arguments in support of central bank independence. It can be shown that by enhancing the independence of monetary authorities, inflationary bias can be reduced, together with partisan variability and the electoral manipulation of monetary policy (see, for example, Alesina 1988).

Solutions to the credibility problem

In order to address the time inconsistency problem economists have proposed different solutions. The first models introduced the concept of reputation. These are generally institution-free models where independent central banks are not explicitly discussed. These models are based on the idea that policy is an on-going process. By acting systematically to keep inflation low, the government (or more generally, a public institution in charge of running monetary policy) can slowly acquire a reputation for a strong aversion to high inflation. In time, as price setters increasingly trust the authority, the economy can eliminate the inflationary bias. These models do not address directly the issue of independence, but make a similar point. A low inflation environment must be gained by acting to signal that there will be no deviation from a price stability policy.

Delegation is another solution to inflationary bias and it is more directly linked to central bank independence. The basic idea is that both the government and private agents can be better off by shifting their power to a third agent: a conservative central banker (see Rogoff 1985). 'Conservative', in this case, means that she has a distaste for inflation greater than society at large. This would eliminate the inflationary bias at once as price setters would know and trust that there would be no deviation from low inflation policy. Monetary authorities also need to address the issue of short-term output fluctuations. If the central banker is solely concerned with inflation, she might disregard the need for policies aimed at limiting output fluctuations. Such an attitude might not be desirable for society. In this sense, society's best bet would be to appoint a central banker who is tougher on inflation than society at large, but not solely concerned with inflation. In other words, the right degree of 'conservativeness' should be sought.

The delegation approach begs the question of how to find the right degree of anti-inflationary preference. The definition of 'conservative central banker' is also somewhat vague. An alternative approach is the following. The government could design a contract which offers a reward to the central banker when inflation reaches a level which is considered optimal (we refer to principal–agent models). The contract could be designed in order to limit the inflationary bias, but at the same time respond to the need for some flexibility. The relationship between the government and the New Zealand central bank is posed as an example of this kind of contract. The governor of the reserve bank agrees on a target inflation path with the government, with his job on the line if she fails to achieve the target. Still, it is difficult to think of real world institutions able to mimic the optimal contract. Even in the case of New Zealand there are several escape clauses in the no-inflation contract, and it is not obvious how the dismissal clause is applicable and when. At present, the main incentive is that the governor may not be re-appointed if the target is missed. The possibility of relating the bonus payments of senior central bank officials to the outcome relative to target, has also been suggested, but never implemented. Worries that this would evoke headlines such as 'Governor makes $500,000, for 500,000 out of work' being one of the motivations. (In general, central banks officials are reluctant to have their salaries tied to their own success in meeting targets, even though this would raise their average salaries. This might be because they are relatively risk averse or because they do not think it would enhance credibility.) Although these principal–agent models propose an interesting and witty solution, they seem difficult to implement in reality. Their validity also depends on how important one thinks political pressures might be.

Central bank independence in the real world

Policy goals

Generally central banks share a common goal: price stability (financial stability is inferred). Sometimes this is the sole monetary goal, sometimes the primary one, but it is normally not the only goal (for example, inflation and employment might be equally considered). In principle, having a sole policy goal seems to erode the flexibility of monetary policy: there is no room for discretion or stabilisation of cyclical fluctuations. According to some economists, this lack of flexibility is desirable, but to others, it is not. The paradox lies in the fact that sometimes both streams use similar arguments to advocate different policy goals.

Among the arguments against focusing solely on the price stability goal, there is the question of the real effects of monetary policy. Almost all authors agree on the neutrality of monetary policy in the long run and on its short-run effectiveness. The disagreement lies in the magnitude of these short-run effects and the role of monetary policy in an environment subject to unpredictable shocks. Economies have to deal with exogenous shocks which alter their original equilibrium and, in principle, monetary policy may be used for stabilisation purposes. If central banks are only concerned with maintaining price stability, they could eventually induce recessions or prolonged periods of weak economy activity. Subsuming financial stability to price stability may also become a dangerous practice, as exclusive focus on a numerical target may turn small and moderate financial problems into larger shocks.

In contrast to the above, it is also argued that too much scope for counter cyclical policy would make the central bank vulnerable to political pressures and would create expectations which could not be met. This is the reason why some authors do not favour an active role for monetary policy in countering cycles. In addition, monetary policy works with long and variable lags so that its ability to dampen economic cycles is, at least, dubious. Economists supporting this view think that only the price stability objective should be stated in a central bank's law. The (increasingly) popular inflation targeting approach also emphasises the need to restrict central bank flexibility in order to establish a low inflation policy. Castello-Branco and Swinburne (1991), note that central banks with greater formal independence tend to have a statutory macroeconomic objective with a relative narrow focus. This can be understood in terms of the desire to promote monetary policy credibility. Multiple or unclear statutory objectives are not likely to be consistent with this desire because they could reduce the transparency of monetary policy and the credibility gains associated with a greater accountability from both sides (central bank and government). Thus they suggest a single clearly defined statutory objective of price stability for an independent central bank's monetary policy. In our view, while it seems reasonable to design few but clear goals, it remains a fact that central banks are faced with a trade-off between growth and inflation. It seems therefore that too restrictive a goal – such as the idea that the bank should be solely concerned with price stability with complete disregard for the business cycle – is not desirable.

Most central banks do not normally focus only on price stability. The Federal Reserve in the US has a dual mandate of maximum employment and stable prices. The Bundesbank in Germany is directed to 'safeguarding the currency'. A recent trend in central banking is towards inflation targeting over a certain period of time, either as an operational procedure for implementing policy or as a formally mandated policy objective. Sometimes this has been implemented in the absence of any change in the legislation (e.g. Canada and United Kingdom), or, as in the often quoted case of New Zealand, combined with a greater central bank independence. The common practice consists of targeting an inflation range over the next year or two, or else a path of inflation (e.g. the Reserve Bank of Australia has a self-imposed 2–3 per cent inflation target over the course of the business cycle). The Bank of Italy has also started setting inflation targets as a self-imposed constraint.

A further issue is that governments in democracies are accountable to the electorate and as such they may be justified in feeling that they have the right to exert some influence over monetary policy. In this case, monetary contracts would have to establish a mechanism for adjudicating disagreements between the government and the central bank in a manner that preserves the long-run objectives of monetary policy. Letting the government play a role in setting short-run targets runs the risk of compromising long-run objectives; on the other hand, giving the central bank the same freedom might lead to an overly conservative central bank. One solution could be an emphasis on transparency and accountability, with the central bank judged on its ability to achieve its objectives and the objectives made public (Walsh 1995). Transparency and accountability are two themes which will be discussed more below. Finally, as the policy goals are sometimes vague (and leave more room *de facto* to the central bank than is officially written), the good performance of the central bank seems to depend not only on its formal mandate, but on a mixture of common sense, economic wisdom and social sensitivity.

Low inflation, at what cost?

Lowering inflation, generally, implies some costs in terms of lost output. In fact, in order to lower inflation, central banks undergo restrictive policies, via higher interest rates, which cause periods of lower growth. Literature on independent central banks works on the notion that more independence implies that banks become more credible inflation fighters and can therefore bring inflation down at lower social cost. The extreme version of the credibility hypothesis claims that rapid, costless disinflation is possible, if monetary policy announcements are completely credible. The basic idea is that inflation depends, in the main, on expected inflation and expected inflation can respond very quickly to the central bank's pronouncements as far as people believe them. In this argument, the credibility of announcements is the key issue. The paradox lies in the fact that, although from an empirical point of view there is not much support to the credibility hypothesis, central bankers and academics frequently refer to it.

In terms of empirical evidence, testing the effectiveness of central bank independence can take two forms. First, testing whether countries with more independent central banks have consistently experienced lower inflation rates, and second, whether credibility makes disinflation less costly. On the first issue, evidence points to some correlation between independence (measured on the basis of a number of qualitative criteria) and low inflation (see among others Grilli, Masciandaro and Tabellini 1991). However, the evidence is not entirely convincing and largely hinges on the inclusion of the 1970s and 1980s in the sample period. The independence ranking also appears to be somewhat arbitrary and there are studies which contradict the above results.

The second empirical issue is the 'credibility effect', i.e. whether independent central banks lower the cost (in terms of foregone output) of lowering the inflation rate (the so-called sacrifice ratio). Evidence does not generally support the credibility hypothesis, in fact there appears to be some evidence to the contrary. Independent central banks seem to pay higher costs when following anti-inflationary policies. In any case, empirical work with developed countries still finds a significant relationship between inflation and growth (Fischer 1993). Importantly, the statistical significance is stronger for inflation rates below 15 per cent than for those above it. In practice, low inflation countries appear to have a greater trade off between the short-run costs of lower output associated with the reduction of inflation, and the longer-run benefits of a lower inflation rate. From this point of view, fighting inflation might create a bigger recession in a country with already relatively low inflation rates. It is difficult to know what would be the growth effects of a reduction in inflation from a low rate to an even lower one (let us say from 3 to 1 or 0 per cent). There seems to be no good reason for setting inflation targets below 2 per cent. A little inflation may serve as a lubricant to the economic system and ruthless anti-inflationary policies could be very costly. Finally, note that the same argument suggests that the output costs of deflationary periods will be greater than the output gains during the inflationary periods, an argument in favour of trying to maintain a low inflation environment.

Can a central bank be really independent?

Central banks do not operate in isolation, but are placed within a specific political and economic setting. As such it is hard to expect them not to be influenced by their environment. In general, countries with independent central banks tend to show a higher aversion to inflation. The case of Germany is often quoted. The German experience of hyperinflation during the interwar period built a broad consensus in favour of price stability. One could argue that, as a consequence, the Bundesbank charter assigned its highest priority to safeguarding the currency among monetary policy objectives. The question which arises is whether what keeps control of inflation is the institution of an independent central bank or the fact that the bank operates in an environment which shares the goal of price stability. The idea is that an inflation-fighting central bank is not just an institutional arrangement, but the result of a particular history, a specific financial system and, in general, a low social tolerance towards inflation. This argument (see Posen 1995) suggests that it is not sufficient (or, in the extreme, it is almost irrelevant) to change the law and make a central bank independent if the goal of price stability does not receive a wide political consensus. In this sense, the emphasis of the last few years on central bank independence could largely be the result of a changing social sensitivity following the 1970s high inflation episodes and of a greater consciousness towards protecting savings against price erosion. This is also an argument which instils some doubts on the case for central bank independence in developing countries, if the institutional change is not accompanied by a convergence of policies (such as fiscal or wage policies) towards lower inflation.

A second practical issue regarding the independence of central banks concerns exchange rate policy. Exchange rate policy and monetary policy are interdependent. Normally, it is the task of the government to choose the exchange rate regime. In managed regimes, changes in parity are also usually decided by the government. However, central banks are responsible for executing exchange rate policy because the instruments needed are the same as the ones used in monetary policy. The setting of short-term interest rates is the main weapon used to achieve price stability, but it is also the main instrument available for influencing the exchange rate. This may be a source of conflict that puts the independence of the central bank at risk.

The problems arise in all regimes which impose limits on free currency fluctuations such as fixed, but adjustable, exchange rates or flexible exchange rates managed to a certain degree. For example, the adjustable pegged system normally evolves into a system with an anchor-country with partner-countries; as in the ERM where the deutsche mark represents the anchor. In the non-anchor countries, central banks largely lose control of monetary policy. They might also, at times, suffer speculative attacks on their currencies and be forced to take extreme defensive action (in 1992, the Swedish Riksbank increased short term rates to 500 per cent in an ill-fated attempt to defend the Krona). The anchor country may also experience problems. It could suffer outside political pressures from partner countries and it might be faced with an external/internal conflict if it is forced to intervene in the foreign exchange market. This undermines the feasibility of its domestic targets.

In the extreme, complete independence of the central bank's monetary policy would require that the government abandon any claim to formulating its own exchange rate policy, but no governments seem willing to do so, indeed, it may not even be desirable. Note that in practice, the scope for conflict is lower than we have shown. Generally, managed exchange rates are devised to reduce currency fluctuations and to limit depreciations, both of which are generally bad for inflation. Central banks therefore are often in favour of stricter exchange rate regimes even though they limit their freedom of action.

Finally, other practical reasons which might limit the central bank's freedom of action can be identified. The characteristics of the labour market (e.g. regulations on minimum wages, trade unions bargaining, or any change that might affect the demand for labour) or the tax system might influence the outcome of monetary policy. Perhaps more important is the interaction with fiscal policy. It is obvious that monetary policy will find it hard to achieve its objectives unless fiscal policy is reasonably consistent with them. It is a simple accounting fact that government expenditure has to be financed, either by taxation, by borrowing or by money creation. Variations in the stock of interest-bearing debt can provide a good deal of isolation of money growth from the size of the government deficit. Large and persistent deficits, however, might cause fears that the debt could become unsustainable and that the authorities might resort to exceptional measures such as debt monetisation, in turn causing inflation expectations and currency depreciation. Here again the interaction between fiscal authorities and independent central banks could weaken the link between independence and inflation control.

Democratic legitimacy and independent central banks

The independence of central banks poses a question of democratic legitimacy, because independence takes control of monetary policy away from elected politicians. An issue of democratic legitimacy might arise when the consequences of agents actions involves a 'social trade-off' (see for example Levy 1995). As described above, central banks perform a task which entails a social trade-off: the choice between long-term price stability and short-term employment fluctuations. The central bank action might not reflect what the general public wants. In addition to this, in the early stages of the process of independence, the central bank may forgo its stabilisation role, instead focusing on the need to build up its credibility. Moreover, economists do not fully understand the connections between business cycles and long-term growth performance (for example, European unemployment shows high persistence, a fact which suggests that restrictive macroeconomic policies might exacerbate it, see Chapter 7). For example, if one believes that short-term fluctuations in unemployment could persist over time, the choice between inflation and unemployment may gain a much greater political relevance. Another aspect of the controversy is that central bankers are often appointed by a board of directors who are rarely representatives elected by the general public; they represent the restricted interests of their sponsors. Levy (op. cit.), for example, notes: 'the twelve regional Federal reserve bank presidents ... are more representative of the banking system than of the American people.' A similar argument might actually be extended to the case of bankers nominated by politicians for fixed terms. Without taking position on this issue, it is interesting to note that the fact that central bankers should be seen as 'conservative' is key to their success in the theoretical models sketched above.

The issue of democratic legitimacy is ideological and beyond the scope of this analysis, though it is important and should not be swept aside without some consideration. First of all, there is a difference between 'goal independence' (the ability to set ones own objectives) and 'instrument independence' (the ability to chose the means by which a given objective is achieved). Most observers find the latter more acceptable. However, goals are necessarily vague and general, such as 'currency stability' for the Bundesbank or 'maximum employment' with 'stable prices' for the Federal Reserve. As a result, that distinction does not entirely address the objection. The most convincing answer which is given to questions of central bank legitimacy is accountability. For example, Alan Blinder, a former vice-chairman of the Federal Reserve, defines accountability in the following terms:

A central bank is a repository of enormous power over the economy. And if it is independent, this power is virtually unchecked. Such power is a public trust, assigned to the bank by the body politic. In return, the citizenry has a right to expect – if not demand – that the Bank's action match its words.

(Blinder 1995)

He offers qualified support to independence on the grounds that 'monetary policy, by its very nature, requires a long-term horizon . . . fighting inflation has the characteristic cost–benefit profile of a long-term investment: you pay the costs upfront and reap the benefits only gradually over time.'

Accountability generally means that the central bank is required to openly announce its targets and the means to achieve them. It is transparent in taking decisions and its performance is the subject of on-going scrutiny from the public, the press and elected politicians. The central bank might also be required to explain its action in public debates, for example in front of parliament. In the US, the Federal Reserve is required to report on monetary policy in the bi-annual Humphrey–Hawkins testimony and the chairman is called frequently to testify in front of congressional committees. Other countries show an increasing trend towards accountability, e.g. in Australia, any change in short-term rates is accompanied by a lengthy report explaining the reasoning behind the decision. Still, in practice, only relatively few central banks have the legal obligation to establish accountability or monitoring mechanisms. Surprisingly, accountability is a fairly new idea. It is interesting to recall that as recently as in 1994, the Federal Reserve did not announce its policy decisions with formal communiqués, but let the market guess their policy decisions via market operations. On the other hand, there are very few arguments against accountability. The most interesting is based on the observation that since only unanticipated inflation affects real variables, some ambiguity is needed to enable the monetary authority to influence real variables such as employment and output. On a similar line, one could argue that central bankers who are obliged to account for their action in front of parliament become either less independent or less effective (see Newmann 1992). The objections, however, seem pretty weak relative to the arguments in favour. It seems that a move towards greater accountability does not only address the issue of legitimacy, but is also likely to increase banks' credibility via a clearer assessment of targets and means. Finally, accountability is of increasing importance given an apparent failure of simple monetary policy rules, such as monetary targeting. This apparent failure has forced central banks to assume a more eclectic, and therefore more discretionary, approach to policy. This topic is addressed extensively in the following chapter.

Practical cases

Central bank independence is a long-established idea in many countries, but the appeal of independence has been almost irresistible since the mid 1980s, where a large number of both developed and developing countries moved to establish independent banks. Independent central banks have been the norm in two out of the three of the largest economies (the Bank of Japan has limited legal independence, but considerable *de facto* independence. Changes to its statute are being considered). In the US, the Federal Reserve enjoys independent status in that its decisions do not have to be ratified by the President or any other executive branches. On the other hand, as mentioned above, the Federal Reserve reports regularly to Congress, and all members of the Board which govern the Federal Reserve System (including the Chairman and Vice-Chairman) are appointed by the President with the consent of the Senate. Over the years, the Federal Reserve has established a reputation for substantial independence from government pressures. The Bundesbank is the independent central bank 'par excellence'. It was established in 1957 (under the Deutsche Bundesbank Act). The bank has the aforementioned goal of safeguarding currency stability. The act states that the Bundesbank is required to support the general economic policy of the Federal government, but leaves the bank independent in exercising its powers. Indeed, 'there is no provision for cases where differences of opinion may arise between the bank and the government – although there are general regulations which commit both sides to co-operation and mutual consultation' (Deutsche Bundesbank 1982). Note that the members of the governing body are of political appointment, though they must have special professional qualifications. The Directorate has eight members appointed by the Federal government for a fixed period. Importantly, they cannot be removed from office.

In the rest of Europe, the drive towards independence has been accelerated by the Maastricht Treaty and the process towards monetary union. The treaty makes central bank independence the major inspiring principle in the institution of the European System of Central Banks (ESCB) (the system of institutions which will run monetary policy in Europe after monetary union, see Chapter 2 and the appendix to Chapter 4, for more detail). Several articles refer to independence in terms of a prohibition to take instructions from (or to give overdraft facilities to) governments or other Community institutions (European Commission 1992, Articles 104 and 107). The treaty also states that 'the primary objective of the ESCB is to maintain price stability. Without prejudice to the objective of price stability, the ESCB shall support the general economic policies in the Community ...' (op. cit. Article 105.1). The treaty requires member countries to make domestic central banks comply with the rules set for the ESCB by the time it is established. As a result, in recent years many European countries have moved towards independence.

In 1993, both Belgium and France passed legislation making their banks independent. French legislation on central bank independence, similar to the Maastricht Treaty, emphasised price stability and political independence, prohibiting any form of instruction from the Government to the central bank. Credit to the government was also forbidden. In Italy, where the Bank of Italy already enjoyed a considerable degree of independence, a 1992 law gave it complete control over official interest rates and a 1993 law prohibited the extension of credit to the government (which was already strictly limited, by the so called 'divorce' law of 1981, between the Treasury and the Bank of Italy). Spain made similar provisions in 1994.

Until recently, the most notable exception to the trend towards central bank independence was the UK, where monetary policy was firmly under the control of the Chancellor of the Exchequer. Interestingly, however, even before the Bank of England was made independent, Britain had made steps to increase the autonomy of the central bank. For example, since 1992, the bank independently published a quarterly inflation report with forecasts on price developments, and since 1994, the minutes of the monthly monetary meetings between the Governor and the Chancellor have been made public after a short interval. On those occasions, the Bank of England Governor has frequently voiced disagreement with the Chancellor. In 1997, the newly elected Labour government made the bank operationally independent, though retaining control over the inflation target and the right to override decisions in exceptional circumstances. The Chancellor has told the monetary policy committee to pursue a target of 2.5 per cent underlying inflation (excluding mortgage interest payments). But the Governor of the Bank of England would be required to send the Chancellor an open letter if inflation was more than one percentage point larger or smaller than the target. This letter would have to explain: the reason why inflation had moved so far from the target, what policy actions the bank was taking to deal with the situation, the period within which inflation would be expected to be back on target, and how the bank's monetary policy objectives were being met. This system was met with some opposition, and was interpreted in some quarters as a loosening of the monetary regime. In practice however it adds another dose of accountability, given the vagaries of inflation targeting.

Two interesting cases are those of New Zealand and Argentina. In Argentina, the 1992 Convertibility Law introduced a currency board which committed the central bank to maintaining fixed exchange rates and back all bank reserves with foreign currency. In this case, the central bank lost all independence, with monetary policy entirely under the control of market forces (a more extensive discussion of currency boards is presented in Chapter 10). New Zealand's central bank law is often hailed as the one which better reflects the indications of academic work. The primary goal of the bank is – once again – to achieve price stability. However, the goal is not set by the bank, but by an agreement (the Policy Target Agreement) between the finance minister and the governor of the bank. The bank has complete freedom to take action towards reaching the objectives. The governor is accountable to the Minister of Finance and to parliament as a way of ensuring accountability. Moves towards central bank independence have also been made in many developing countries such as Chile and Mexico. Often greater independence has been promoted as part of IMF sponsored stabilisation plans (e.g. Honduras in 1995). Steps towards bank independence have also been taken in several transition countries in Eastern Europe.

Conclusion

Central bank independence has become a very popular topic among academics and policy makers, viewed as an important institutional arrangement to prevent the resurgence of inflation. Indeed, the move towards the independence of central banks is credited with having given an important contribution to the lower inflation environment of recent years. The underlying idea is that monetary policy is ineffective in improving economic performance in the long term. Instead, if used in an attempt to prop up short-term growth, it might result in a permanent increase in inflation. As a result, it is useful to take this control away from politicians who might be tempted to use monetary policy for short-term purposes. Monetary policy requires an ability to make long-term plans which, according to supporters of independence, are much better implemented by independent technocrats than by elected politicians. Indeed, some characterise independence as a free lunch: the simple announcement – if credible – that a central bank is being made independent should improve inflation in no time and at no cost. In reality, this is not entirely the case. The credibility of a central bank takes time to be established and the reduction of inflation still implies a cost in terms of lower output and higher unemployment. Moreover, an independent central bank is probably less willing than elected government ministers to take action to stabilise temporary output fluctuations. To what degree is this desirable? Finding a central banker with the right degree of conservativeness or shaping a central banker's contract in order to achieve the best outcome for society are appealing theoretical solutions, but difficult to implement in practice.

In contrast to the above, critics note that central bank independence is as much the result, as the cause of a public distaste for inflation. If the preference for price stability is strong, the central bank, the labour market, fiscal policy, tariff policy, etc. are likely to be shaped in order to reflect an anti-inflationary bias. In this sense, establishing an independent central bank in a country with a history of high inflation might be almost irrelevant if society at large does not adopt behaviour conducive to lower inflation. Another crucial argument is that an independent central bank is in contradiction with democracy. To counter this, most central bank laws contain provisions for accountability, for which actions taken by the central bank need to be explained and evaluated publicly. In practice, independent central banks have been established in a very large number of both industrial and developing countries. In industrial countries, a growing distaste for inflation has been accompanied by the increasing globalisation of financial markets. Bond and stock markets are very responsive to inflation expectations. Low credibility of monetary policy can cause large fluctuations in financial variables such as exchange rates or bond yields, which in turn might affect the real economy. An independent central bank, with strong credibility, provides 'fortification' against large market fluctuations. In developing countries, things are more complicated. Firstly, legal independence does not always correspond to real independence, particularly when political pressures on central bankers are strong. Also, it is doubtful whether central bank independence is effective if it is not accompanied by broader policies conducive to lower inflation. Still, in some cases, independence could represent a first step towards greater financial discipline, particularly against a government's financial profligacy. Overall, the independence of central banks is not a cure-all or a magician's wand against inflation. It is, however, an important complement to a policy orientated to price stability. In this sense, it seems an unstoppable trend.

6

CENTRAL BANKS GET ECLECTIC

The fine art of setting interest rates

> Given the greatly diminished importance of the monetary
> aggregates in the policy process, a major policy challenge cur-
> rently confronting the FOMC [Federal Open Market
> Committee] is to guarantee that short-term decisions designed
> to address cyclical concerns are consistent with the long-run
> low inflation objective.
>
> (Gary H. Stern, President of the Federal Reserve of
> Minneapolis, 1996)

Introduction

The fall from grace of monetary targets as the anchor of monetary policy has
opened a whole new debate on how central banks should conduct themselves. Central banks have to combine their prime objective of maintaining
stable prices in the long term with the need to respond, in the short term, to
cyclical fluctuations. Below we argue that central banks have progressively
moved to view monetary policy as a more complex game, where they have to
use greater flexibility in interpreting facts and figures and have to take
greater account of the behaviour of other subjects, such as markets, governments, and wage and price setters. This implies that central banks have to use
greater discretion and are subject to a greater risk. An issue of accountability
and transparency of their behaviour also emerges. Below, we describe how
this change has come about, how it has affected the main central banks and
what options are now left to them. We conclude that acknowledging this
change is necessary to read how central banks have reacted to varying external conditions.

Central banking, monetary targeting and
the Bundesbank

Monetary targeting has been very popular with academics for some time,
though it appears to have gone out of fashion recently. The monetarist rationale behind money targeting is that if the money stock grows faster than GDP,
the price level will soar accordingly. Also, setting a binding rule seemed a

good way to avoid 'discretion', with the dual benefit of avoiding the temptation of trying to engineer higher than potential growth, thus fuelling inflation, and of being an effective way to shield monetary policy from political
interference, thus protecting central bank independence.

In a 1995 report, the Bundesbank presented a discussion of the monetary
targets for 1995 and stated that:

> The Bundesbank is thus abiding by its tried and tested strategy of
> monetary targeting, and underlines that, despite the disruptive influ-
> ences of the past few years, it still regards the money stock M3 as
> the key reference variable for its monetary policy.
>
> (Deutsche Bundesbank 1995: 23)

Such a clear restatement of the Bundesbank reliance on monetary targeting
represented a divergence with the prevailing central banking opinion in most
other industrial countries and, particularly, in Anglo-Saxon ones. The
Bundesbank also affirmed that the recent, poor, performance of M3 (a measure of money supply) as a predictor of nominal growth was due to special
factors unlikely to reappear regularly in the future. Since the beginning of
1995, however, ten-month volatility has increased about four-fold.

A second wave of M3 overshooting occurred in early 1996 further under-
mining the reliability of monetary indicators. The Bundesbank itself, while
still mentioning M3 as a key policy variable, seems to have widened its
view. It cited several one-off distorting factors in 1996 justifying high M3
growth. These included a temporary shifting out of long-term bonds as
domestic non-banks avoided investing in longer-term assets. As financial
markets become more international, money supply is becoming increasingly subject to the vagaries of foreign bond markets. It seems likely that
such distortions will reappear time and time again. The Bundesbank seems
to have gone pretty far down the road to ignoring M3 completely, cutting
the discount rate in April 1996, when M3 stood over 12 per cent against the
target corridor of 4–7 per cent. Notable in this respect is the Bundesbank
council member Krupp's statement that 'the former relationship between
money supply and price developments is no longer recognisable' (Reuters
April 1996).

Fall from grace

There are two main reasons why money targeting has gone out of favour: the
relation between nominal GDP growth and money growth has become much
less stable in recent years as money's velocity of circulation has decreased
significantly, but has become a lot more volatile; and different definitions of
money supply have tended to show diverging behaviours, thus making it difficult to define which one should more appropriately be used for monetary

targeting. Mussa (1994) for example cites several instances in the 1980s in which monetary aggregates have given divergent indications of the stance of monetary policy. For example, in 1985–6 in the US M2 was growing roughly in line with the previous few years, while M1 was growing at an extremely fast pace.

In Germany, in the last ten years, the slightly wider definition of 'M3 extended' grew at a much higher annual rate than the narrow M3, with the gap, at times, as wide as 3 per cent. The main factors blamed for the observed instability of the relation between nominal growth and money are financial innovation and restructuring, the acceleration and increasing flexibility in capital flows and the fact that demand for hard currencies might be subject to sharp changes with no immediate rationale in economic fundamentals. An increasing degree of currency substitution has, in fact, contributed to increasing non-transactional demand for foreign currency (the IMF (1995–7) cites studies which argue that two-thirds of the US currency is circulating outside the US. A smaller, though fast rising, level is likely for Germany). Michael Mussa concludes his discussion of monetary policy during the 1980s, arguing that

> there is no unique quantitative guide to monetary policy which best serves the generally agreed, and intrinsically related objectives of promoting maximum sustainable growth and assuring reasonable price stability. Instead, the central bank needs to examine a variety of indicators of the current and prospective economic performance and to assess several measures of the stance of its own monetary policy.
>
> (Mussa 1994, p. 138)

The Federal Reserve and others

After adhering strictly to monetary targeting during the persistent inflation of the early 1980s, the Federal Reserve has taken a more discretionary attitude. B. Friedman writes

> In 1987 the Federal Reserve gave up setting a target for the narrow money stock but continued to do so for broader measures of money. In 1993 the Federal Reserve publicly acknowledged that it had 'downgraded' even its broad money target – a change that most observers of US monetary policy had already noticed long before.
>
> (Federal Reserve 1995)

Similar shifts in strategy have occurred in the UK, where monetary targeting was first, rather briefly, substituted by currency pegging in the EMS and then by the current inflation target. Inflation targets are the rule also in Sweden, Canada and New Zealand. Clearly, considering the generally recognised fact that bringing inflation down implies high output costs, the central bank's job must be the one of anticipating any tendency to increasing inflationary pressures, before these actually appear in the economy. Central banks should therefore concentrate on a broad range of indicators, from leading indicators of inflation, such as capacity usage, labour market slack, wage dynamics, to financial indicators, such as interest rate expectations, the yield curve and, where indications are available, expected inflation. A consequence of the more eclectic attitude to central banking is that it leaves central banks more open to political scrutiny. However, central bank independence is, by now, a fairly universally recognised principle. Moreover, market scrutiny tends to punish governments which interfere with central bank decisions with currency weakness or high long rates, therefore making governments more cautious over taking confrontational attitudes.

The Bundesbank

Up until quite recently, the Bundesbank referred to a number of both internal and external studies according to which the relation between the money stock and nominal GDP growth is still remarkably stable in Germany. As an example, the OECD estimates a money demand function and finds that the relation held until then. They include a structural change variable due to unification (OECD 1994). The Bundesbank argues that while changes in velocity – estimated at roughly 1 per cent a year in their calculation – remain reasonably steady, M3 has been distorted by special factors which do not hinder the long-term relationship.

The special factors can be broadly summarised in two categories:

1   Tax distortions. Changes in taxation might cause one-off changes in demand for money or cause temporary liquidity logjams. Two of the special factors which have contributed to the fast growth of M3 since the end of 1993 fall into this category. Tax changes have caused a large repatriation of funds from Luxembourg which have boosted domestic liquidity. Also anticipated changes in residential taxes had caused a sharp boost in lending to individuals which also temporarily boosted liquidity holdings. These tax related factors should not jeopardise the long-term money/GDP relation as they are relatively rare and their effect is, generally, predictable

2   Financial market related factors. In the recent case of M3 overshooting, other reasons were blamed: uncertainty over interest rates development have caused investors to shift funds down the yield curve towards shorter maturities thus reducing monetary capital formation. In fact, contrary to conventional wisdom for the control of excess supply of money, at times, the Bundesbank seems to adopt the strategy of reducing rates to convince investors to increase the maturity of their funds

Strong growth in short-term savings deposits was also a factor from 1996, as many different kinds of savings deposits become more common. These deposits cannot wholly be regarded as 'money', even though they are a component of M3. The distinction is problematic, as short-term savings deposits both act as a way to hold 'money' or cash, and as a way to build up assets/savings, and therefore can over-inflate the money supply numbers. Other M3 boosting factors have been, at different times, the increase in demand for DM for speculative reasons and the heavy foreign exchange intervention following the ERM crisis. These reasons seem to argue that the money–growth relationship has indeed become more unstable due to financial innovation and increased currency substitution.

Identifying distortions

The key question to assess, in order to establish if the Bundesbank can continue to use monetary targeting to design interest rate policy, is whether it is possible to identify special distortionary factors *ex-ante*. From past experience, identifying special factors means looking at monetary developments within a broader framework, i.e. taking account of recent financial market developments, of investors expectations, the yield curve, the international environment, the real economy etc. After all, one could argue that this does not differ significantly from the 'discretionary attitude' used by other countries. In both cases, engineering interest rate policy does not follow an automatic and binding rule, but uses discretion in interpreting a broad range of elements. In this environment, Krupp talked of an 'increasingly problematic indicator function for M3 in practical monetary policy'. He added: 'It is true that the Bundesbank has never understood money supply as a monthly indicator but the distortions have now been occurring for a longer period of time' (Reuters April 1996). With the Bundesbank, acknowledging the difficulties, German M3 seems to have lost its appeal as the main leading indicator of Bundesbank policy shifts.

Current options

With the fall from grace of direct monetary targeting, central banks are left with three options, all of which imply a greater discretion in the running of monetary policy. These are: long-term monetary targeting, direct inflation targeting, and interest rate targeting.

Long-term monetary targeting

This is largely based on the rationale described above for the Bundesbank, i.e. that the long-term link between prices and money is still the safest way of predicting inflation and that targeting intermediate indicators remains the most efficient strategy. Naturally, this view needs to become more pragmatic in taking into account the high variance in money growth indicators. In this sense it does not differ enormously from inflation targeting. Indeed, in the presence of low inflation, the Bundesbank has dismissed M3 as distorted several times in the latest rate cycle as showed by Figure 6.1.

Inflation targeting

This can be achieved both by targeting inflation for a particular period of time or by setting intermediate targets for a longer time span. The rationale is that lack of intermediate measures able to be both good predictors of infla-tion and which can be manipulated by the central bank, suggests that target-ing inflation directly is the best option. As noted above, it certainly seems to be very popular at the moment. Naturally it contains a number of problems. Targeting current inflation contains two risks. Generally, inflation results from higher than potential growth and tends to follow high levels of capacity usage, tight labour markets and high wage settlements, production bottle-necks, etc. Once inflation shows in the numbers, the process might have started and might be difficult to stop. Monetary policy acts with a lag – up to six months in the US – which is both long and variable. Central banks have to take action with that in mind. As a result, inflation targeting has to be car-ried out based on a forward-looking view of inflation, rather than on current performance. In the UK, for example, where the central bank's lack of inde-pendence (until 1997) made credibility a particular important concern, the Bank of England published an inflation report, where a wide range of indi-cators was analysed. The Bank of England became operationally independ-

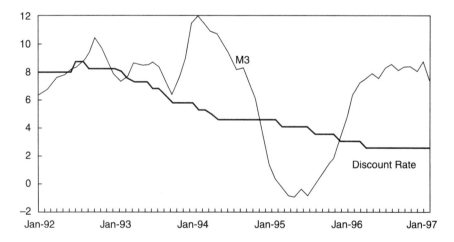

Figure 6.1 German M3 and the discount rate
Source: Deutsche Bundesbank Monthly Reports 1996

ent only in 1997, one of the first steps taken by the new Labour government. Before then, the report was both a good way to assess inflationary progress and risks and to increase accountability. In fact, transparency and accountability become more important issues as most central banks – independent, but depositories of large power on the economy – need to use greater discretion in their action.

Interest rate targeting

Another way of conducting monetary policy might be based on targeting short-term interest rates. In general, targeting real interest rates is preferable. However, this poses a question of implementation as there is no agreement on how real interest rates are calculated or on whether they can be controlled. For countries of smaller proportions, an external anchor, generally in the form of exchange rate pegging, is a fairly widespread option. It has proven successful in many cases, though its sustainability is dependent also on the consistency of domestic economic policies.

In search of rules: recent proposals

The search for rules has not been abandoned following the failure of monetary targeting, but a number of new rules have been devised which try to encompass a broader number of indicators. According to their authors, these rules have a very satisfactory explanatory power for past history and can therefore be a good rule for the future. The most popular is the Taylor rule, under the name of its proponent in 1993 (see *The Economist* 1996). Taylor suggests that monetary policy should be the sum of four elements. Firstly, short-term interest rates, which are neutral relative to economic growth. Secondly, the expected inflation rate. This is often inferred from financial market variables, such as the shape of the yield curve, or in some cases, from bonds indexed to the consumer price level. Surveys or other indicators are also used. The central bank should then follow a rule for which interest rates are increased (decreased) by about 0.5 per cent for every percentage point by which expected inflation is above (below) the central bank target. Finally, some adjustment should be made for the output gap, i.e. the difference between GDP and its long-term trend. GDP above its long-term trend implies that growth is exceeding what is its potential rate. Growth above potential could put pressure on resources, in terms of utilised capacity or unemployment, and signal that future inflation is in the pipeline.

The Taylor rule is appealing in that it is fairly comprehensive. On the other hand, it contains a number of flaws. Firstly, there are many ways to calculate expected inflation, or the neutral interest rate. Secondly, estimates of the output gap can vary significantly and are based on assumptions which are not always realistic. Finally, even if one chooses to adhere strictly to the Taylor rule, this does not provide a single level at which interest rates should be set. A fairly wide range would result depending on how the variables above are calculated. The Taylor rule has been found to explain with reasonable accuracy how central banks have run monetary policies in the past. Even in the case of the Bundesbank, which has long been following a policy of monetary targeting, policy fits a pattern described by the Taylor rule quite closely.

On the other hand, the rule begs the question of why the central bank should limit itself to using a limited number of indicators, even if those are among the most important. There are a much great number of indicators that the central bank can use, for example, to measure inflationary bottlenecks, wage pressure or whether policy is expansionary or contractionary. Such indicators are often contradictory or, at times, flawed by special factors. Another popular rule is the McCallum rule based on targeting narrow money (M0) with some amendments. This rule, however, does not appear to differ too profoundly from the monetary rules mentioned above (the Taylor and McCallum rules are discussed, from a practitioner's point of view, in Dicks 1996). It seems that the best way of following the Taylor rule is to adopt an eclectic attitude to monetary policy, concentrating on a broad number of indicators.

Three interesting cases: UK, Italy and EMU

UK: the Chancellor and the Bank of England

In spite of the increasing trend towards independent central banks, the Bank of England remained under the control of the Chancellor of the Exchequer until 1997. Perhaps partly as a result of that, consumer price inflation in the UK had been historically more volatile than other EU and OECD countries. The more cyclical nature of UK inflation could in part be explained by a political business cycle, though on average inflation levels did not seem to be much higher than in the rest of Europe.

In 1979 a Conservative government was elected with a pledge of monetary control, in the form of a target for M3, as the centrepiece of its counter-inflation policy. In the March 1980 budget the Chancellor (HMSO 1980) unveiled the Medium Term Financial Strategy (MTFS) which set objectives targets for M3 over the next four years and which placed other variables as secondary:

> The Government has announced its firm commitment to a progressive reduction in money supply growth. Public expenditure plans and tax policies and interest rates will be adjusted as necessary in order to achieve the objective [p. 16] . . . there would be no question of departing from the money supply policy, which is essential to the success of any anti-inflationary strategy [p. 19].
>
> (HMSO 1980)

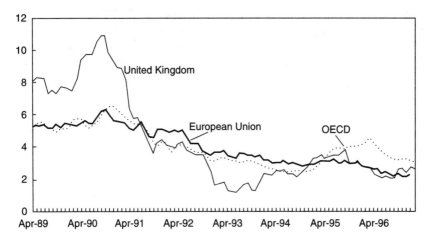

Figure 6.2 UK inflation in comparison with OECD and EU averages
Source: OECD Statistics 1989–96

M3 was already running well above its target in the first year of the MTFS. In the UK, shifts in the velocity of money seemed to be the main problem, and were simultaneous with the start of the MTFS. From 1979, velocity began to decline rapidly, i.e. M3 rose faster than nominal incomes. Target ranges, however, were set on the assumption that the previous trend in velocity would resume. By 1982, it was increasingly clear that this was not going to occur. The statistical relationships that had existed between M3 and nominal incomes could no longer be relied upon. By 1985 the government effectively stopped targeting M3. After a brief attempt by Chancellor Lawson to shadow the DM, policy resorted to assessing a wide range of economic indicators (including the exchange rate). In October 1990, the UK joined the wider ERM band (+/−6 per cent) with the intention of signalling its commitment to maintain price stability.

In September 1992, the UK came out of the ERM and monetary policy continued with the introduction of a new framework, adopting an explicit inflation target for the first time in the UK. The initial target was a 1–4 per cent range over 1992–7, with the intention of a 1 to 2.5 per cent target by the end of that period. The primary 'target' however is the assessment of future inflation. This was supported by surveys of private forecasters collected by the Treasury. Monetary targets have taken a back seat, though 'monitoring ranges' for M0 and M4 are used (0–4 per cent and 3–9 per cent respectively). In addition, the Chancellor followed exchange rate and asset price developments. An important development for the transparency of Bank of England actions was the publication of a quarterly report on inflationary developments and prospects in comparison to the government's 2.5 per cent target. As in the US, the minutes of monetary meetings are also published after a delay of six weeks.

In 1997, when the new Chancellor, Gordon Brown, gave the Bank of England operational independence, he set up a new Monetary Policy Committee, to act on the basis of a majority vote. This would include four 'expert' members from outside the Bank of England. Openness about decision making was to be ensured by the continuation of publication of minutes of proceedings (after six weeks), which would now also include the votes of the Committee. The requirements for the Bank of England to report to the Treasury Select Committee of the House of Commons were to be enhanced, with the Court of the Bank of England also to review the performance of the Committee as well as that of the bank generally. The Court itself was to be reformed to make it more representative of the UK, particularly its industrial and business sectors. The government would retain the right to override the operational independence of the bank in extreme economic circumstances, for a limited period only and subject to ratification by the House of Commons.

The Bank of Italy

The Director General of the Bank of Italy, Padoa-Schioppa, noted that:

> Italy has adhered for over thirteen years to the European exchange rate agreement . . . in that experience the reference to the exchange rate has been the essential support in the search and defence of monetary stability . . . in the meantime, the central bank has always indicated that – without coherent action on the domestic front – in the income policy and Budget adjustment – the exchange rate position could not have been maintained indefinitely
>
> (Padoa-Schioppa 1995)

The statement summarises the Bank of Italy's attitude before the 1992 lira exit from the ERM. Since then, the Bank of Italy has first, it seems, followed a policy of monetary co-ordination with the rest of Europe. This was changed, quite explicitly, with an announcement of inflation targeting. In the 1995 'Final Considerations' the Bank of Italy Governor stated that 'the average annual rate of inflation of consumer prices – net of indirect taxes – will have to be below 4.5 per cent. It will have to fall below 4 per cent in the following year'. Among the indicators selected by the Bank of Italy are: trend inflation (measured by data such as three month annualised average inflation), and inflation expectations (as measured by various surveys and for longer-term expectations, long-term bond and swap yield spreads between Italy and other countries). In its early stages, the main characteristic of the Bank of Italy's version of inflation targeting was targeting current, rather than future, inflation rates. The bank tended to change rates almost exclusively in response to inflation reaching its targets, in an attempt to reduce the difference in inflation between Italy and other European countries. There is a risk however, that if the specified level of inflation is not reached, the Bank of Italy may be faced with a dilemma. Cyclical weakness could justify rate easing, but inflation may not be entirely satisfactory. In November 1996, the lira returned to the ERM in its new form with 15 per cent wider bands. The Bank of Italy has reiterated that the inflation target remains the top priority. The need to respond to lira fluctuations will, however, represent a constraint to its freedom of action.

The European Central Bank

The characteristics of the European Central Bank (ECB) will be an important issue in the run up to monetary union. The Maastricht Treaty (article 105 on Monetary Policy) says that 'the primary objective of the ESCB (European System of Central Banks) shall be to maintain price stability. Without prejudice to the objective of price stability, the ESCB shall support the general economic policies in the Community.' The latter establishes – among other objectives – the promotion of 'harmonious and balanced development of economic activity and of sustainable and non-inflationary growth'. The objectives are not far from those established by the Bundesbank where the primary objective of the central bank is to promote monetary stability, though within the framework of the general economic policy of the Federal government. Note that, for the Bundesbank, there is a further caveat: that the government policy is not in insoluble conflict with the targets of monetary policy. Also, the Bundesbank is in charge of currency stability. This direct reference is not present in the Maastricht Treaty. Nevertheless, the emphasis on price stability and on the federal structure of the ECB are a direct reference to the Bundesbank structure – and so is the clear reference to independence – in the hope that the ECB will be able to inherit the Bundesbank anti-inflation credibility and the considerable success in obtaining currency stability. The debate is still open on what the ECB will be like, but an eclectic attitude, with an eye to monetary growth, is to be expected. These indications were confirmed by the Bundesbank's Chief Economist, Issing, who stated that the ESCB will have to look at monetary developments in conjunction with a number of other objectives (reported by Reuters October 1996).

The make up of the ESCB

The final decision on how the European Central Bank will conduct policy will remain in the hands of its Governing Council, which will comprise of the ECB's Executive Board and Governors of participating countries' central banks. The Executive Board will comprise a President, a Vice-President and four other members. The members of this Board will be appointed from among persons of recognised standing and experience in monetary or banking matters by a common accord of the governments of the Member States on a recommendation from the European Council after it has consulted with the European Parliament and the Governing Council. The General Council will consist of representatives of all fifteen EU countries, and not just EMU countries. Though the ECB is the central policy making body, the system of member-state central banks which will obviously work closely with the ECB, and which will conduct day-to-day operations, is the ESCB. The Maastricht Treaty states 'The ESCB shall be composed of the ECB and of the national central banks ... the ESCB shall be governed by the decision-making bodies of the ECB which shall be the Governing Council and the Executive Board' (Article 106). 'The national central banks are an integral part of the ESCB and shall act in accordance with the guidelines and instructions of the ECB.' (Chapter III, Article 14.3).

The Councils of the ECB

The General Council:

Central bank governors from all fifteen EU countries

The Governing Council:

The Executive Board (President, Vice President and four other members)

+

Central bank governors from participating EMU countries

How will monetary policy decisions be made?

Only the members of the Governing Council will have a vote in setting monetary policy with each member allocated one vote. Decisions will be taken by a simple majority, and in the event of a tie, the President will hold the casting vote. The Governing Council will meet a minimum of ten times a year but the proceedings of the meeting are to remain confidential. This could have repercussions for the transparency of ECB policy, especially if target indicators are unknown, and given the uncertainty which will surround the new central banking system. On certain matters, such as capital requirements and foreign exchange reserves, the Executive Board will not be allowed to vote and central bank governors will cast weighted votes according to the national banks' shares in the subscribed capital of the ECB and on a qualified majority basis.

Although the ECB Governing Council will decide the precise formulation of monetary policy, it will be left to the national central banks to conduct day-to-day operations. The operational framework will also allow national central banks to manage the liquidity of the interbank market and contribute to the smooth running of the payments system. The money markets will be unified throughout the euro area by the TARGET system. The main instrument of the national central banks will be open market operations, used to steer interest rates and influence liquidity (for more details see the appendix to this chapter: the operational framework of the single currency).

Conclusion

Central banks have become more eclectic. First the Federal Reserve and other Anglo-Saxon central banks progressively moved away from strictly targeting the growth of monetary aggregates; then other European central banks, including the Bundesbank, have shifted away from monetary targeting as internationalisation and financial innovation have made them less reliable indicators. Now central banks need to be more eclectic, looking at a wider number of indicators and at the response to their actions by other agents such as governments and markets. The search for a new, systematic way for conducting monetary policy continues, though the recent trend seems to be a direct targeting of the ultimate goal – inflation – with an attitude which requires a more pro-active style.

APPENDIX: THE OPERATIONAL FRAMEWORK OF THE SINGLE CURRENCY

The ECB will be set up in 1998, after the meeting in early 1998 which will decide which countries will be participating in the first wave of EMU. The framework, prepared by the EMI, will then be submitted to the ECB for decision. In the remainder of 1998, the ESCB will prepare for its full operation. January 1997 saw the release of the European Monetary Institute's (EMI) framework plans for the operations of the new European System of Central Banks. The EMI is the fore-runner of the European Central Bank, which will come into existence in the first half of 1998. The document entitled 'The Single Monetary Policy in Stage Three – Specification of the operational framework' (EMI 1997) contains the guidelines for monetary policy strategies as well as for monetary policy instruments and procedures. Arrangements for foreign exchange intervention and ERM II are also detailed. Here we outline the main points in this important document. Though not all the details have been decided upon, the documents give us a clearer picture for the monetary arrangements for the single currency. All quotations come from the EMI document itself, unless otherwise stated.

The EMI's guiding principles for monetary policy strategies

Of the guiding principles mentioned in the EMI paper, the most interesting are:

1   *Accountability*: involving the composition and communication of targets 'so that the ESCB's actions can be held accountable to the public'
2   *Transparency*: 'The process of setting targets and making decision on the basis of the strategy must be clear to the public'
3   *Medium term orientation*: 'providing an anchor for inflation expectations, but nevertheless providing the ESCB with some discretion in response to short-term deviations from the target'

Other guiding principles include: effectiveness, continuity (with the experience of NCBs), and consistency with the independent standing of the ESCB specified by the Maastricht Treaty.

The possible monetary policy strategies of the ECB

1   Exchange rate targeting
2   Interest rate pegging
3   Nominal income targeting
4   Monetary targeting
5   Direct inflation targeting

The EMI dismiss the first three possibilities fairly rapidly: exchange rate targeting is not considered suitable due to the potential size of the euro-area and the consequent possibility of endangering internal price stability. Interest rate pegging is also thought to be inappropriate by the EMI, given difficulties in identifying the equilibrium real interest rate that accords with price stability. A nominal income target could provide a clear framework for targeting, and could be consistent with price stability but the paper states that it would be difficult to control by the ESCB, which could lead to some misinterpretation of the price stability goal. Data could be problematic, given the number of revisions which occur.

The EMI states that the crucial factor distinguishing the other two strategies is the part played by monetary aggregates. Though no real decision has been reached yet, the EMI document states that:

> a particular strength of the monetary targeting strategy is that it clearly indicates the responsibility of the ESCB for developments which are both easily observable and under its more direct control and, therefore can be interpreted by the public in a transparent manner.

(EMI 1997)

The EMI also admits that the long-term stability of money demand has to be assured in order to ensure effective monetary targeting: 'stability of money demand is important to guarantee that the ESCB's actions can confidently be interpreted by the public as following a consistent scheme, thus ensuring that the strategy provides a clear anchor for inflation expectations.' The new environment of an EMU may make money supply targeting subject to further vagaries, though the EMI states that empirical studies still show that money demand in the euro area has the 'desirable properties' to be used as a target indicator. The potential volatility of M3 understandably concerns the EMI, and they state that this, if it occurred in Stage III, could seriously damage the credibility of the ESCB under a monetary targeting strategy.

The advantage of an inflation targeting system, as identified by the EMI, is that 'it directly stresses the responsibility of the ESCB for achieving and maintaining price stability. Furthermore, policy actions under such a strategy can be consistently and directly linked to prospective price behaviour, which if the strategy is credible, will affect public expectations in a favourable way.' In the EcoFin meeting of 27 January 1997, Alexandre Lamfalussy, president of the EMI stated that there was a 'basic agreement' that stability of the future EMU meant 'inflation of 2 per cent or less'.

The disadvantages of an inflation targeting system are similar to those of a monetary targeting system in that 'to be successful inflation targeting also required stable relationships between various economic and financial indicators, on the one hand, and future inflation, on the other'.

Key elements of a monetary policy strategy in stage III

The EMI suggest that the following five key elements should be an essential part of the strategy adopted by the ESCB:

1   'The public announcement of a quantified definition of the final objective of price stability'
2   'The public announcement of a specific target (or targets) against which the performance of the ESCB can be assessed on an ongoing basis by the general public'
3   'The use of all available information relevant to the final target of monetary policy', i.e. the monetary strategy should be based on a broad set of indicators, which should all be considered. These should include 'financial variables (in particular the money market yield curve, money and credit aggregates, credit market conditions, bond yields, exchange rates and other asset prices) and various non-financial variables (such as price and cost variables, indicators of aggregate demand and supply conditions including the output gap, the balance of payments and expectations surveys)'

4   If money demand is sufficiently stable in the long run, monetary aggre-
     gates should be assigned a principal role within the set of indicators
     studied by the ESCB, with targets/ranges set for their growth. In this
     way, monetary strategy will use many different variables though with a
     higher weight for monetary aggregates
5   'The ESCB should be in a position to make its own forecasts for infla-
     tion and other economic variables'

Thus the ESCB should have a framework whereby whatever final choice is
made on the actual targeting system, that other variables should also be followed, as important but supplementary elements. This is an approach which
we would encourage, as we have cited the problems of money supply and
inflation targeting in this chapter.

The communication strategy of the ESCB: The EMI state that the communication strategy of the ESCB should involve the following elements:

• The publications of its target(s) and details of their derivation
• The regular publication of data and analyses relevant to monetary policy
• The explanation of deviations from target and of policy
  responses by the ECB

(EMI 1997)

The ESCB's monetary policy instruments and procedures

Open market operations

The ESCB will use open market operations to steer interest rates, manage
liquidity and signal the monetary policy stance. It will use five main types of
instruments, particularly reverse transactions, but also outright transactions,
debt certificate issues, forex swaps and the collection of fixed-term deposits.
These procedures would be used by the ESCB to carry out the following four
types of monetary policy operations.

Monetary Policy Operations

Main refinancing operations   Regular liquidity providing reverse transactions every week, with a maturity of two weeks. These will be executed by
NCBs, with standard tenders. These will be used to provide most refinancing
to the financial sector.

Longer-term refinancing operations   These will represent a limited part of
the global refinancing volume, and will be carried out by liquidity providing
reverse transactions every month, with a maturity of three months. The ECB
would not use these to intentionally signal to the market.

Fine tuning operations These may also be carried out by the ECB, on an *ad hoc* basis, to control the liquidity situation and to steer interest rates; in particular to smooth the interest rate effects of unexpected liquidity fluctuations. Fine-tuning operations will mainly be carried out as reverse transactions, but may also be outright transactions, foreign exchange swaps and the collection of fixed-term deposits. Fine-tuning operations will normally be accomplished by NCBs through quick tenders or bilateral procedures. The ECB Governing Council will decide if, under exceptional circumstances, fine-tuning operations may be performed in a centralised or decentralised manner by the ECB.

By issuing debt certificates, the ECB will also be able to affect the structural liquidity position of the banking sector with regards to the ESCB by issuing debt certificates, using reverse transactions and conducting outright transactions. Reverse transactions operations and the issuance of debt will be executed according to standard tenders. Clearing and settlement of those instruments will be performed by NCBs on a decentralised basis. Outright transactions will be carried out through bilateral procedures.

Standing Facilities These aim to provide and assimilate overnight liquidity, so signalling the prevailing stance of monetary policy. Two standing facilities will be available to the ESCB's eligible counterparties:

1   The marginal lending facility: permitting counterparties to procure overnight liquidity from the NCBs at a pre-specified interest rate against eligible assets. There will usually be no credit limits or other restrictions to access. In typical circumstances, the interest rate on the marginal lending facility will provide an upper bound for the overnight market interest rate
2   The deposit facility: allowing counterparties to make overnight deposits at a pre-specified interest rate with the NCBs. There will usually be no limits on the corresponding deposit accounts or other restrictions to counterparties access to it. In typical circumstances, the interest rate on the deposit facility will provide a floor for the overnight market interest rate. The terms and conditions of both facilities will be set by the ECB and will be identical throughout the euro area

Minimum reserves

The ECB may require credit institutions to hold minimum reserves on accounts with the NCBs within the framework of the ESCB. These minimum reserves available to the ESCB could be used for stabilising money market interest rates, producing or expanding a structural liquidity shortage and possibly aiding the control of monetary expansion. To help to stabilise money market rates, the ESCB's minimum reserve system will include an averaging mechanism, implying that compliance with reserve requirements would be determined on the basis of an institution's average daily reserve holdings over a one month maintenance period. No carrying over of reserve shortfalls or surpluses to the next maintenance period would be allowed. The legal framework for the ESCB minimum reserve system will be laid down in Community legislation at a future date, the ECB will need to submit a recommendation to the EU Council to this effect following its establishment.

Size   The size of minimum reserves held by each institution would be determined in relation to the liability positions of its balance sheet.

Application   Should the ECB decide to have a minimum reserve system, all appropriate institutions established in the euro area would be legally subject to it. This implies that branches in the euro area of institutions with no registered office in the euro area would also be subject to the system. For institutions with establishments in more than one Member State, each establishment would be required to hold minimum reserves on reserve accounts with the NCB in the relevant Member State in relation to its liability position. The ECB may need to impose reserve ratios on a extensive range of liabilities and institutions. There may be a uniform reserve ratio for the whole reserve base or differentiated reserve ratios across categories and maturities of eligible liabilities.

Foreign exchange intervention by the ESCB

From the start of Stage III, the ESCB will be able to conduct foreign exchange intervention. Such operations might be done to influence exchange rate movements between the euro and other currencies. The ESCB will conduct forex intervention by means of transactions on the foreign reserves transferred from the NCBs to the ECB. Article 30 of the Statute of the ESCB detailed the conditions under which NCBs in the euro area shall provide the ECB with foreign reserve assets, up to an amount equivalent to 50 billion euro.

Organisation of foreign exchange intervention in the ESCB   Decisions relating to intervention will be taken by the ECB. The implementation of such decisions will be either centralised or decentralised within the ESCB, though there has not yet been any final decision. For the former, intervention operation will be carried our exclusively by the ECB, using its own technical infrastructure. For the latter, all participating NCBs will execute intervention following instructions given by the ECB.

The final decision on the appropriate degree of centralisation/decentralisation will be taken by the Governing Council of the ECB. Depending on the centralised or decentralised nature of the intervention operation, the role of NCBs and the ECB may differ.

The EMI's proposals for ERM II

Though may of the details of ERM II were already known, we show here that 'as part of the future exchange rate policy co-operation between the euro area and other EU countries, a new exchange rate mechanism will be established'. Membership will be voluntary, EU Member States with a derogation can join the mechanism once achieving a satisfactory degree of economic convergence. Interventions will be supportive, along with other policy measures, including appropriate fiscal and monetary policies beneficial to economic convergence and exchange rate stability.

Box 6.1 Main features of ERM II

The standard fluctuation band is expected to be relatively wide, around central rates. Participating non-euro area Member States could establish, on a bilateral basis, fluctuation bands between their currencies and intervention arrangements aimed at limiting excessive bilateral exchange rate volatility. Central rates would be set by agreement between the ECB, the Ministers of the euro area Member States, and the Ministers and Governors of the central banks of the non-euro area Member States, following a procedure involving the European Commission and after consultation of the Economic and Financial Committee. The Ministers and Governors of the central banks of the other EU Member States not participating in the ERM will not have the right to vote in the procedure.

The stability of exchange rates in the new mechanism will be closely watched to ensure that any adjustment of central rates is conducted in a prompt fashion to avoid significant misalignments. Against this background, all parties to the agreement, including the ECB, will have the right to initiate a strictly confidential procedure aimed at reconsidering central rates.

Forex intervention and financing at the standard margins will in principle be automatic and unlimited. However, the ECB and the participating non-euro area NCBs will have the possibility of halting intervention and financing if these were to encroach upon their primary objective of maintaining price stability.

The possibility of co-ordinated intramarginal intervention (decided between the ECB and the respective NCB), along with other appropriate policy responses by the NCB in question, will be maintained.

The present Very Short Financing facility (VSTF) will be continued, following some appropriate adjustments.

The exchange rate policy co-operation between non-euro NCBs and the ECB could be strengthened further. The procedure to be followed would depend on the form of the closer link.

7

EUROPEAN UNEMPLOYMENT

A thorn in the side

The concept of full employment, suitably updated, should
remain as a principal objective of economic and social policy.
(The International Labour Organisation 1996–7)

Introduction

There is a striking difference in the recent employment performance in the
US and Europe, with Europe experiencing significant job losses even in the
presence of some economic growth and the US creating large numbers of
new jobs. There is little doubt that the bulk of the reduction in unemployment in Europe needs to rely on structural reforms. In particular, different
steps towards increasing labour market flexibility were implemented in all
EC countries. Below, we describe some of these steps and comment on the
effectiveness of such measures in reducing unemployment. Currently, however, in light of low confidence and of the persistent nature of European
unemployment, we believe any structural measure should be accompanied
by solid economic growth.

Estimates suggest that high levels of growth are needed in order to reduce
unemployment. Maastricht and bond market pressures strongly limit the
scope for expansionary fiscal policy. As a result, a mixture of a high level of
cyclical unemployment, and scope to aid a structural reduction in unemployment, suggests room for proactive monetary policy.

In 1995, the US grew by 1.3 per cent while Germany grew by 1.9 per cent.
These are quite similar figures. Yet, by comparison, the performance of
employment in the two economies could hardly look more different. The US
created over one million jobs between March 1996 and March 1995.
Germany however has destroyed over 200 thousand jobs (January
1995–January 1996) while in Europe as a whole, the unemployment rate
rose by 0.2 per cent to 11 per cent. In European OECD countries, unemployment has persistently exceeded the OECD average since 1993 (OECD 1996).

In what follows, we briefly address the unemployment issue and finish by
looking at: whether, unemployment might represent an obstacle to monetary
union as argued by many in Europe (e.g. the German Social Democrats); and

97

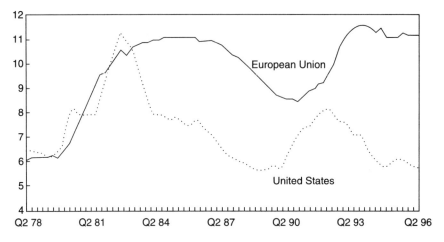

Figure 7.1 Unemployment rates in Europe and the US
Source: OECD *Economic Outlook*, June 1996, Paris

also whether the different unemployment performances could cause a persistent difference in economic performance between the US and Europe.

Unemployment in Europe and in the US: some facts

During the recession of the early 1990s, the US unemployment rate reached 7.7 per cent. Since then it has fallen to below 5.5 per cent, a historically low level. By comparison in Europe, the end of the 1993 recession produced very little in terms of lower unemployment. Unemployment has started to grow again in most of the main European countries and particularly in Germany, where it went as high as 11.1 per cent in February 1996. The European problem is essentially one of low job creation, rather than one of job market newcomers. If anything, the growth of job market participants seen in the 1980s (when women in particular entered the job force) has fallen. Moreover, the general pattern is for countries experiencing large rises in participation to record very small increases in unemployment (Norway, Sweden, apart from the US and Canada) while countries lagging behind in the participation trend experienced large increases in unemployment (in particular Spain, Italy and Greece). The growth in the population has also slowed, with those approaching work age (18–24 years) peaking during the 1980s in the OECD.

During the 1970s and 1980s, the net destruction of jobs in Europe largely came from the reduction in employment in manufacturing industry. Employment also exhibited an asymmetric pattern, with the jobs destroyed during recessions being only partially restored during expansions, therefore leading to a net destruction of jobs in the manufacturing industry. Interestingly, on a long-term perspective, one of the key differences in employment trends between the US and Europe does not lie in the expanding sectors, but in the contracting ones. It is not the job creation capacity of the service sector in the US that accounts for such a different behaviour of employment (in fact, averaging during the last two decades, the contribution to job growth made by the service sector has been roughly comparable in US and Europe). Of course, in comparison with the US, a larger proportion of jobs in Europe are related to the evolution of the public sector: during the 1980s the share of public jobs rose sharply (from 18 per cent to 25 per cent in France). A trend inversion has taken place, with fiscal consolidation leading the public sector to often become a net job destroyer (e.g. in Italy).

Finally, another interesting difference between the US and the European labour markets, is that the former has a much higher degree of labour mobility than the latter. This applies to geographical mobility, accessions and separations, job turnover, inflows and outflows from unemployment. Higher mobility is related to a greater ease of hiring and firing, as well as changing work organisation. A key difference is also that, whereas in Europe most labour turnover takes place within employment, in the US labour flows in and out of unemployment and non-participation are much higher. This explains one of the most unfortunate characteristics of European unemployment: that it is highly dominated by long-term unemployment (see our German example in Chapter 8). Within Europe, countries with the lowest flows in and out of unemployment (Spain and Italy), are also those which register the highest shares of long-term unemployment (see Centre for Economic Policy Research 1995)

An upward trend over the business cycle

A particular feature of European unemployment is that it shows a considerable amount of persistence, i.e. cyclical increases in unemployment which do not reverse entirely. The problems, therefore, seem to be both of a high level of structural unemployment and of unemployment persistence. To illustrate the former factor, EU unemployment in the 1980s was constantly above that in the US, in the last 12 years European unemployment has been 3.5 per cent above the US on average. One must allow for the role of persistence, and thus the history of shocks, in explaining such high structural unemployment. In Germany, in particular, this trend is very clear as each German cycle has been associated with highs and lows of unemployment above those in the previous cycle (see Chapter 8). Similar trends are present in most European countries, one of the most dramatic and documented being the Spanish case.

Moreover, European unemployment does not seem to be very responsive to the economic cycle. Employment does expand or contract with the cycle, but total registered unemployment has been steadily increasing (except in 1983–90). In other words, labour demand reacts somewhat to the economic cycle, but in practice unemployment does not. Thus, the persistence of unemployment arises. Labour responses to increases in demand are elastic, i.e. employment rises with increases in production (good examples of this are the European expansion in the second part of the 1980s, the German unification boom and northern Italy's post-1992 export-led reflation) but these increases do not seem to be big enough to absorb the increasing existing stock of unemployment. This is the reason why some economists argue that we need high and persistent growth in order to reverse the upward trend in unemployment. There is also a pure statistical reason for explaining the lack of reaction of unemployment to the cycle. There is causality running from unemployment to labour force participation. When unemployment levels are high, people get discouraged and avoid participating in the labour force (they might want to, but they do not because they consider it too difficult to find a job). On the contrary, during expansions when labour demand increased, they return to the labour force. Thus, although new jobs are created and some people flow out of unemployment into employment, the ex-discouraged join the unemployment figures.

Long-term unemployment is also a specific feature of European unemployment (especially in those countries with a high level of unemployment persistence). Those who have been unemployed for a long period of time find it more and more difficult to get a job; as their level of skills (human capital) falls, they tend to be considered less productive. Both Italy and Spain are dramatic cases: along the decade 1983–93, long-term unemployment (twelve months and over) never went below 50 per cent of total unemployment.

According to some interpretations, apart from growth rate considerations, some of the difference between the US and the European employment records may lie in the tough policy stance of European governments towards inflation and the external balance. This has been partly induced by the EMS exchange rate policy, which has been responsible for the more volatile and unpredictable character of expansions in Europe. As aggregate demand shocks have played a key role in explaining the recession of the 1990s, some question the convenience of aggressive disinflationary policies in economies which suffer from high unemployment persistence (e.g. Spain) (Simonazzi and Villa 1996).

Uncertainty regarding growth and a more protective legislation on hiring and firing can also explain why European firms prefer to increase hours of work instead of hiring in periods of high demand. In Italy, GDP growth in 1995 could largely be explained by increases in productivity and in hours worked of those already employed, rather than with fresh job creation. Higher hours worked and lower use of the wage supplementation funds (for temporary layoffs), coupled with higher productivity, accounted for all output growth. The number of employed workers dropped by 0.5 per cent (110,000 people), even though the amount of total work input remained flat. Meanwhile, the output per unit of labour grew 4.2 per cent in the first three quarters of 1995.

Why such a low employment rate?

There are different explanations for the large absolute decline in European industrial employment, the main two being technology and globalisation. Understanding the main causes of the European industrial unemployment pattern is one of the first steps to implementing proper measures to tackle it. First, there is the notion that technological progress is labour saving: independently from the level of real wage and the rate of growth of output, demand for labour would be reduced as technological progress takes place. In practice, two opposite effects on employment interact while new technology spreads over the economy. Firstly, there is an increase in aggregate demand since the same output can be produced at a lower cost, therefore generating increases in the demand for labour. Secondly, there is a labour displacing effect, this is normally assumed to be offset by the first effect. Under a high-growth regime (like that of the 1950s and 1960s) higher productivity is accompanied by higher real wages and a higher demand for goods and services, so that, as a net result, new technology should not have an adverse impact on the level of unemployment. In a low-growth environment, technology may destroy more jobs that it creates. This effect could be solved by simple demand management policy as in old-style Keynesianism. However, evidence shows something different: Europe has a high level of unemployment at which growth in demand causes inflation, rather than a rise in output. More precisely, Europe has a high natural level of unemployment. A simple boost in aggregate demand – with no changes in the working of the labour market – would therefore be likely to cause a rise in inflation with little unemployment impact (a phenomenon generally known as eurosclerosis).

Technology still offers a convincing explanation for the unemployment problem, but the terms are slightly different. The argument is that technological change has not only increased productivity, but it has crucially also increased the skills premium in production. The productivity of skilled workers relative to unskilled has risen faster as new technology has been introduced. This explanation of the composition of unemployment and the evolution of relative skill wages in flexible labour markets (like the US and the post-Thatcher UK) seems the most accurate. The spread of new technologies (especially information technology) seems to have benefited those with higher skills (those more educated) and to punish those who are unskilled or less educated. A low level of unskilled worker protection (US and recent UK history), has been attached to upward trends in skill wage differentials. On the contrary, European wage dispersion (with the UK exception) indicates non-increasing patterns. Krugman states that 'many people on both side of the Atlantic believe that the United States has achieved low unemployment by a sort of devil's bargain, whose price is soaring inequality and growing poverty' (Krugman: 1994). In Europe, as we discuss further below, the trend to higher wage inequality has been countered by policies which, directly or indirectly, have prevented a significant fall in unskilled wages. The European Commission notes that 'the relatively high cost of unskilled labour is encouraging investment in rationalisation and holding back job creation in services' (European Commission: 1993).

The second explanation for rising wage differentials deals with the increasing competition faced by the European manufacturing sector coming from less developed countries (LDCs). In general, the so called 'globalisation' of the world economy would also include an increasing internationalisation of the production, distribution and marketing of goods and services. In essence, the ability of Western capital to locate almost anywhere around the world. The political evolution that has opened the former Eastern bloc should also be mentioned. Foreign trade with (mainly) Asian countries and the increasing innovations prompted by external competition does seem to explain a shift from labour-intensive activities towards skills-intensive ones. This would partially explain the observed fall in the share of manufacturing in total employment. Finally, some suggest that the increasing volatility of labour demand, and not only the trend towards higher demand for skilled workers, may be a common cause of increasing wage dispersion in the US and higher unemployment in Europe (Bertola and Ichino 1995).

To study the composition of European unemployment (long-term and unskilled unemployment) gives useful hints for the economic dynamics leading towards it. Most economists (see, for example, Malinvaud 1994) agree on the interpretation that the European unemployment problem is one of relative wages. The high cost of low-skilled labour compared with skilled encourages a rapid substitution of capital for unskilled labour. Though re-training low skilled workers could help to increase the demand for them, this would be a medium-run solution (the emphasis on education as an economic policy tool is discussed in Robert Reich's interesting book 'The Work of Nations', 1991). The only way of encouraging higher demand for unskilled workers in the short run would be by reducing their relative costs. Reductions in wages, however, were and are much more difficult in Europe than in the US. Thus alternative measures (such as subsidies to enterprises) should, in principle, be implemented. Again, if we consider the increasing trend of skilled wage differentials in the US and more recently in the UK (which has a labour market close to the American one), a clear trade-off between employment and wage inequality emerges.

The US seems therefore to react to negative labour market shocks via wages while Europe has tended to do it via employment. This suggests the convenience of looking at the different functioning of the labour markets from an institutional perspective. The notion of 'inflexible European labour markets' was very popular during the 1980s. Experience made it clear that Europe was not as able as the US to reduce unemployment by decreasing wages. Nominal wage resistance (due to a high union power, high degree of centralisation in wage setting, etc.) and real wage resistance (due to employment protection, unemployment assistance and wage indexation) were blamed for this lack of European response. Other rigidities, such as high hiring and firing costs also make companies unwilling to take on new workers. In addition, the higher level of taxation and of social security contribution create a 'wedge' between the salary paid to the workers (which they compare with their reservation wage, the minimum level at which a worker is prepared to accept a job) and the one offered by the firm (see Chapter 8).

It is difficult to quantify the relative importance of all these different factors to the absolute degree of inflexibility in the labour market. Indeed, although generally accepted as the main cause for the different pattern of unemployment in the US and Europe, empirical studies on the role of such inflexibilities are not conclusive. For example, it is normally said that high income taxation and generous welfare benefits distort worker's labour supply decisions. However, as pointed out by the OECD Job Study (1994), most studies fail to find any cross-country correlation between unemployment benefits and aggregate unemployment (with even a negative correlation between benefits levels and unemployment in the 1960s and early 1970s). When time series evidence is considered, unemployment rates do seem to react to benefits entitlements, but with such a long lag (from five to twenty years) that a potential causation seems to be diluted. The International Labour Organisation also questions the idea that empirical evidence unequivocally points to labour market deregulation as the solution to the high unemployment problem. Their 1996/1997 report argues that 'there is no basis for a blanket presumption that these regulations are invariably sources of rigidity and that deregulation is automatically the optimal solution'. Despite doubts, a fairly wide consensus has grown among academics and policy makers that at least part of the solution has to be found in greater labour market flexibility.

Trying to avoid hysteresis: a more flexible European labour market

By the mid 1980s, most economists seemed to agree that the hysteresis phenomenon (high actual unemployment leading to an increase in equilibrium unemployment) could be explained by a too rigid labour market with unemployment behaviour mainly caused by different versions of the insider–outsider model. In insider–outsider theory, only those in work contribute to setting wages, therefore causing an upward bias: positive demand shocks are preempted by higher wages for those already employed while negative demand shocks translate into more unemployment without affecting insider power, leaving insider wages intact.

The 1980s were the decade where emphasis progressively shifted in favour of increasing the flexibility of the labour market: from the mid 1980s to the beginning of the 1990s, legislation aiming to increase the flexibility of the European labour markets was implemented in all countries, following OECD advice. These measures mainly covered three aspects of the labour market: rules regulating the transactions taking place in the labour market, rules governing the price-setting process and social security provisions for job-seekers.

Among the first set of rules, we can distinguish those trying to reduce the dismissal of workers and facilitate hiring, the encouragement of so-called atypical employment (part-time, temporary work, self-employment) and of temporary contracts (with a more flexible use of fixed-term contracts) as well as different working time arrangements in order to allow a more flexible use of working time. Rules governing the price setting process in the labour market were related to wage bargaining systems (increasing decentralisation) and protective legislation on pay (both minimum wage and other legislation). The trend has been towards a reduction of the minimum pay relative to average wages in all countries with legally binding agreements protecting workers. Finally, social security provisions were approved concerning unemployment benefits (duration and quantities reduced) as well as increasing training for long-term unemployment.

Despite significant differences in economies and institutions, all European countries moved in the same direction. They all trusted deregulation policies in order to expand employment and, hopefully, decrease unemployment. Britain seems to be the only case in which unemployment has sensibly decreased. Some authors even talk about a structural break in the UK labour market in the sense that the fall in unemployment from 1994 to date has not led to a rise in inflation. Critics note, however, that much of the progress has been paid with a fall in job security and a massive rise in atypical work contracts, such as part-time employment.

These deregulation policies did not have the expected effect on unemployment in other European countries. Some would argue that this was because they were not strong enough (or because the positive outcome has yet to arrive). Interestingly, however, the same institutional changes had different results depending on which country adopted them. Two good examples (proposed by Simonazzi and Villa 1996) are Spain and Germany. In Spain, the government introduced fixed contracts in 1984, shortly before the economy entered a period of rapid expansion (1986–90). Over that period, 80 per cent of the registered contracts were fixed-term, with the result that by 1995, over one-third of all employees had temporary jobs. As a consequence, employment became more volatile over the business cycles, firms used these contracts to cover themselves from the cycle, labour turnover increased dramatically and wages for temporary workers declined in relative terms. This increased labour market segmentation since it did not modify the better paid positions of the permanent workers.

In Germany, the Employment Promotion Act of 1985 (among other things) relaxed legal restraints on fixed-term contracts. However, by 1995, data on temporary employment did not show any significant increase in proportional terms. German enterprises did not substantially change their behaviour of favouring stable, long-term relationships (see Chapter 8 for other changes in the German labour market).

What has been done recently?

If the explanation outlined above is accepted, despite mixed results, the main long-term solution to the employment emergency would be to implement further structural reforms. Some steps in this direction have been taken in all European countries. Many such reforms were suggested by the 1994 OECD job study. Some examples of the measures implemented over the last few years follow.

Italy

In Italy, various reforms have been implemented at different times. In 1991, the job allocation scheme (which limited employers' choice of prospective employees) was terminated, with small firms allowed to choose employees. In July 1993, the Income Policy agreement followed the abolition, a year earlier, of the *Scala Mobile* (wage indexation scheme) introduced a two-year system of centralised wage bargaining with forward-looking wage settlements and limits on other wage rises to profit-related indicators. The agreement also introduced indications, some of which still need to be implemented, in favour of more flexible contracts such as temporary and part-time work. In 1993, the use of wage supplementation funds (*Cassa Integrazione*) was extended to some service sector companies. Some tax breaks for the employment of the young or long-term unemployed were introduced in 1994. Note that steps towards greater labour market flexibility figured prominently in the programmes of both sides for the 1996 general election. Policies for the south (including the limited scope for regional wage differentials) are also prominent given huge unemployment differentials. In 1995 alone, the south lost 2.2 per cent of its jobs, while the industrial northeast gained 0.6 per cent.

Spain

Spain passed fairly widespread labour market reforms in 1994, ten years after the similar round of labour market reforms which failed to invert the trend of growing unemployment. The new reforms included various measures, with the aim to lower hiring/firing costs. The main measure was an easing of the rules for collective dismissal, though leaving the rules for individual dismissals and the level of severance payments (among the highest in Europe) unchanged, additional measures were agreed in 1997 addressing these issues. On top of that, rules were relaxed in order to allow greater internal flexibility, whilst rules for fixed-term contracts were tightened (they still represent a very high share of new jobs). Work-time regulations were eased and apprenticeship contracts for school-leavers were introduced. Wage bargaining has remained centralised at regional and industry level, though retaining some elements of automatic indexation. These were suspended in 1994–5, but have never been formally repealed. In 1995, a reduction in the social security contributions of 1 per cent was financed with a 1 per cent rise in VAT.

France

In France, unemployment has also risen over successive cycles, despite the government taking a number of measures, shifting the weight towards active labour market policies. For example, the use of 'employment-solidarity' contracts has risen sharply since 1990. A five-year programme was introduced in France in 1993 and was centred around job creation, training and entry into employment. One of the identified problems has been the SMIC, the level of minimum wages (which was around 50 per cent of the average wage in 1994). Despite some attempts, it has been judged politically unfeasible to reduce the level of the minimum wage, although some action was taken to reduce the weight of social security contributions (at almost 30 per cent of total wages in 1994), thus reducing the tax wedge on the SMIC. Other measures in this direction were contained in the 1995 budget. Finally, measures have included an easing of the rules for part-time employment, more working time flexibility and the introduction of a time limit for unemployment benefits. The 1995 budget also contained measures in favour of the long-term unemployed and the Juppé government endorsed measures promoting apprenticeship positions (partly state subsidised, contract initiative employment). Some social security reforms were planned for the future. In 1997, the newly elected government led by Jospin pledged to reduce the working week to 35 hours to help reduce unemployment – the controversial proposal caused strong opposition from employers.

Germany

In Germany, at the end of January 1996, the government released its 50 point action plan for jobs and growth. These plans include:

1 Cuts in supplementary unemployment benefit by 3 per cent per year
2 Limits on unemployment benefits (cutting payments, so they cover only those over 45 years instead of those over 42, and raising the age from which one can start claiming maximum benefits, to 57 rather than 55)
3 Lowering social security contributions by employers and employees, to under 40 per cent of income levels
4 An increase in protection against lay-offs, and an extension of permitted job contracts to twenty-four from eighteen months (designed to make

firing more difficult to prevent more increases in unemployment). Prior to this, the level of unemployment benefits were lowered moderately in January 1994, and the 1995 budget saw marked cuts in the duration of benefit payments (cut from unlimited benefits, to 1–2 years, depending on the claimants circumstances). Unification has been an important exacerbating factor for unemployment, though high wages, high unemployment benefits, and the sector-level system of wage bargaining are seen as crucial structural issues which have led to a reduction in the tracking of unemployment to economic growth (see the following chapter on the German case). Note, however, recent years have seen unions agreeing to moderate wage rises in a concerted effort to reduce further lay-offs

Wage moderation

Most of the debate on unemployment focuses on the rigidity of real or relative wages, linked to regulatory or institutional features. Another argument is based on the idea that labour costs are too high in Europe, particularly in the manufacturing sector. Germany is the most often mentioned case: in comparison, US wages are 55 per cent and Japanese wages 75 per cent of German levels. The United Kingdom wage levels are just 45 per cent of Germany's. Note that in Germany the non-wage labour cost – mainly social security and pensions – accounts for 45 per cent, as opposed to 29 per cent in the US (BIS 1996). Clearly, terms of trade and exchange rate considerations make these comparisons a little dubious. Still, anecdotal evidence and investment data point to the fact that there might be some labour cost effect. In the first half of the 1990s, the net outflow of investment from Germany has amounted to DM180 billion, equivalent to more than 10 per cent of domestic investment in machinery and equipment. While some of this might be marketing or network services, the data represents evidence of some shift to production abroad.

Figure 7.2 plots unit labour costs in the US and the EU. This highlights the fact that, over a fairly long period of time, there appears to be only moderate evidence that aggregate wages have been growing at a significantly faster pace, given differences in productivity (at the aggregate economy level) in Europe in comparison to the US. Non-wage costs and wage dispersion might represent a problem, but European wage inflation is not striking.

In recent years, apart from the post-unification wage rises in Germany, coming out of the 1993 recession, wages might have become part of the problem, especially when combined with the DM appreciation. Though, the growth of aggregate real wages cannot account for a significant rise in German unemployment as it was no faster than in the US over the last three years. Wage agreements in most countries in the last couple of years have confirmed the trend to wage moderation, while unions have acknowledged that unemployment must figure on the top of agendas, alongside, or above,

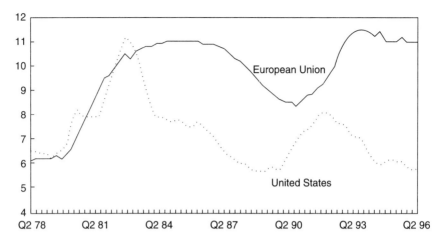

Figure 7.2 Unit labour costs in the US, Germany and France
Source: OECD *Economic Outlook*, June 1997, Paris

wage requests (departing therefore from the insider–outsider model). A continuation of the trend to wage responsibility seems key both to address the unemployment level and to determine central banks behaviour. However, initiatives such as the Income Policy agreement in 1993 in Italy, and the 'Alliance for Jobs' talks in Germany have highlighted a growing awareness among wage setters of the link between excessive wage growth and unemployment.

Unemployment and growth

The European job destruction process in the last few years is serious, worsening an already alarming situation. A strong correlation between growth, employment and unemployment is normally observed along the business cycle. But taking into account the fact that European unemployment as a whole does not seem very sensitive to the business cycle, we might want to consider other non-transitory relationships between growth and unemployment. On the one hand, the nature of the European unemployment (highly persistent and based on long-term unemployed) suggests the need to keep with structural policies which might help to break the trend. On the other hand, employment levels are still sensitive to economic activity. Indeed, although not a solution in itself to the extent that it cannot be freely chosen by European countries, high rates of growth might eventually help to reverse the trend if they are sustained over long enough periods. That unemployment has recovered less than in other post-recession periods is significant, but it does not necessarily mean the old Keynesian medicine is no longer working.

In the recent European business cycle, the low level and weak recovery of consumer confidence pointed to low expectations of future improvement, somehow unusual at the early stages of a recovery, and which empirical evidence tends to associate with low or unstable job prospects. Even in the British case, where job creation was higher, some evidence shows that there is a rising share of bad, low-quality jobs in the stock of entry jobs. Real entry wages have fallen relative to the wages of those already holding jobs. Entry jobs are mainly part-time, temporary work and self-employment. There seems to be a trend towards employment polarisation. Thus the composition of employment across households during this recovery (at least in Britain) can be thought of as being more polarised than during the previous one.

Monetary and fiscal policy is unlikely to foster the long-term economic growth needed to absorb unemployment. Under certain conditions, however, economic policy can help create an environment favourable to lowering unemployment. For it to be the case, certain conditions need to be in place, notably mechanisms for moderating wage inflation via wage bargaining, social pacts or other forms. Also, it is important to redesign the labour market in a way which increases its efficiency, from measures to increase flexibility, reforms of the benefits system, and reforms of the payroll taxes or the provision of training. A brief description of such measures follows.

What else could be done?

As an alternative to labour market deregulation, active labour market policies have been popular, particularly when looking at ways to deal with the long-term unemployed. Active labour market policy is a term which encompasses a number of measures designed to improve the efficient workings of labour market and its degree of equality. Four main types of programmes can be distinguished: firstly, measures to improve the matching between jobseekers and notified vacancies, counselling for those looking for work and enhancing the extent and quality of job search; secondly, measures to raise the stock of skills, which aim to provide training courses in order to reduce any mismatch due to an imbalance of skills in the labour market, and sometimes to influence the incidence of training for those already in employment; thirdly, measures to directly increase the demand for labour which either take the form of work programmes in public or voluntary agencies offering low skilled marginal jobs or recruitment subsidies which aim to spur private employers to hire the unemployed; finally, measures to promote the equality of opportunity in employment, which usually target groups likely to be marginalised in the labour market, such as the young (see Robinson 1996).

The main rationale behind these programmes is that the long-term unemployed play no role in holding down wage inflation. Therefore, if active labour policy reduces the level of long-term at the expense of the short-term unemployment, this would cause a reduction of wage inflation. In turn this would allow for an expansion of the demand for labour and an absorption of the workers who have been previously substituted. Once the programme ends some of the previously long-term unemployed could find themselves unemployed again, but as they have joined the short-term unemployed, they place downwards pressure on wage inflation, possibly, causing an increase in labour demand. Empirical evidence does not fully confirm these arguments, hence re-routing attention towards the microeconomic evaluation of the specific programmes on a case-by-case basis. Still, at times, these programmes might be important as a solution to the unemployment problem and as a way to enhance the efficiency of the labour market. With the employer/employee relationship tending to become more transitory and fluid in many sectors, ways to fashion a more efficient market assume increasing importance. Note that labour market flexibility might also be enhanced at times by measures which do not directly concern the labour market. For example, in the US, from mid 1996, employees who change jobs are allowed to retain their insurance coverage from their previous employers (Health Insurance Portability and Accountability Act, August 1996). Pensions system in Europe should, in many cases, also be redesigned to account for greater labour mobility.

Among the alternatives to the policies aimed at reducing unemployment, there is one which receives both dramatic support and criticism. Namely, the work-sharing solution. The basic idea is that workers are not worse off with lower pay providing they value leisure. By dropping hours of work in order to enjoy leisure, workers free potential job places which will be added to by the unemployed. The EU is currently legislating for a maximum working week of 48 hours. It cannot be denied that the trend is towards less hours of work per person. According to the OECD (Maddison 1995) the number of total annual hours worked on average in the EU is the same in the 1990s as it was in the 1970s, but now there are roughly twice as many people in employment. Nevertheless, many authors talk of the 'lump of labour fallacy': it is a mistake to assume that there is only a fixed number of jobs available. The number of jobs can grow over time. The fallacy is very well solved by Ormerod (1996), by fixing the share of labour in national income which is required to sustain any given medium-term growth rate. The growing real value of this share can be taken up entirely by those in employment, leaving the number of jobs constant, or, at the other extreme, entirely by new jobs leaving the level of real wages constant.

The US labour market has frequently been considered the benchmark when structural reforms have been implemented in Europe. It has been argued that countries suffered from wage rigidity and reacted to negative demand shocks via employment instead of by reducing wages. Nevertheless, the American model has showed to imply the well-documented rise in wage inequality which seems to be the other side of the low unemployment coin. The changing economic conditions of the last two decades have imposed a redistribution of income that the American labour market solved by paying less and the European by paying to less people. While that choice might be to a certain degree inevitable, the search for alternative ways to address the unemployment problem is worthwhile.

Conclusion

There is little doubt that much of the unemployment progress in Europe needs to come from structural reforms. As we have briefly highlighted, some steps in that direction have been taken in most European countries, though much of the measures are still only pretty tentative. Note that the design of such rules needs to be adequate to the particular circumstances and cultural factors of each country. Not all policies work the same everywhere. Many US style deregulation policies are unlikely to be effective in continental Europe. We would also argue that the effectiveness of such measures, in light of low confidence and of the persistent nature of European unemployment, need to be accompanied by solid economic growth. These policies should be maintained for a sustained period. Firstly, greater flexibility without growth in demand can, at times, have a negative impact on employment, e.g. if companies take advantage of greater freedom to shed workers. In addition, mimicking the American labour market structure has clear costs in terms of inequality and social discomfort. Also, the persistence shown by Europe's unemployment suggests that there is a role, albeit limited, for aggregate demand to bring unemployment permanently down. Finally, we seem to detect greater awareness among policy makers and wage-setters both of the need to pursue structural reforms and to accompany those reforms with wage moderation. In short, institutional changes, both in the present and future, might make the non-inflationary level of unemployment progressively lower, opening an opportunity for demand to take advantage of that.

The National Institute for Social Research in London has undertaken a number of studies of sustainable unemployment in Europe. The estimates suggest that sustainable unemployment is around 8 per cent in France and the UK and 7 per cent in Germany. When countries with a high unemployment history are included in the analysis (Spain, Italy), the sustainable unemployment rate in the EU goes up somewhere between 9 and 10 per cent (in Barell, Pain and Young 1994). Thus, unemployment in many European countries does not seem likely to reach its long-run level until the end of the century. In addition, estimates suggest that growth as high as 4 per cent is needed to have an impact on unemployment (the Delors White paper envisaged a growth rate of 3.5 per cent). Maastricht and financial market pressures have strongly limited the scope for expansionary fiscal policy. As a result, a mixture of a high level of cyclical unemployment, and scope to aid a structural reduction in unemployment, suggests room for proactive monetary policy. Worries about the high level of European unemployment were behind the new French Socialist government (which came to power in June 1997) demanding some procedures to counterweight the focus on fiscal balance in the Stability Pact. A jobs summit was held in the autumn of 1997. Though it is difficult to find agreement on legislation to increase employment, and the German government was adamant that employment policies should remain *national* concerns, the Jobs Chapter was designed to put procedures in place where EMU countries would examine and discuss their employment policies at least once a year (see Chapter 2).

8

GERMAN UNEMPLOYMENT

Bargaining, benefits and other inflexibilities

> Unemployment matters ... It erodes human capital. And
> finally, it involves psychic costs. People need to be needed.
> Though unemployment increases leisure, the value of this is
> largely offset by the pain of rejection.
>
> (Layard, Nickell and Jackman 1991)

Introduction

We devote this section to examining the German unemployment problem,
which has seen a sharp deterioration since the 6.2 per cent unemployment
rate of 1990 to over 10 per cent for 1996. The situation is probably even
worse than this indicates, as many have left unemployment, but are on job
creation schemes, retraining or early retirement (accounting for about 1.5
million in 1995). Sharp increases in unemployment in 1995 and 1996 have
catapulted the issue of employment into the political limelight in Germany,
and in other European countries where the costs of the efforts to reach EMU
are being questioned by workers and trade unions. Strikes were also seen in
France in 1995–6, as well as protests in Greece and Spain against government austerity measures to reach the 3 per cent deficit to GDP target for
EMU entry. These actions highlighted the concern that the measures to reach
EMU could end up turning popular opinion against the project entirely.

The 1990s also, however, saw increased understanding between employers
and trade unions on the need for wage restraint and on the relationship
between wages and unemployment. This has led to some small but remarkable steps in labour relations adding to the structural changes seen in the
1990s. German trade union proposals such as the 'Alliance for Jobs',
although largely unsuccessful, have marked a profound change in European
labour practices.

The German example is one that can advance lessons to the rest of Europe,
both in terms of bargaining and benefit system changes, and in terms of
negotiation and employer–employee accord. Though some parts of the bargaining and benefit system have been reformed, much more can be done.
There have been many small steps made by employers and employees in the
right direction. Regional contracts in Lower Saxony in 1996 to reduce

layoffs by installing flexible hours which change with demand, could be the way of the future, and could eliminate much cyclical unemployment. Company rejection of government sick pay cuts, though after widespread union protests, and though the government's ruling was to some extent illegal, was also a sign of increased willingness of firms to listen fairly to workers' wishes.

Alliance for jobs

1996 saw the 'Alliance for Jobs' proposals by IG Metall (the largest union in Germany), reciprocatory proposals and plans from the Bundesvereinigung Deutscher Arbeitgeberverbände (or BDA, the national grouping of 1000 employers associations), the Federation of German Industry (BDI), and even the Christian Democrats (CDU) government followed, but talks broke down fairly quickly and there were some repercussions. Chancellor Kohl's pledge to make employment his political priority this year resulted in the governing Christian Democrats launching an economic growth and job-creation plan. This includes tax cuts for companies (lower business taxes, concessions to new companies in production and service sectors), abolition of the local trading capital tax and the wealth tax effects on companies as well as cuts on social spending. Some companies pledged actual employment increases. Volkswagen promised to add 1,000 of the 300,000 jobs demanded by unions in a trade for real wage freezes, but few other guarantees were forthcoming, as the economic climate did not lend itself to such ambitious economic fore-planning. This type of national wage talk however could show the way to more progress on limiting unemployment in the future.

Wage bargaining

The German unemployment problem seems to be caused mainly by a lack of flexibility of their labour market rather than relatively high wages alone. In many ways their recent history of unemployment is worse than in other European countries. Wages tend to be slow to change to the economic climate. Secondly, unlike in France and the UK, the employment rate in Germany has been on a downward trend since the beginning of 1995. The German unemployment problem is due in part to the German wage bargaining system which, by its nature, tends toward higher wage growth, and tends to hinder adjustment to economic changes by encouraging uniformity of wages across sectors, regions and occupations. The relationship between unemployment and growth in Germany is breaking down; unemployment more or less mirrors the cyclical nature of growth but has been on a clear upward trend since the 1960s, despite a fairly flat trend in GDP growth. More flexible wage adjustment in the face of shocks will allow German industry to counteract some of the detrimental effects of the strong DM, helping ailing export growth.

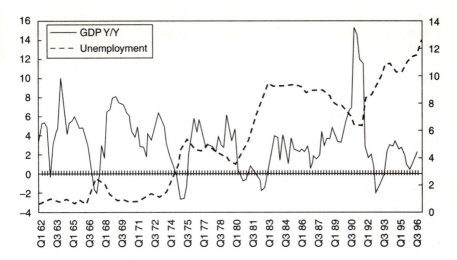

Figure 8.1 German GDP growth and unemployment rate (RH axis)
Source: Federal Statistics Office, Germany

The real problem

'Hourly labour costs are amongst the highest in the world, while the adjustment speed of employment to labour demand is amongst the slowest' (OECD Economic Survey on Germany 1996). Though unemployment in Germany has increased so much in the 1990s, the German system of wage bargaining has not resulted in excessively high wage growth in recent times, due in part to the 'responsible' attitude of trade unions in Germany on the need for productivity rises to finance wage rises.

The main problem in Germany is not really high wage growth, but the German wage bargaining system itself, which hinders the adjustment of wages to excessive demand/supply of jobs. With a fairly flat and inflexible wage structure it is almost impossible to even out the demand and supply of labour in certain regions or occupations using changes in wage rates. The German labour market therefore tends to have high structural and regional employment, the latter exacerbated by unification, due to the adoption of fairly similar wages, and wage bargaining, in East Germany as in the West. It is this type of unemployment which will be most prevalent in EMU, and therefore the German example gives us some guidance on how to approach these present and future problems.

Wage bargaining theory

Economic theory suggests that national-level bargaining causes the most moderate wage growth outcome. Firm-level bargaining also results in a moderate wage growth outcome, but in Germany, wage bargaining is on an industry-wide level. Industry-level bargaining is more inflationary than firm-level bargaining, because labour supply at an industry level is from a fixed pool. Employers do not have the choice of bringing in workers from elsewhere in an industry-level bargain, therefore they have less bargaining power against union wage demands. Firm-level bargaining means if workers are pushing for high wage claims, employers are able to threaten to bring in other workers from outside the firm, if the present workers get too 'costly'. This threat, whether explicit or implicit, translates into lower wage growth. National-level bargaining on the other hand internalises some of the problems of firm-level bargaining, as employment issues are incorporated in the bargain. There is also a reduced risk of 'leap-frogging' (i.e. when employers try to outbid each other for better quality workers or when firm-level unions are able to achieve better and better differential wages in comparison with workers in other firms, thereby causing upwardly spiralling wages) (see Layard *et al.* 1991 for a detailed explanation and model).

The German system

Collective bargaining is enshrined in the German Constitution, and in the wage contract law of 1949. It takes place without government intervention and the partners to the negotiations are on the one side the nineteen national unions organised by sector (without occupational distinctions) and on the other side the one thousand employer associations, which together form the BDA. Only unions can represent employees in collective agreements, but employers can negotiate as associations or individually.

These sector-level wage negotiations result in minimum basic wages by job grade, and include provisions on working hours, holidays, employment protection and training. Deviations from these basic provisions are only allowed if they are in favour of the workers (this is known as the 'favourability principle' or Günstigkeitsprinzip). The problem the German government faced, when it wanted to cut sick-pay levels at the end of 1996, was that they could not do so without it being agreed at the sector-level wage bargain. Since it was not beneficial to workers, it could not be implemented immediately. It is due to the favourability principle that there is room for upwards wage drift at the level of the firm, even though wage bargaining is industry-wide. In fact, most employers pay wages some 10–20 per cent above the basic wage. This makes the industry-level bargaining system a little like the firm-level system, resulting in slightly more wage flexibility, but this is upward flexibility and therefore tends to be more inflationary. These supplements to the basic wage are finalised at informal firm-level wage negotiations between management and Workers Councils, but industrial action is prohibited at this stage. This therefore adds an extra inflationary bias to an already inflationary wage bargaining system. There is no increase in wage disparities either, therefore there is no equilibrating factor to even out unemployment disparities between different sectors/regions.

Problems and proposals

The 'Alliance for Jobs' talks that started in January 1996 between the IG Metall union and the engineering employers attempted to solve Germany's unemployment problems. At that time pan-German unemployment was at 10.8 per cent (January 1996). It subsequently reached a high of 12.2 per cent in early 1997. The proposal of the unions was to trade wage rises for new employment: the unions sought 330,000 jobs to be created between 1996 and 1998 including 30,000 specifically for the long-term unemployed (see below). In exchange, unions offered to agree to a wage increase in line with inflation in 1997, i.e. no real wage increase. There was disagreement however on how this should be achieved. The metal employers federation, Gesamtmetall, instead proposed a three-step programme to increase the flexibility of the labour market in the metal industry. These would include letting companies offer lower entry-level wages for job starters, allowing deals for lower wages in exchange for job guarantees and providing incentives to cut overtime. The talks failed, with only a few companies able to offer job guarantees. German unions have shown a great deal of sophistication in dealing with their employers, but the harshness of the economic climate, exacerbated by moves to attain the EMU criteria, made it difficult for firms to come up with any job guarantees.

On the other hand, the proposals by the BDA (in reply to the union 'Alliance for Jobs' proposal) advocated a three pillar system whereby workers' sectoral wages would be topped up by two extra elements: one reflecting the profits earned by the specific company and another reflecting the workers' performance. This proposal is notable by the use of a profit-sharing segment of wages. Profit sharing is little used in Germany. Bonuses are paid at the employers discretion but these are generally unrelated to profits. This system would have increased wage differentials between firms, as more profitable firms would have paid higher wages. The Federation of German Industry (BDI) also put forward their own proposals. Their package called for social security contributions to be cut to 37 per cent of incomes from the present record 41.1 per cent. Local workers councils would be guaranteed a bigger role in negotiating wages and conditions, which at present are negotiated nationally. The BDI have called for government action as well, including lower taxes and less government spending.

Regions, sectors and occupations: differentials

Even though wage negotiations take place regionally for one sector, in Germany wage contracts are typically also the same nationally for that sector. The regional negotiations have the advantages that strikes can be limited to regional areas, though the uniformity of the wage contracts means that regional wage cost competition advantages are eliminated. Thus with little regional differences, the price mechanism does not give enough incentive to encourage labour mobility, thereby leading to regional unemployment. This, as we discuss in Chapter 2, is an important problem under a monetary union. European labour mobility is generally low, and regional wage differences will be needed to encourage labour mobility to prevent the build-up of regional pockets of unemployment.

East Germany is experiencing unemployment because of the relatively high wages there, though these are justified by an attempt to limit migration from the East to the West. Direct and indirect labour subsidies are widespread in East Germany helping to stall the adverse effect of high wages on investment and growth, but they are insufficient. Relatively high wages look set to continue as in most sectors of the East German economy, management and labour have agreed clauses to adjust negotiated wages and salaries to the level in West Germany. Therefore the higher wage round settlements of 1995 became automatically effective in the new Länder too. Indeed, in some instances the agreed basic remuneration has been increased to a higher proportion of the corresponding West German wage level e.g. in 1996, in the metal-working and electrical engineering industries, remuneration was raised from 87 per cent to 94 per cent of the West German level.

Wages across different sectors also turn out fairly similarly. This is because the German system is often characterised by 'pattern bargaining'. The metalworking industry, represented by the IG Metall union with its 3.5 million members (about 25 per cent of all union members in Germany), as well as the public and construction sectors tend to be the wage trendsetters, with the other sectors following their pattern fairly closely.

With this 'pattern bargaining' or 'convoy behaviour' wage moderation is achieved through the internalisation of the consequences of aggressive wage bargaining behaviour. The effects of the 'trade-off' between higher wages and greater unemployment is seen on a sector-wide scale, and therefore internalised in that sector's decision on its wage claims. This duplicates to some extent the national-level bargaining system. In a pattern bargaining system, the effects of the leaders' wage bargain on the rest of the sectors is direct and therefore there is little room for differential wage increases.

Although wages have been kept reasonably low in Germany despite the industry-level wage bargaining system, there is little wage flexibility as far as wage differentials are concerned.

> Germany (together with France) is exceptional among the major seven economies in that there is no tendency over the 1980s for the earnings distribution to widen ... A marked dispersion in regional unemployment rates in the context of a rather narrow regional dis-

persion of wage increases suggests a high degree of inter-sectoral wage rigidity.

(OECD 1996: 115)

Differentials are important to equilibrate employment across regions, occupations and sectors. Germany, however, is characterised by uniformity of wages. This uniformity reduces the ability of wages to respond to conditions in different parts of the labour market, regions, occupations etc. Even though real wages are not high as a whole, if the wage dispersion or wage differentials are too low, the mechanisms that equilibrate labour demand and supply may be prevented, resulting in regional unemployment, or unemployment concentrated in certain industries or occupations.

Developments to increase wage flexibility

Some developments to increase the flexibility of the bargaining system which have already been introduced are discussed below.

The introduction of 'opt-out' clauses (Harteklausel) in wage contracts in East Germany allow below-tariff wages to be paid if a firm and its workforce agree that there is a financial crisis. This allows the individual employer seeking an exemption to bypass the employers federation, but the regional/national union is still responsible for negotiating the exemption on behalf of the workforce. These have been little used due to union opposition, but placing the authority to negotiate exemptions at the level of the firm's Workers Council might make such clauses more useful.

Employers have been pulling out of, or just not joining, employers federations. It is estimated that a quarter of eastern German employment is in firms which are not members of employers federations. In addition even some firms that are members of employers federations have been paying below tariff wages, with the tacit agreement of their workforce, therefore avoiding the need to seek union agreement on the use of an opt-out clause. It is estimated that over one-third of firms in east Germany pay below-tariff wages.

As we have mentioned above, there have been regional wage deals in the metal sector in Lower Saxony, which have agreed to have lower working hours instead of layoffs in times of low demand. Thus, though workers experience lower take-home pay at these times, they do not have to face cyclical unemployment. This also prevents the build-up of the long-term unemployed, as workers are not allowed to lose their skills, and become 'discouraged' in this type of system. Some increased wage flexibility has been introduced in the chemical sector, with lower wage agreements for new workers who were previously unemployed for a long period.

It is clear that the main way forward is to inject greater wage flexibility at the firm level, giving firms more autonomy to set wages themselves at rates below (or above) the tariff wage. This would require a lower basic wage in order to be feasible, thus reducing the marginal cost of labour generally. These ideas amount to an increasing decentralisation of wages which implies less overall wage growth, and more flexibility of wages. With lower wages, German industry will receive a boost from these cost advantages on an international scale. These new wage tendencies should mean a healthier trade outlook. Germany should be better able to compete with countries with decentralised wage bargaining such as the UK and Switzerland, which have more firm-level bargaining, and Scandinavia, which has national-level bargaining.

Persistent unemployment and the benefit system

Germany historically has a falling employment trend; it comes out of every recession with a long-term unemployment increase. This employment persistence might be encouraged by long-duration benefits. Though German employment is heavily cyclical, the level tends to fall through time. High ratios of wages to benefits also prevent a quick improvement in the unemployment situation after a recession. Social assistance and high benefits push up the wages at which people are able to leave unemployment.

Employment protection is also a hindrance to the flexibility of wages in Germany. With procedures which make hiring and firing very difficult, it makes employers slower to employ new workers. Employment protection legislation in Germany is harsh and is characterised by uncertainties surrounding court proceedings and different legal interpretations of the relevant legislation. The uncertainties over the legislation cause a reluctance to hire by employers, as employment mistakes can be very costly to the firm. The discretion of the courts is used a great deal in the area of employment protection, which has created considerable uncertainty for employers. The fact that the German economy is characterised by considerable amounts of overtime even in periods of recession is indicative of the lags involved in cyclical changes in employment, due to employers' reluctance to hire.

Collective dismissals at larger firms are subject to even more stringent conditions. If more than five employees are to be dismissed within thirty days, the Labour Office must be notified of the dismissal and can delay it by up to two months. If more than 20 per cent of the workforce or more than sixty employees are to be dismissed, management and the Works Council must agree on a 'social plan' that compensates the workers who are to lose their jobs. It has been estimated that payouts under the social plan average four to six months of wages for a worker with average blue collar industrial earnings.

There are three different types of unemployment assistance in Germany: unemployment benefit (Arbeitslosengeld), unemployment assistance (Arbeitslosenhilfe), and social assistance (Sozialhilfe) which is also for others whose income is inadequate. Unemployment insurance is compulsory for all employees except civil servants and soldiers. Unemployment benefits and unemployment assistance are paid to those who have contributed to the unemployment insurance scheme for at least one year out of the three years prior to unemployment, who have involuntarily lost their jobs, and who are actively seeking work. Those who voluntarily quit work must wait twelve weeks before drawing benefits. Until recently, unemployment benefits were payable at rates as high as 68 per cent of previous net earnings for a claimant with children and 63 per cent for a claimant without children; from January 1994 these replacement ratios were lowered to 67 per cent and 60 per cent respectively. After unemployment benefits have expired unemployment assistance is available.

The unlimited duration of unemployment assistance was a particularly generous feature of the unemployment insurance system, but unemployment assistance was limited to two years in the 1995 budget. This assistance is also payable to most people who are in need and have lost their jobs, but are not entitled to unemployment benefit. For them, the period of eligibility, which was also unlimited, was reduced to one year from January 1994. Unemployment assistance is payable at the rate of 57 per cent of previous net earnings for a claimant with children and 53 per cent for a claimant without children. Finally, social assistance is available, for an unlimited period, to those whose income is inadequate to meet basic needs, although social assistance recipients who are able to work are required to register with the labour office and to accept appropriate job offers. The payments consist of cash allowances, contributions to housing and heating costs and special one-off payments for necessary purchases. For many, the ratio of social assistance to average earnings is over 70 per cent, and in some cases in east Germany it is at about 87 per cent.

A 1996 OECD study indicates that the three benefit systems taken together account for a wage replacement rate of 70 per cent for about two-thirds of the unemployed, with about one-third receiving around 80 per cent of their median earnings. This is very high indeed, and must act as a disincentive for effective work search. We explore problems of work search and long-term unemployed in the next section. These issues are very intertwined with the high-benefit system.

The long-term unemployed and effective job search

A feature of the [German] wage adjustment process which is of particular importance is that wages appear to be negatively influenced by both the level and the change of unemployment, indicating a substantial degree of hysteresis: after an initial impact the unemployed have only a weak influence over the wage formation process, so that unemployment tends to persist. Indeed, econometric estimates suggest that the impact of long-term unemployment is only one-third of the influence of unemployment of shorter duration, suggesting a market insider/outsider effect at the aggregate level.

(OECD 1996: 113)

The benefit system in Germany is unusually cushioning. It is also the unlimited (until recently) duration of unemployment assistance, as well as the high payments, which might provide little incentive for active work search, thus reinforcing the tendency toward increasing unemployment. Long, high unemployment benefits have advantages in aiding the unemployed find the most appropriate job for their own skills, and provide a much needed social safety net, but they also tend to discourage active work search as they reduce the difference between wages and unemployment benefits.

Employment persistence is partly due to the growing numbers of long-term unemployed who become increasingly discouraged, with deteriorating skills and confidence. Employers too take long-term unemployment as a negative signal and are reluctant to take on the long-term unemployed. Unemployment can be reduced without increasing inflation if these long-term unemployed are encouraged to get back to work, with training and assistance, as due to their lack of work search efforts they tend to exert less, if any, downward pressure on wages by their presence in the body of unemployed. We can see in Figure 8.2 that though there has been a marked rise in unemployment, the downward pressure on wages has been less pronounced. This may be partly due to an increase in the long-term unemployed.

One measure for the effectiveness of the job search is the number of vacancies being left unfilled. This can be seen in Figure 8.3. More recently we can see that although unemployment has been increasing, so too have vacancies. An increase in the number of vacancies matched by an increase in unemployment shows that either workers are not finding jobs they are happy

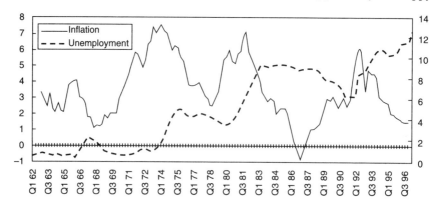

Figure 8.2 German unemployment and inflation
Source: Federal Statistics Office, Germany

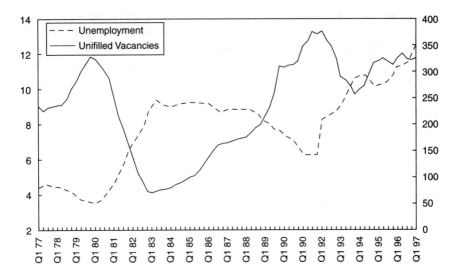

Figure 8.3 Unemployment and unfilled vacancies
Source: German Labour Office

with or that employers are unable to find the right vacancy fillers. This tendency may be because workers or employers are becoming more fussy, or because workers are becoming less active in their job search. Thus the inclusion in the 'Alliance for Jobs' of proposals to reduce the long-term unemployed, and the reciprocal measures of Chancellor Kohl in this area, are beneficial. The German government's 50 point 'Action plan for Jobs and Investment' (see Chapter 7) included many cuts in taxation and steps to promote the development of new technologies. The points which were more labour-related included cuts in supplementary unemployment benefit, cuts in the duration of unemployment benefit payment, and the reduction of social security contributions by firms and employees. More measures along these lines are needed however to really tackle unemployment persistence and to boost consumption, without increasing inflation.

Work-time flexibility

Methods of dealing with unemployment (before unification, in the 1980s) included efforts to reduce the working week to thirty-five hours and attempts to increase the number of people in employment, more recent attempts have also focused on reducing working hours and overtime. German employers make substantial use of overtime to adjust to times of higher demand. This is expensive, but is due to fairly restrictive conditions in industry wage agreements. In 1996, regional wage bargains even allowed for some reduction of hours worked in times when demand is low, an attempt to maintain labour levels and eliminate cyclical changes in employment. The 1996 wage round was notable for its moves to increase work-time flexibility. The working week has become more flexible, and overtime above a certain level is now being compensated by free time. This reduces some of the expense of overtime for employers and should reduce overtime in favour of increased employment. Hiring costs have also been reduced, making it easier for employers to answer extra demand with extra jobs.

Conclusion

The moves toward greater flexibility of wages should be encouraged in Germany. Moderated wage growth moves do not provide a long-term solution to the German unemployment problem. There should be some concentration on unemployment persistence (such as helping the long-term unemployed), and improving the sensitivity of wages to shocks. These moves will improve the adjustment of the German economy to shocks and provide long-term benefit. The pure 'jobs for wages' deal proposed by the unions, though unsuccessful, and the resultant attempts by the government to improve the unemployment situation indicates a small, but important shift in focus. The move toward the decentralisation of wage bargaining methods should aid the flexibility of wages, lower wage growth as well as improve Germany's competitiveness. These problems, some a result of unification and others of antiquated bargaining systems, are experienced elsewhere in Europe also and provide a valuable idea of the unemployment problems which may be experienced under EMU, and some possible solutions. Reducing unemployment, however, needs many other measures. The upgrading and changing of skills and education is also needed. Though Germany has a long history of good vocational and academic education and training, this has to be duplicated in East Germany, and this will be difficult to achieve with government spending so restricted by the 3 per cent deficit target for EMU and the Stability and Growth Pact.

9

BUBBLES, CRISES AND INTERVENTIONS

Some flaws of free floating

Introduction

Since the break-up of Bretton Woods, currency volatility has increased. Its effects on an economy can be devastating, as uncertainty makes investment decisions almost impossible. This is one of the main justifications for the move towards EMU as many European countries have suffered due to this currency volatility. Given large speculative capital flows, the exchange rate regimes which seem most durable are floating exchange rates and monetary unification (the two ends of the spectrum). Intermediate regimes which involve explicit exchange rate targets (pegged but adjustable rates, target zones, currency bands, crawling pegs) invite attack and perform well for only short periods. Given this, one can assume that countries will in the long term tend to one end of the currency spectrum or the other. It seems likely that large countries like the US, Japan and Germany will continue to float one against the other, whereas smaller countries will seek to establish fixed rates with their larger trading partner. This implies that we are moving towards a world of three currency zones: the dollar, yen and EMU. Though the process will be a slow one, its roots are already very much in place.

The many different events which affect free-floating currency rates make markets very bad predictors of exchange rate movements. Currency markets are prone to mispricing and overshooting which may be due to the use of short-term 'technical' methods of forecasting rather than a reliance on fundamentals. Interventions in foreign exchange markets can help to reduce volatility, but they must be handled in a clear and pragmatic way and using macroeconomic fundamentals as justifications for reversals of mispricing.

Out of the woods, into volatility

There was a dramatic difference in exchange rate volatility before and after the break-up of the Bretton Woods system in the early 1970s.

With fixed nominal exchange rates, it is price and wage changes which lead to changes in the real exchange rate. However, prices and wages tend to change only slowly, so that real exchange rate volatility is fairly low. On top of this, it is argued that fixed exchange rate regimes tend to cushion themselves from real shocks by using trade restrictions, capital controls or import/export taxes, reducing the effects of the shocks on the real exchange rate. The Bretton Woods system of fixed exchange rates therefore contained very little real exchange rate volatility.

Flexible exchange rates with instant price adjustments, in practice, prove to be much more volatile. In this case, a positive monetary shock leads to increasing domestic price levels. This leads to a (short-term) real depreciation of the currency. It is argued however that this should not be the case, i.e. that real exchange rates (nominal exchange rate adjusted for differences in prices/costs) should be unchanged by purely nominal monetary shocks. This 'classical' view (that monetary shocks are adjusted to quickly and with little or no real effects) is contrary to what was actually seen in the move from Bretton Woods to flexible exchange rates. After the break-up of Bretton Woods, expectations were that real shocks would be dominated by the size of nominal ones and that both real exchange rate movements and nominal exchange rate movements would be independent of each other. The opposite proved true in the 1973 to 1986 period. With floating exchange rates a relatively new concept post-Bretton Woods, the reality was that real exchange rates fluctuated more than nominal exchange rates. The two most notable cases were the appreciation of sterling (1976–81) and the US dollar (1979–85). In both cases unit labour costs rose more quickly than their competitors but appreciation still took place. Thus, the new flexibility of exchange rates led to real economic shocks, rather than just monetary ones.

Exchange rate determination

In the light of the increased volatility of exchange rates since the break-up of Bretton Woods, exchange rate determination has become a topic of much debate. We examine some of the most popular theories, old and new, and examine why exchange rate markets are often not very good predictors of currency trends.

Purchasing Power Parity

At a very basic level the exchange rate is said to obey purchasing power parity (PPP). PPP is a 'law' by which the exchange rate should be equal to the ratio of the price levels of the two countries. The direction of causation is ambiguous however, and PPP allows for a two-way cause and effect with exchange rates adjusting to changes in price levels, and vice versa. The PPP hypothesis only really holds under fairly strong assumptions, which makes it difficult to use in reality. These conditions are that:

1　Each equivalent tradable good must have an identical price (when in a common currency) in each country
2　Factor prices, and production functions must be the same
3　Each good must receive the same weight in the price index in both countries

PPP as a short-term equilibrium　Given wide product diversification, and imperfect competition, with firms facing different demand reactions to price changes, the conditions above are fairly unrealistic. Differing transportation costs, trade restrictions and taxation systems make prices difficult to compare between countries. There are limits to the ability of prices to change, given wage contracts and unit production costs which are fairly downwardly rigid. The latter fact means that firms are less likely to accommodate exchange rate changes, especially when exchange rates are volatile, and movements uncertain. All of the above suggests what is widely held to be true, that shifts away from PPP are likely to be slow to correct. Therefore PPP does not provide a good determinant for short-term behaviour.

PPP as a long-term equilibrium　PPP as a long-term equilibrium is not so easy to dismiss however, and has been supported by arguments despite doubts on the validity of conditions (2) and (3) above. The arguments are that the differences in consumer preferences, production functions, etc., are likely to be reflected in international differences in relative prices, and in price index weightings. Changes in consumer preferences and in production technologies are likely to alter relative prices with a resultant change in real exchange rates. Thus PPP could hold in the long run when firms have had a chance to change their prices accordingly. For the very long run, the case for PPP becomes even more watertight. It is argued that the dissemination of knowledge and technologies, production methods, as well as capital and labour mobility all point towards a strong tendency towards PPP in the very long run.

PPP and hyperinflation　The reliability of PPP is very much dependent on what causes an exchange rate movement. If price indices are changing due to purely monetary developments rather than structural shocks, then PPP is more likely to hold true. Changes in productivity are less likely to affect price levels in countries as there tends to be an equilibration between similar workers in different countries.

Interest rate currency determination

In the 1970s, contrary to what occurs now, it was usual for interest rate increases to be associated with a depreciation of the currency. This may have been due to the fact that central banks seemed to increase interest rates in response to weakening of exchange rates rather than to curb inflationary pressures. However, after monetary targeting became the fashion in the US and UK, the relationship tended to be the opposite. A rise in interest rates occurred with an appreciation in the exchange rate. One can see from Figure 9.1 that the lower the interest rate differential between the Federal Funds rate and the German discount rate the weaker the dollar tends to be.

One would expect, given fairly accurate market expectations, that moves in the exchange rate would lead changes in interest rate differentials, but this is not really the case. Interventions, real or verbal, give strong signals to the currency markets, but events may only occur with a long lag. This inability of markets to predict currency moves is a signal of how difficult it is for other economic agents, such as firms, to predict and prepare for currency trends. This is one uncertainty that would be reduced in EMU.

Forward rates as predictors of future spot rates

Given rational expectations, the forward market rate should be a good predictor of the actual future spot rate, but evidence shows the contrary. Empirical evidence (Isard 1978, Mussa 1979, Frenkel 1981) shows that interest differentials explain only a small proportion of changes in exchange rates. The predicted changes were generally much smaller than the actual changes in exchange rates. In fact Fama (1984) showed that the explanatory power of the forward rate in predicting future changes in the spot exchange rate was negligible. As described above, assuming random walk behaviour over periods of up to three months (Mussa 1979) one should conclude that the best estimate of the future spot rate should be the current spot rate, and

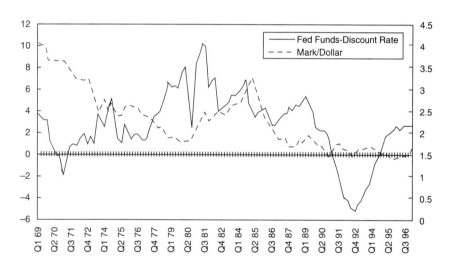

Figure 9.1 US Fed Funds/German discount rate against DM/US$ (1969–97)
Source: Datastream

128

not the three month forward rate. Market expectations actually often predicted the wrong direction of a currency change.

There has been much debate over why the predictors of exchange rates via the forward rates have been systematically incorrect. If the market were 'rational' systematic mistakes should not be made. There are many different possible explanations. The 'peso problem' is a popular one, whereby even if expectations are formed rationally, and are correct, they may predict an event which may fail to occur over a long period, but which eventually happens. Connected to this is the argument that market participants are rational 'students' of changes in policy setting rules, and other structural shifts influencing currencies: they do not have complete information about how policy is set, and may therefore make repeated mistakes in interpretation and forecasting. Prediction bias may also result from speculative 'bubbles', the self-fulfilling prophecies of investors.

Random walks

Empirical evidence on currency paths have mostly rejected the hypothesis of exchange rates resembling a random walk, i.e. having no tendency to revert themselves over time. Random walk behaviour means that the best predictor of a future exchange rate would be its current value. Mussa showed that exchange rates exhibited a random walk behaviour, but mainly over shorter time periods, i.e. less than three months (Mussa 1979). Studies have shown that instead exchange rates exhibit a certain amount of 'mean-reversion', though means tend to change through time.

Exchange rate expectations and overshooting

The notable lack of predictive power of forward rates for actual exchange rates was noticed fairly early on after the beginning of the flexible exchange rate system following the break-down of Bretton Woods. Models then evolved which modelled expectations of exchange rates, and the reactions of currencies to new data or events. The sharp over-reactions to news spawned Dornbusch's overshooting model (see Dornbusch 1976, 1983 and 1987). Dornbusch assumed short-run price stickiness, so that PPP held only in the long run. With short-run price stickiness, nominal and real interest rates would be lowered by an expansion in money supply, but only for the time it takes for prices to change. Dornbusch therefore attributed overshooting to sticky price adjustments, but many other, newer explanations are also interesting.

Amidst the madding crowd: heterogeneous speculators

The modelling of the exchange rate market on the basis of fundamentals or using one particular model or theory could be seen as misplaced. Speculation and investment takes place on the basis of many theories and methods. Frankel and Froot (1986) and Goodhart (1988) talk of a 'heterogeneous' group of speculators in action on the currency markets, all using a wide range of techniques from longer-term fundamentals to short-term mean-reversion, and 'technical analysis'. They argue that many different methods and the shifting balance of these groups, given new data and events, leads to apparent overshooting and mispricings.

Trading strategies based on 'technicals' rather than fundamentals can make significant profits. When there are no changes in expectations of what the fundamentals hold, chartists tend to reign. Short-term fluctuations are the result of speculators with shorter time horizons, who tend to rely on short-term forecasting methods. In these cases technicals provide more justifications for short-term trends, but can tend to exacerbate short-term movements over a longer period, leading to exchange rates becoming mispriced.

Overshooting may also occur as market participants often cannot immediately divulge the importance of news releases, new data, etc. They therefore take some time to digest news. A market participant uncertain on how to interpret news may use the market as its guide. It provides instant feedback on the thought processes of other participants, e.g. if a speculator does not know how a particular piece of news will affect an exchange rate, she may wait to see the market reaction and then follow it, thereby exacerbating the original trend. Currency markets are prone to 'herd instincts' precisely because they embody more uncertainty and volatility. Market movements themselves may therefore provide signals and new information which can lead to overshooting and extra volatility. Exchange rate interventions should be used to remind market speculators of the fundamentals, especially considering the long-term impacts that short-term volatility can have on the real economy.

Budget deficit reduction: the effect on the exchange rate

Both empirical evidence and theoretical argument are ambiguous when it comes to the resultant effect of budget deficits on the exchange rate. This ambiguity stems from the many different smaller effects deficit reduction can be seen to have on an exchange rate, some of which are positive and others negative. When a government is attempting to reduce a budget deficit, it generally needs to borrow less (as it no longer has to pay so much for the excess of spending over taxes). This causes the demand for funds and consequently domestic interest rates to fall. With interest rates falling, this has a weakening effect on the domestic currency. This is seen as the main direct effect from deficit reduction to the exchange rate. There are other smaller indirect effects, however, which may, in combination, counteract this direct effect. This abundance of different effects, makes currency prediction, and therefore planning for the consequences of currency changes even more difficult.

The decline in demand for funds by the government could be replaced by an increase in funds demanded elsewhere, e.g. by private investors. This would occur due to indirect effects from the budget deficit cutting effort, via either lower expected inflation, lower foreign exchange risk premia or a greater expected rate of return on domestic securities.

Lower expected inflation is seen as a result of reducing budget deficits, as lower budget deficits reduce investor fears that the government would resort to monetizing the deficit. The counter argument to this is that a fall in inflation expectations leads to a reduction in the inflation premium on long-term interest rates, thereby reducing the long-term interest rate, leading to a weakening of the exchange rate.

Deficit reduction could also reduce the risk premium of domestic securities in comparison to foreign securities. When the foreign exchange risk premium falls, the demand for domestic securities rises and the currency strengthens. This could happen via a fall in the stock of domestic government securities due to deficit reduction or via a lower probability of default, or other indirect effects. Though default is usually fairly unlikely for industrial countries, a remote chance still has an effect on the demand for domestic securities.

By cutting government spending, deficit reduction shifts demand from the government to the private sector (via lower interest rates). Consequently, productivity and long-run potential economic growth could rise, especially if some of the resources are shifted from public spending to private investment. This would have the resultant effect of increasing the expected return on domestic assets, perhaps increasing demand and inducing a stronger exchange rate. By running a budget deficit, given that the government should eventually raise taxes to make interest payments in the future, this implies a higher rate of tax on capital gains, and a lower after tax return. Therefore, when a budget deficit is being *reduced*, the demand for government debt should *increase*, as a lower tax rate, and a higher after tax return are expected in the future, one would therefore expect a firming of the domestic exchange rate.

The question remains whether these indirect effects, which tend to strengthen the exchange rate, offset the direct effects that tend to weaken exchange rates. The indirect effects are more likely to dominate if deficit reduction is seen as long term and sustainable. In this case, deficit reduction is expected to reduce inflation expectations considerably, also the risk premium, and the after tax expected rate of return, thereby strengthening the exchange rate. Otherwise, if there is a large risk of monetisation, or a large risk of default, or the expected return on domestic assets increases significantly, then the reduction of budget deficits will have a positive effect on the exchange rate.

A recent IMF study (IMF 1996) showed that the real exchange rate rose 5.4 per cent on average in fourteen 'successful' periods of fiscal consolidation, while the exchange rate fell in the forty-eight 'unsuccessful' cases (a period was determined as being 'successful' if the gross public debt as a share of GDP fell by at least 3 per cent by the second year after the end of a fiscal tightening). The IMF study showed that 'successful' cases tended to have a larger fiscal contraction of about 4 per cent of GDP compared to unsuccessful cases of about 3.2 per cent. Unsurprisingly successful cases relied more on spending cuts rather than revenue increases. Average expenditure cuts for the successful episodes was about 3–3.75 per cent of GDP as opposed to only 2 per cent for the unsuccessful episodes (see Chapter 4 for more on fiscal policy).

Currency effects on growth

Large fluctuations in exchange rates make it more difficult to maintain stability in growth and inflation. A large fall in the exchange rate increases inflation through relatively more expensive imports. A weakening of the exchange rate will also tend to shift income (in the short run) away from wages towards larger profits. This is due to consumers facing a negative income effect from more inflation, with domestic firms benefiting from consumers substituting out of imports in to domestically produced goods. An appreciating currency, however, has a strong adverse effect on manufacturing. The trade balance may not always reveal this effect directly as currency fluctuation effects on trade can be cushioned to a large extent by profit margin changes.

Added uncertainty

Exchange rate changes induce an upheaval of inflation and growth allocations between different countries. Firstly, the increased uncertainty which derives from currency fluctuations has dampening effects on investment and consumption decisions. With inflation affected by currency depreciation, uncertainty about inflation rises, affecting consumption decisions made. Uncertainty about the path of exports has a resultant effect on employment decisions, leading to a strong reluctance to employ even when an upturn in foreign demand is seen. Secondly, there is an imported inflation effect. For countries where the currency is weakening, a short-run increase in growth comes hand in hand with an upturn in inflation, and vice versa for strengthening currency countries. The European Commission note that:

> firstly, short-term (exchange rate) movements may – because of the uncertainty they engender – lead to a fall in the volume of trade. Secondly, certain medium-term movements can also affect trade flows and international specialisation on account of the changes in competitiveness that they engender.
>
> (European Commission 1995: 2)

These latter, more long-term structural effects on industry are more visible and can be devastating to an economy.

Temporary appreciation, long-term problem.

Currency movements limit forward planning, holding industry hostage to whatever fluctuations take place. Sterling's and the dollar's appreciation in 1979–81 and 1981–5 respectively left industrial and manufacturing output greatly weakened. The currency movements had reversed themselves by the mid (UK) to late 1980s (US) in both countries, but industry in the meantime went through substantial change. The adjustments needed to cope with these currency changes was almost entirely a waste of resources. Substitution away from firms that are made less competitive by currency changes can have dramatic effects on various sectors and regions. In particular smaller firms suffer as they are less able to diversify either as far as products are concerned or on a geographical basis. Diversification by larger firms, and closure of smaller firms, means that the resultant adverse effect on domestic employment can be very large.

In the next few sections we look at examples from Germany, the US and Japan. Though examples from the last two may seem to be less relevant to the European case, they are important, well-known examples of the effects of currency changes on economies which may be considered more able to cope with fluctuations than the smaller, often less diversified economies of the EU.

Dollar appreciation, US consequences (the mid 1980s)

In the 1980s the dollar appreciated about 60 per cent resulting in widespread economic consequences, the loss of important export markets, with production moving abroad where costs were relatively much cheaper. The policy response was to increase relief to US sectors from the effects of the stronger dollar. The real impact on traded goods was large, as the strong dollar made imports more attractive compared to domestically produced goods. The ratio of the volume of retail imports to total US goods produced rose from 19 per cent in 1980–2 to 26 per cent in 1986. In manufacturing the rise in the ratio of imports to US manufacturing output was even more dramatic. It rose from 19.7 per cent in 1980 to 32 per cent in 1985, while the ratio of manufacturing exports fell from 25.5 per cent to 17.2 per cent between 1980 and 1986. These changes were not only notable for the magnitude of effect but for their rapidity. The effect on employment was also marked. Manufacturing employment fell from 23.4 per cent in 1979 to 19.8 per cent in 1985, with no benefit attained from the economic recovery of the mid 1980s.

Twin deficits: the US problem

The rise of the dollar in the 1980s was initially a result of rises in interest rates at the end of 1979. This increased the real interest rate and reduced the risk of runaway inflation making dollar securities less attractive on the international market. Reagan's election and the plans for cutting taxes and increasing defence spending increased expectations of large future budget deficits, thereby once again increasing interest rate expectations. The correlation between a large budget deficit and an appreciating dollar was unusual, compared to past experiences. In this case however, the large budget deficit was not associated with rising inflation. The Federal Reserve's fairly tough anti-inflationary stance meant that higher interest rates might not be concurrent with higher inflation. The dollar however continued to increase in 1982 and 1983, even after inflation had stabilised and the Federal Reserve had let short-term rates fall. The problem of twin deficits then became an issue. With the large budget deficit reducing total domestic savings and private sector savings not rising (or investments falling) to fill the gap, the trade deficit worsened. In the US, although savings fell relative to GDP, net private investment increased, making the rise in the trade deficit, and in the dollar, inevitable.

German competitiveness worsens (the 1990s)

The stronger DM in the 1990s as well as high wage deals have worsened the competitiveness of German industry. Calculations by the European Commission show that German production prices increased 4.7 per cent compared to the Community average between 1987 and 1994. In the same period, export volume fell 15.7 per cent compared to the Community average. These factors caused substantial loss of export market share, with the German intra-EU trade share falling from 30.95 per cent in 1987 to 24.26 per cent in 1994. The export market share of extra-EU trade, fell from 38.37 per cent to 35.16 per cent between 1987 and 1994 (European Commission 1995). Germany's cost disadvantages can be illustrated clearly by its lack of benefit from the general world trade increase in 1995. The increase in world trade was estimated at 8 per cent, but Germany's rise in real exports was estimated (by the Bundesbank) at only 4 per cent in 1995.

Japan begins to re-emerge

In Japan, economic perspectives remain weak for 1996–7 and far below standard Japanese rate of growth. After 0.5 per cent in 1994 and 0.9 per cent in 1995, GDP growth should record 2.5 per cent in 1996 and 2.7 per cent in 1997 (OECD 1996, forecast). Even if these rates are high compared to Western industrialised countries, they are far below the average GDP growth of 5 per cent recorded in the period 1988–91. The recovery follows the extra-ordinary expansion in fiscal and monetary policy adopted by the government and the Bank of Japan. The yen has seen steady strengthening since 1990. The OECD notes that the correction of the overvaluation of the yen should reduce the losses experienced in export market shares. In 1994 and 1995, manufacturing export growth was 10 per cent below the growth of export markets. The reversal in the yen, seen since mid 1995 should help profits in export industries to increase especially in the chemical and car industries which were hit very hard. Exports recorded a sharp decrease due to the shift of manufacturing sites in satellite countries (Korea, Taiwan etc.) which increased imports of once exported goods and due to a strengthening of the yen against the dollar, the yen/US$ exchange rate fell from 144 in 1990 to 85 in mid 1995.

Trade

The links between macroeconomic and trade policies run in two directions. Fiscal, monetary and exchange rate policies have substantial effects on trade volumes, limiting the ability of domestic industry to compete. For example excessively high interest rates can reduce companies incentives to invest, also high taxes may make a firm less able to compete on the world market. On the other hand, a healthy export market can often be the key to push an economy into more robust growth, assisted by a weakening currency.

Developments in world trade since 1992 show, unsurprisingly, that relative export prices have been responsible for changes in world export shares. Japan's loss of export share has followed their relative price increases since then. Germany has experienced a similar process, but its relatively smaller

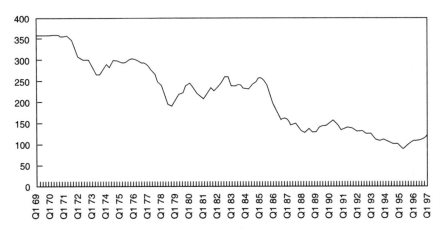

Figure 9.2 Japanese yen to 1 US dollar (quarterly average)
Source: Datastream

loss in competitiveness has meant a large drop in export share. On the other hand, in order to keep its large market share, the US has seen a fairly substantial fall in relative prices.

One solution to eliminating a trade deficit is of course a depreciation or devaluation of the domestic currency. This would make it easier for domestic firms to compete with those abroad. This tends to be inflationary however,

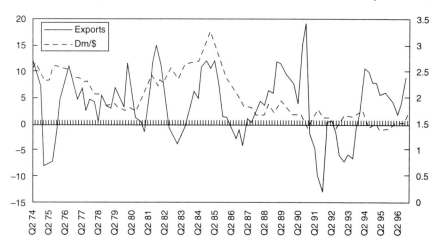

Figure 9.3 German exports Y/Y and the DM/US$ exchange rate
Source: Datastream and Federal Statistics Office, Germany

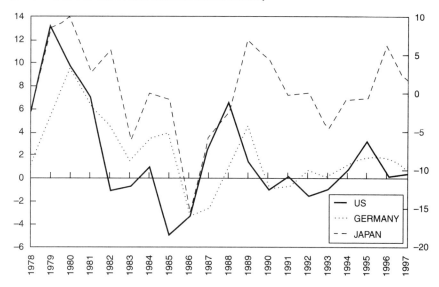

Figure 9.4 OECD relative export prices
Source: OECD *Economic Outlook*, June 1996, Paris
Note: 1996–7 data are OECD projections

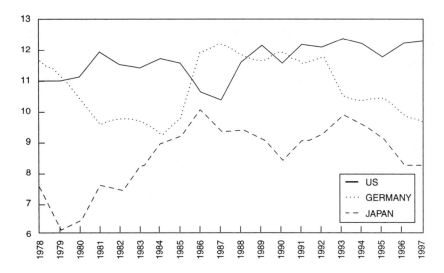

Figure 9.5 OECD share in world exports
Source: OECD *Economic Outlook*, June 1996, Paris
Note: 1996–8 data are OECD projections

which in turn reduces competitiveness in the medium term, so defeating the initial goal. The solution to a trade deficit has two parts, people first have to be persuaded to shift their demand from foreign to domestically produced goods. But these measures must be taken alongside policies reducing the level of domestic demand, so that there is some counterbalance to inflationary pressures. The first part of the solution, shifting demand from foreign to domestically produced goods can be done by reducing the demand of the domestic currency or by imposing tariffs or import quotas. Cruder methods such as the 'Buy British' advertising campaign in the 1970s have also been tried but have not proved very successful.

Recent trade policy developments

Modern trade policy is based on the fact that increased trade, in an environment of loosening trade barriers, should act as a strong stimulus to economic growth. Trade literature emphasises that trade liberalisation leads to higher economic growth through many channels. This was, of course, part of the justification for the common market in the first place.

European trade and the EEC

The establishment of the EEC in 1958 led to a quick reduction of intra-EEC tariffs and quantity restrictions. The EEC also became more powerful in trade negotiations, a force to contend with for the US. Many empirical studies point to a close connection between EC integration and the growth of trade, with the dominant part of that increase due to trade creation rather than diversion from other trading partners. Muller and Owen show that in 1970, 30 per cent of intra EC trade in manufactured goods was due to new trade creation. More recent studies have shown that growth in trade has increased plant size and improved economies of scale, the cost savings induced amounted to about 3–6 per cent of GDP for the six countries (Belgium, France, Germany, Italy, Luxembourg, Netherlands) for 1980. There were also indications of increases in investment particularly from the US. These results do have to be digested with caution however, as much of the increases in GDP and trade noted were aided by a favourable macroeconomic environment. In the 1990s, the Internal Market programme of the European Union was a major initiative to stimulate growth. Though there were some worries that this might create a impenetrable European trade area, this has not come about, with fairly limited trade diversion (estimated at about 2.5 per cent of extra EU imports).

Trade theory

General trade liberalisation theory has shown that the import of more efficient capital goods, and the reduction of monopoly power are two main areas which have improved with greater trade liberalisation. Several channels of transmission from trade to permanently higher growth rates are generally cited, these include the increased international diffusion of knowledge, and stimulated innovation and growth by expanding the effective market size for producers. Trade may also provide access to a large variety of specialised inputs and production techniques. Against this emphasis on open trade, with liberal trade policies to stimulate trade and improve efficiency, is the tendency of governments, when faced with the increased globalisation of trade and increasing competition accompanied by currency volatility, to tend towards protectionist trade policies. Trade volumes in the early 1990s grew more than real GDP. Trade development in industrial countries was accompanied by significant regional liberalisation, with continued escalation of trade friction.

The Uruguay Round

The international trading environment came under some strain in 1990–3, the Uruguay Round sought to create the most ambitious multilateral trade negotiations in history; but difficulties in discussions worsened trade tensions and undermined confidence in multilateralism. The trend towards regional integration intensified, partly reflecting frustration with the multilateral process, but also as a result of political and economic wrangling of regional partners. Protectionist pressures and trade frictions persisted, and escalated in some areas given slow growth and high unemployment, which led to governments increasingly desiring to shelter their economies. Delays in the Uruguay Round exacerbated this trend.

The conclusion of the Uruguay Round in late 1993 substantially improved the prospects for restoring the credibility of the multilateral trading system. Large strides were made in market liberalisation (estimated to add 1 per cent to real world GDP and 12 per cent to world trade upon full implementation of the agreement); the creation of the World Trade Organisation to adjudicate disputes more efficiently; and the inclusion of areas such as services, intellectual property rights, and traditionally sensitive sectors such as agriculture, textiles and clothing into the multilateral trading system.

For the future, the list of areas for which trade policies are needed continues to grow. The links between trade policy and environmental and labour objectives are undoubtedly important, and more negotiations should be seen in areas such as agriculture, steel, and civil aircraft. In general however there is some worry that overloading the trade policy instrument to serve too many objectives may be damaging. With trade policy now balancing the weight of responsibility for revenue, balance of payments, income distribution, competition policy, environment, labour standards, and human rights this may lower its efficiency as a resource allocator, thereby making increased trade liberalisation less able to emerge.

Some empirical results

Studies of the impact of protectionist policies on growth have shown that many microeconomic inefficiencies resulting from various types of protectionism tend to lead to high capital–output ratios and reduced economic growth. Cross country studies generally show that lowering trade barriers stimulates exports and hence growth, but Krueger (1978) shows that the direct effect of trade liberalisation on growth is not statistically significant. Edwards (1992), shows to a high degree of robustness that countries with more liberal trade policy regimes have grown more quickly than those without.

Does central bank intervention work?

Currency volatility can impose large economic costs on the economy in question, as we discussed above. It is also an inconvenience for policy makers. When foreign exchange markets are not seen to be portraying the correct picture in terms of fundamentals, central bankers may intervene to redress the balance. Given the strong real economic outcomes from exchange rate mispricing, interventions should be pursued to limit the long-term damage. Volatility is a function of the certainty with which views on economic fundamentals are held and interventions, actual or verbal, can clarify market expectations, thereby reducing market volatility. Foreign exchange volatility can also affect the stability of the financial markets, by making all asset prices subject to more volatility. Speculative bubbles can also occur, for the reasons described above.

Arguments for intervention

If the external balance is affected by an internal shock then with flexible exchange rates the internal shock is usually exacerbated in order to restore external balance, e.g. internal deflation will strengthen the real exchange rate, depressing domestic activity further via falling demand for exports. Lower export demand would tend to lower the nominal exchange rate to equilibriate the trade balance. Given that internal shocks occur fairly frequently, there is a case for limiting the damage done by exchange rate movements via intervention. Flexible rates therefore provide a buffer from external shocks but exaggerate internal ones.

Fully flexible exchange rates tend to mean more overshooting and mispricing. Greater short-term variations in rates are also seen in a fully flexible system, this volatility is more than is necessary for the long-term adjustment of the external balance. If interventions were to reduce this volatility, they would reduce market mispricings and speculative 'bubbles'. Foreign exchange volatility can also affect the stability of financial markets, by making asset prices subject to more volatility. Monetary policy goals could then be more difficult to achieve.

Difficulties of intervention

Intervention can be effective in moving the exchange rate to a more desired level, but it is becoming more and more difficult. Central bank reserves are very small, and the ability of currency imbalances to be financed by fluctuations in reserve levels or by small variations in interest rates relative to other countries, is limited to a great extent. When reserves are too small, there are also problems in arranging large-scale borrowing on reasonable terms. The size of short-term capital flows can now offset the reserve position of most countries very quickly. The scope available to finance an imbalance without taking other steps to correct it are very small and can be non-existent.

Do interventions reduce volatility?

1 Central bank intervention can reduce volatility if it succeeds in lessening uncertainty, e.g. by emphasising central bank commitment to a certain monetary policy, or if it curtails speculative movements before profits can be made out of them. Speculators may be more reluctant to take positions if they perceive that the central bank would intervene in the opposite direction. By limiting selling pressure when a currency begins

to fall, central bank intervention could reduce speculative bubbles, there-fore leading to a fall in volatility

2 Central bank intervention could increase volatility however by encour-aging more speculation, e.g. if the intervention is not sufficiently explained, the market's expectations of future moves may become more uncertain

3 Intervention may have no real effect on the currency, e.g. the Federal Reserve can only intervene by a small fraction of the amount of capital flows in the market. Therefore Federal Reserve interventions may have little effect on the market

Evidence on volatility

One can use implied volatility to measure the markets expectations of future volatility. Implied volatility is derived from the price of a foreign exchange option. An increase in volatility of the exchange rate increases the value of the option, and its price. A paper by Bonser-Neal (1996) using this technique is particularly interesting.

The study looks at the dollar during 1985–91 and shows evidence that interventions led to an actual increase in volatility. The period was divided into three phases:

The first period is the 'Plaza' phase which was from 1 January 1985 to 21 February 1987. Then the goal of intervention was a gradual depreciation of the dollar. This goal was formalised in the Plaza agreement of 22 September 1985, by the finance ministers of the G5 countries. This represented the shift from a relatively laissez-faire policy during the first Reagan administration to a more flexible policy of activism during the second administration. Some intervention was agreed upon at a G5 meeting on 17 January 1985, and took place soon afterwards, though for the US this was fairly small. The German monetary authorities intervened heavily to sell dollars in foreign exchange markets in February and March. Intervention was particularly strong on 27 February, and appears to have been the catalyst to the following depreciation. By the time the G5 had met at the Plaza Hotel on 22 September 1985, the dollar had already depreciated by 13 per cent. The meeting agreed that 'some orderly appreciation of the non-dollar currencies is desirable' and that 'they stand ready to co-operate more closely to encourage this when to do so would be helpful'. A 10–12 per cent depreciation of the dollar had been specified as the aim and seems to have been accepted by the G5 ministers. The dollar immediately fell 4 per cent against a weighted average of other currencies, but then it resumed to a gradual depreciation at a similar rate to the preceding seven months. The slow fall of interest rates in the US had lit-tle effect, and the Plaza agreement was regarded as a success. For this period however the study shows that there seems to have been no effect from cen-tral bank interventions on volatility.

The second period studied was the Louvre phase (22 February 1987 to 31 December 1989) where the intention was to stabilise the dollar at existing levels. The G7 finance ministers at Louvre on 21–22 February 1987 agreed that in return for a more stable dollar, Japan should agree to expand domestic demand and Germany and others agreed to reduce levels of taxation. The US commitment at Louvre showed up in three ways : an absence of the statements by the Secretary of the Treasury talking down the dollar; purchases of dollars in foreign exchange intervention operations; and a tighter monetary policy (reversing a three-year trend of lower interest rates). Though the last part was really spurred by a desire to lower inflationary pressures, rather than any dollar motivated strategy, the results seem to have been fairly positive (as can be seen from Figure 9.6).

There is evidence to suggest however that central bank interventions in this period caused increased volatility. Academics have suggested (Krugman 1988a) that international policy co-operation during 1987 was incorrect to resist further downward pressures on the dollar, through interest rate increases which in the end may have caused the stock market crash of October 1987. The third period under study was the post-Louvre period, when Federal Reserve intervention became less frequent and less likely to be co-ordinated with other central banks. During this period there was some evidence of a fall in volatility although most of the evidence pointed to minimal effect.

Though currency intervention can be of little use, and may even be self-defeating, it is often better than nothing. The 'hands off' policy of the US from April 1981 led to a sharp dollar appreciation. Perhaps some improvement in the way interventions are carried out, and more transparency of intention could lead to better intervention policy. In fact the dollar plunge

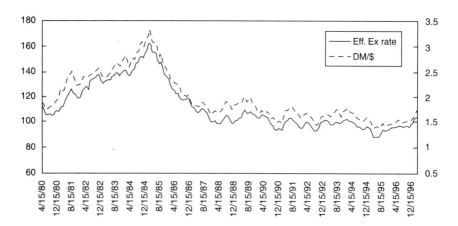

Figure 9.6 US effective echange rate and DM/US$ rate
Source: Datastream

seen in 1994 was undone by concerted and consistent signalling by international policy makers, notably at G7 meetings early in 1995. Thirty-day dollar volatility fell from nearly 20 per cent to about 8 per cent between April and July 1995. It is arguable as to how much these signals directly reduced volatility, but they did have some effect in pushing the dollar back to reasonable levels, and stabilising dollar movements. The G7 meeting (28 September 1996) noted the success of the 1995 interventions in pushing up the value of the dollar, notably against the DM.

Europe and the ERM 1992–3

Much has been said about the explosion of internationally mobile private capital in recent decades, and its fast speed of movement. Though these developments create problems, they also enable a country to smooth its consumption through growth cycles. In theory international capital mobility also means that savings can move from where productivity is relatively low toward countries where productivity is higher.

This year-long drama forced a major re-think of transition plans to monetary union. International capital mobility was a major factor in the problems experienced. Other factors were also at play, most importantly the unification of Germany and the constraints imposed on European countries by the Maastricht criteria. German unification resulted in a substantial increase in fiscal expenditure at a time when the West German economy was experiencing near potential growth rates. The increases in expenditure therefore caused the Bundesbank to keep interest rates high in order to reduce inflationary pressures. The result was that though other countries experienced an initial impetus from increases in exports to Germany, the Bundesbank's high level of rates meant that given the commitment to exchange rate stability against the DM both in the ERM or pegged to the ECU (for Finland, Norway and Sweden) European countries suffered substantially domestically.

The emergence of a one-way bet on realignment between higher yielding currencies and the DM put extreme pressure on all the countries with relatively high short-term interest rates. Pressure began in earnest after the Danish referendum narrowly rejected the Maastricht Treaty in early June 1992. In August, matters worsened with French voters looking like rejecting it also in a vote on 20 September. Confidence weakened very rapidly, with a full range of institutional investors and non-financial corporations applying pressure. The first currency to fall off its peg was the Finnish markka (8 September 1992). Market pressures then attacked the Swedish krona, though it defended the first attack, it fell in November. Days later on 13 September the lira was devalued by 7 per cent. On 16–17 September, sterling and the lira were both withdrawn from the ERM. On 17 September the peseta was devalued by 5 per cent. Pressures continued on and off through until August 1993 when the bands were widened substantially. From June to December 1992, total official intervention sales of DM by European central banks were DM284 billion net, of which DM188 billion was sold in defence of ERM currencies.

Transitionary problems towards EMU

These events have caused much discussion about transitionary problems towards EMU. The possibility of further speculative attacks needs to be tackled. One of the important issues is whether the current fairly wide ERM bands should be maintained until the move to a single currency, or whether there should be a gradual narrowing of bands. Wide bands have many advantages, they obviously reduce the likelihood of parity changes, whilst being a small safety valve to ease short-term financial pressures. They do not however rule out the possibility of speculative attacks due to large financial shocks.

Target zones

Target zone models were very popular until the ERM crisis of September 1992. They were introduced to describe the functioning of the EMS, its sustainability and its credibility. A target zone is a quasi-fixed exchange rate regime where the rate fluctuates around a central parity ($+/-2.25$ per cent in the EMS case). When the exchange rate touches the upper and the lower bound, it reverts to the central parity (in this case the exchange rate becomes a mean reverting process) given that the system is credible and the markets do not believe that the bounds will be overshot. The key assumption of this model is that the two central banks, whose currency is under attack, commit themselves to keep the exchange rate between the admissible fluctuation range. In this scenario, the credibility of the commitment by central banks and the connected intrinsic nature of the mean reversion by the currency are a self-fulfilling mechanism. The breakdown of the EMS in September 1992 showed that this kind of system could not work without capital controls and with a lack of co-ordination in fiscal policies (as happened after the expansionary fiscal policy which followed German reunification).

The Mexican currency crisis

The main currency event in recent times was the Mexico crisis. This was a good example of the fragility of currency markets. Though there were good reasons for a weakening in the Mexican peso, the actual weakness seen was greater, and had a larger effect than fundamentals would have implied. In the early 1990s capital from abroad started to pour into developing countries, to take advantage of what was seen as a higher marginal productivity of capital. Net capital inflows to Latin America went from under US$11 billion between 1985–9 to over US$60 billion in 1992–4. These capital inflows represented more than 2 per cent of GDP for many developing countries. By the end of 1994, however, sentiment towards Mexico changed suddenly, with the resultant fall in capital inflows and a sharp fall in the Mexican peso. This had a strong effect on the Mexican economy, with contagious effects on other currencies and countries. Changes in capital flows are the result of many different factors, often out of the control of monetary authorities. The causes often have short-term horizons but long-term impacts. Growth in Mexico remains very hesitant, and the future relies on the ability of the large risk premia currently incorporated into interest rates to fall. Assistance from the IMF was crucial to putting Mexico back on the road to recovery.

There are many hypotheses about why the Mexican crisis came about (see Teunissen 1996). The three main reasons generally cited are:

1   due to an unsustainable external position
2   due to relaxed fiscal policies
3   due to a series of political and criminal events

The timing of the crisis was unfortunate, coming after years of macroeconomic stabilisation and structural reform efforts including strengthening public finances, deregulation of economic activity, financial reform, privatisations, restructuring of external debt, trade liberalisation and the signing of the North Atlantic Free Trade Agreement (NAFTA). Economic activity had recovered (to about 3.1 per cent GDP average between 1989 and 1994) and inflation was down to single digits. All these moves attracted flocks of investors, with capital flows reaching unprecedented levels (US$104 billion between 1990 and 1994). The Mexican peso appreciated as a result with the corresponding effect on the current account.

The stronger Peso led to a reduction in exports, a large increase in imports, with a large current account deficit. In fact the current account went from a surplus of 2.7 per cent of GDP in 1987 to a deficit of 7.7 per cent of GDP in 1994. This external balance soon became unsustainable, and led to the collapse of the exchange rate. The origins of the current account deficit were both an increase in investments and a fall in savings ratios. The increase of foreign capital flowing in, and the reduction in US interest rates at the end of 1990 meant a surge in external resources being sucked into Mexico. This was used to increase investment and consumption and resulted in increased imports and in an accumulation of international reserves. The outcome was added inflationary pressure and a large current account deficit.

Many argue that the collapse of the Mexican peso was due to its overvaluation, but this seems unreasonable in the light of the fact that it had already been the subject of several depreciating influences in the late 1980s:

1   The price of oil, Mexico's largest export, dropped sharply in 1986 causing a loss of revenues of about 6 per cent of GDP; this in combination with a public sector deficit of 15 per cent of GDP led to an adjustment which required a peso depreciation by 60 per cent in 1986

2   In 1987, as recovery was beginning, the collapse of world stock markets
    in October 1987 caused a crisis of confidence, and a 20 per cent devalu-
    ation in the Peso; with a much weaker peso than in 1985, the effect on
    inflation was large

The Peso underwent substantial appreciation from the end of 1990 to
January 1994 but these moves were based on changes in fundamentals.
Mexican firms in tradable sectors were forced to compete internationally,
which meant an upgrade of technologies, and an increase of the productivity
of labour in those sectors. This in turn pulled up wages in other sectors, and
increased inflation. Secondly, the inflows of capital had a natural appreciating
effect on the Peso, especially in comparison to the previous period in which
the country was a net exporter of capital. In this period Mexico was using a
pre-announced exchange rate band, as part of its concerted strategy to reduce
inflation. In 1991 the speed with which the band was widened was increased,
and the inner intervention band was abandoned towards the end of 1993.

The data suggests that Mexican fiscal policy in 1994 continued to be fairly
solid. The non-cash deficit was at -0.3 per cent of GDP compared to a surplus of 0.7 per cent of GDP in 1993. When privatisation funds are included
the deficit turned into a surplus of 0.1 per cent. Given this, the final factor
that led to the currency crisis seems not to have been fiscal laxity, but instead
a series of unpredictable political and criminal events, the most important
being the assassination of the ruling party's presidential candidate and the
Chiapas uprising. The former caused a large loss of international reserves as
a result of the increased uncertainty. After the assassination an 8 per cent
depreciation of the exchange rate was allowed, with interest rates increasing
sharply and Tesobonos issued. Nominal and real interest rates remained high
during 1994, the money market's leading rate doubled from 9 per cent to 18
per cent. Higher interest rates put added pressure on the private sector. The
post-assassination devaluation was seen as a betrayal, after so much optim-
ism on Mexico leaving the developing world and making it as a First World
nation. The Chiapas uprising was also crucial in changing sentiment towards
Mexico. This showed that Third World poverty still existed in some regions
of the country, which in turn caused a serious questioning of the political stability of the government. The violent reaction of domestic and institutional
investors was surprising, but was a culmination of many factors.

Large current account deficits can be financed for a long time, but they significantly increase an economy's vulnerability to variations in international
capital flows. When a large amount of those funds used to finance the deficit
are short-term volatile resources, vulnerability is even greater. Increased
awareness of this potential danger should lead authorities to limit current
account deficits to certain levels. Abrupt and massive changes in capital
flows leave policy makers and private agents little time to adjust. Countries
such as Mexico face a paradoxical problem, as large inflows eventually tend

to lead to growing current account deficits, the same investors who were eager to bring in their capital may be put off by the size of the deficit and become concerned. This may lead to a withdrawal of funds and may contribute to a payments crisis. Reducing the exposure of the country to the volatility of external capital, while sustaining a healthy level of investment required an increase in national savings. One way to accomplish this which has been seen to be useful in countries such as Chile is through the development of pension programmes.

The reverberations from the reversal in capital flows makes the adoption of measures to discourage the entrance of large capital inflows useful. The Bank of Mexico had imposed a limit on foreign currency denominated liabilities that commercial banks could take on. In hindsight, additional measures were needed, e.g. limits on the acquisition of public debt instruments by non-residents. In fact such a restriction had applied to foreign purchases of government paper from December 1980 to December 1990, but was eliminated in the liberalisation efforts.

The three currency zone world

In a world of liquid markets and efficient financial markets, the exchange rate regimes which seem the most durable are floating exchange rates and monetary unification (the two ends of the spectrum). Intermediate regimes which involve explicit exchange rate targets (pegged but adjustable rates, target zones, currency bands, crawling pegs) invite attack and perform well for only short periods. Given this, one can assume that countries will in the long term tend to one end of the currency spectrum or the other. The division is likely to be allocated by country size, as smaller countries suffer much more from currency swings than larger ones, and are therefore likely to want to fix their currencies. This is due to the fact that a larger proportion of the production in small countries is sold on international markets. Also, the financial sector of these countries will be smaller relative to the global financial markets, meaning that they are more susceptible to shifts in market sentiment or in the level of relative interest rates, causing large disruptive swings in inflows and in currency rates. Therefore, large countries like the US, Japan and Germany will continue to float one against the other, whereas smaller countries will seek to establish durable pegs with the larger trading partner. This implies that we are moving towards a world of three currency zones: the dollar, yen and EMU.

Conclusion

Currency markets are the most opaque and volatile of financial markets. The two case studies we looked at, the appreciation of the dollar and the ERM crisis of 1992–3, show that both too much rigidity in an adjustable peg system and a 'benign neglect' exchange rate policy can cause problems. What is most important in providing more stability in exchange rates is good macroeconomic stability. But in the example of the Mexico crisis a country experiencing wide ranging reforms and advances fell foul of a sharp turn-around in investor sentiment and the resulting currency volatility. International policy co-operation is needed on currency issues, individual countries should not be forced to pursue foreign exchange policies which are not in their interests. Currency stability is generally most at risk when authorities seek to maintain currency levels that are not in line with healthy macroeconomic outcomes. Time and greater experience have meant that recent exchange rate policy has become more transparent, and many of the problems of, for example, excess speculation or badly conducted policy are known and are being addressed. When exchange rate policy is faced with so many problems, the fundamental lesson should perhaps be that one can only do good when one works with, rather than against, the market. With currency markets apt to mis-price and to over-react, and given the very severe effect this can have on an economy, the move towards a three zone currency world seems to be an inevitable, and desirable one. EMU is very much part of this process.

10

LIFE OUTSIDE EMU

What currency regime for EMU outs (and is Argentina's currency board an option?)

Introduction

The recent debate on EMU has highlighted a conflict of interest between core and non-core EU members: most non-core countries, in particular Italy and Spain, have shown a strong willingness to be part of EMU from the outset (1 January 1999). Core countries view this with some scepticism or with outright opposition (as occasional Bundesbank comments have shown). In the event that Italy and other peripheral countries were to remain out, an increasingly unlikely scenario, there would be considerable pressure to devise forms of associate participation, particularly as the 'outs' have made considerable efforts to be part of EMU and would not want such efforts to go completely unrewarded. 'Links' to EMU will also become interesting as the EU pursues a gradual enlargement towards the East. Here, we look at possible options. We concentrate on the idea of a currency board, the strictest form of currency pegging. This system contains several interesting properties, particularly the fact that it provides a strict, but unilateral and reversible, form of fixed exchange rates. We conclude, however, that the risk of financial instability is so high that the system cannot be considered a viable option. A weaker alternative form of bilateral currency pegging with some borrowing facilities and intervention obligation within wide bands seems the only possible solution. This is discussed below. ERM II would not differ much from its predecessor. The lack of intermediate regimes between monetary union and a loose ERM system constitutes a problem for EMU and explains non-core countries' insistence on being part of the first wave.

The risk of being an 'out'

It is difficult to foresee the reaction of financial markets to a core-only monetary union. In particular, the effects on countries that are left out could be large. One possibility is that the impact will be moderated by expectations that those countries will be allowed in the union at a later stage. However, there is an undeniable risk that:

1   Investors will be attracted to the newly created and stronger currency

2   Failure to join in the first wave will be perceived as lowering non-core country incentives to pursue adjustment policies
3   The latter scenario implies higher interest rates in the non-core countries, weakening their economic growth and posing questions of debt sustainability that could reinforce market pessimism

The countries included in EMU suffer the risk of an appreciating euro which would worsen their competitiveness. If this was followed by uncertainty and volatility in financial markets, countries that were part of EMU might suffer from additional spillover effects. This would be particularly damaging if the launch of EMU was already associated with difficulties due to the introduction of the euro and the phasing out of domestic currencies.

The need to address the issue of how to deal with countries which do not qualify for EMU at the first stage was discussed in Chapter 2. There is controversy over what solutions can be devised and policy options appear limited. Below, we review the main options available to countries that wish to limit the fluctuations of their exchange rates, describing the possible exchange rate regimes and their main characteristics. We highlight where the ERM II proposal stands in our classification. Also, we note that the strictest form of currency pegging is the institution of a 'currency board' and we describe its main characteristics, discussing whether it is suitable for countries that are keen to join EMU, but do not quite qualify.

Exchange rate regimes: the IMF classification

We present a list of possible exchange rate regimes, short of monetary union, as described by the IMF (IMF 1995: 18). The list goes from the least flexible regime to the most flexible regime, practically a free float. This includes all the options available to countries which remain outside EMU to link their currencies with the euro, short of more comprehensive institutional arrangements or of bilateral regimes. All the regimes described below are unilateral (in the sense that they involve a commitment only from the country that is targeting its currency).

Peg: single currency   The country pegs to a major currency with infrequent adjustment of the parity.

Peg: currency composite   A weighted composite is formed from the currencies of major trading or financial partners. Currency weights are generally country specific and reflect the general distribution of trade and services or capital flows. The composite can also be standardised, such as those of the Special Drawing Rights (SDR) and the ECU.

Flexibility limited vis-à-vis single currency   The value of the currency is maintained within certain margins of fluctuation around a *de facto* peg.

Flexibility limited: co-operative arrangement This regime refers to countries in the Exchange Rate Mechanism (ERM) of the European Monetary System (EMS). It is a conceptual cross between a peg of each EMS currency to others in the system (currently within wide margins) and a float of all EMS currencies jointly against non-EMS currencies.

More flexible: adjusted according to a set of indicators The currency is adjusted more or less automatically in response to changes in selected quantitative indicators. A common indicator is the real effective exchange rate which reflects inflation-adjusted changes in the currency with respect to major trading partners; another is a fixed, pre-announced change.

More flexible: managed float The central bank quotes and supports the rate, but varies it frequently. Indicators for adjusting the rate are broadly judgmental including, for example, the balance of payments position, international reserves or parallel market developments; adjustments are therefore not automatic.

More flexible: independent float Rates are market-determined, with any intervention aimed at moderating the rate of change rather than establishing a level for the rate.

Multilateral agreements after EMU

The regimes described above would be strengthened if they were accompanied by multilateral agreements in which both sides were committed to respect certain fluctuation limits for their currencies. These would clearly be more complex to run, involving a bilateral arrangement rather than a domestic policy decision. There may also be times when the regime might imply a trade-off between the currency commitment and domestic policy needs. For example, an obligation to intervene against one's own currency may cause an undesirable increase in domestic money supply. On the other hand, bilateral agreements might have considerably greater credibility. (For a simple listing of these regimes see, among others, Spaventa 1996: 142.)

The weakest form of multilateral arrangement is one in which there is no mutual obligation to defend any specific currency level but in which the parity is set by multilateral arrangements. This is essentially equivalent to the case described above under the title 'flexibility limited *vis-à-vis* another currency', but the country involved gives up the right to unilaterally set the level or the band at which pegging takes place. In the case of Europe, for example in a new ERM, countries would have to agree on their central parity and on fluctuations bands together with their partners (the decision would be taken by the monetary committee, formed by economic and finance ministries and central bank officials). If an agreement is not reached a financial ministers meeting might have to be called. There would also be an obligation from each participating country to notify and submit for approval any parity change. In this weakest form of multilateral arrangement, however, there would be no obligation from partner countries or, in this specific case from the European Central Bank, to defend the parity.

The same arrangement as above could be strengthened by other commitments. In the European case, there have been several proposals. One is to give the currencies of the 'outs' some form of associated membership to the system. This could imply, for example, having a non-voting member in the policy setting council of the European Central Bank. Apart from representing a fairly limited concession, this arrangement would require a change in the Maastricht Treaty, which is legally very complex. Other, more interesting proposals imply some form of conditionality. The 'out' country would be required to satisfy some of the conditions required for countries in EMU, particularly with respect to maintaining the budget deficit within the limits set by the Stability Pact. In exchange, the ECB would selectively commit itself to defending the parity. In any case, this agreement would imply discretion by the ECB.

The strongest form of multilateral agreement is one in which both parties are committed to maintaining their currencies within a certain grid, and in which there are clear and binding intervention obligations and support facilities. This is essentially an attempt to correct the asymmetrical character of normal pegging arrangements. Some of the EMS rules attempt to move in this direction. The EMCF (European Monetary Co-operation Fund), a short-term financing facility, allowed countries to use a foreign currency credit facility made available by the other European countries during a speculative attack. The degree of asymmetry in this system can vary significantly, with both formal and informal arrangements. For example, within the EMS, the Bundesbank was clearly more strongly committed to offer support to the French franc than to other currencies.

ERM II: viable but weak

The EU summit in Dublin in December 1996 agreed a proposal on the arrangements for ERM II, based on European Commission proposals released in October 1996. The agreements are that the fluctuations between the euro and the currencies left out will be limited to 15 per cent on each side of their central rate in the ERM II system. When the currency of a country that is left out of EMU knocks against the 15 per cent band, the European Central Bank (ECB) will be required to intervene in the foreign exchange market to push it back into the band. However, this support would not be unlimited. It seems that intervention would be dependent on attempts by the country in question to retain its macroeconomic stability.

The newest element in ERM II is the fact that the ECB might offer its support in the form of open market intervention, depending on a set of convergence indicators. In particular, governments would present new 'convergence programmes' with targets for variables such as inflation, government deficit and debt. These would include proposed measures for the achievement of objectives. Compliance with the convergence programmes would be monitored by the Council and the Commission. A good performance on convergence would strengthen the case for support for a 'pre-in' currency if it came under attack (see the appendix to Chapter 6 which details the EMI's 'Operational Framework of the Single Currency' including arrangements for ERM II).

The ECB is likely to have the right to initiate realignment discussions if it appeared that the central rate of a currency was out of line with fundamentals. ERM II could also allow a narrowing of fluctuation bands, which could remain secret or be announced publicly. Known narrow bands would require 'automatic intervention' whereas secret bands would only be supported by 'co-ordinated' intervention, which is likely to be fairly limited. This system is very much as in the current ERM system. Marginal intervention would be only nominally compulsory as central banks (both the European Central Bank and national ones) have the right to suspend it if it clashes with their domestic policy objectives.

The European Commission proposal states:

> Given the linkage between exchange rate stability and convergence, the Commission would foresee a role for reinforced convergence programmes in the management of the new ERM. For example, the progress achieved by a 'pre-in' toward its convergence objectives might be used as a reference in deciding on the sustainability of central rates. A favourable performance relative to convergence objectives would be expected to strengthen the case for support for a 'pre-in' currency in the event of speculative pressures. However, the use of convergence programmes as a reference in the context of the new ERM would not interfere with the ECB's prerogative to safeguard its price stability objective with respect to its intervention obligations. This convergence-based approach to operating the new ERM would preserve flexibility while ensuring an appropriate level of exchange discipline.
>
> (European Commission 1996)

Note that this system, in practice, would differ little from the current ERM. In fact, even now, countries submit convergence programmes to the EU and bilateral intervention is largely discretionary. As a result, countries not joining EMU in the first wave would not really experience a change in the management of their currencies.

153

Club Med dancing the tango: is a currency board an option?

Probably the strongest form of unilateral currency commitment is represented by the institution of a currency board. This implies profound institutional changes. In its strictest definition, a currency board is an arrangement in which one country pegs to another currency at a fixed level and the issue of domestic currency is fully backed by the foreign currency. One could even say that a currency board is a form of unilateral and reversible monetary union. In a currency board regime, even more than in a fixed exchange rate regime, a country gives up sovereignty in monetary matters. Currency boards have normally been used by small countries, often ex-colonies. More recently, different versions of currency boards have been adopted by developing countries such as Argentina (since 1991), Hong Kong and Singapore among others.

A currency board is, to a large extent, similar to a gold standard system (this was the prevalent system in the US with a varied history up to the early 1970s when Bretton Woods collapsed). It is a system in which the exchange rate against another currency is fixed. In addition, the monetary base (represented by coins and notes in circulation, plus the amount of deposit at the central bank held as reserve requirement) is fully backed by convertible foreign currency reserves held by the central bank. In the gold standard, the monetary base was backed by gold holdings. As a result of this arrangement, the monetary base becomes endogenous (in the sense that it is determined by supply and demand of the currency). An increased supply of domestic currency must be met by sales of forex reserves via the central bank. This reduces the monetary base and leads to an increase in domestic currency interest rates. The Argentinean convertibility law makes the point very clearly: 'at all times, the freely available reserves of the central bank of the Argentine Republic in bullion and foreign exchange shall be equivalent to at least one hundred per cent ... of the monetary base' (Article 4, Title 1, Convertibility of the Austral, Law 23, 928, March 1991).

Currency board: main features

Two characteristics of the currency board are interesting (the following discussion draws partly from Rojas Suarez and Weisbrod 1995. See also, Goldman Sachs Economic Research 1995).

A currency board differs from a fixed exchange rate system. In the latter, the central bank cannot influence the monetary base but can determine its composition. For example, suppose that a country has a monetary base equivalent to its currency reserves. If the central bank is faced with a one-off outflow of funds, it can respond:

1   by shrinking the monetary base by the equivalent of the loss in currency reserves, thus allowing a rise in domestic interest rates

154

2   by increasing the monetary base by raising the supply of domestic credit. This puts downward pressure on the currency and forces a drop in currency reserves

In the end, the central bank has unchanged interest rates, but the monetary base is only partially backed by foreign currency, the rest is backed by domestic credit. The asset composition of the monetary base has changed. A currency board only has option 1. Note that in the case of Argentina, 20 per cent of the monetary base can be backed by credit. This has been allowed to permit more effective management of day-to-day liquidity fluctuations. The features of the currency board mean that the central bank cannot fund Treasury liability. In normal circumstances, in fact, a central bank would increase liquidity by purchasing government bonds.

The currency board system works differently under strain. Suppose that the market expects a devaluation of the currency. Normally this would lead to a rise in domestic interest rates. In the extreme case, however, if the devaluation expectations are very high, all holders of domestic currency would go to the central bank to have their holdings converted into foreign currency at the current fixed rate. Somewhat counter-intuitively, the central bank would still be able to satisfy all of its liabilities, despite the fact that the monetary base (usually M0) is much smaller than liquidity (M1). In fact, the central bank is only committed to convert the monetary base. The strain would fall on domestic banks via the monetary multiplier. Domestic banks' liabilities are only partially backed by deposits at the central bank. A run on the currency would impose on them a sudden massive increase in the cost of their liabilities. To the extent that they would not be able to decrease or convert their assets (for example it would be difficult to sell their portfolio of badly performing loans) the banking system could experience a significant fall in profitability.

Dollarisation and the banking system

Faced with massive withdrawals of domestic currency, there are two possible outcomes for domestic banks.

The financial market does not see a systemic risk for banks, but only for the value of the currency. In this case, domestic banks might face the withdrawal of domestic currency deposits with an increase in foreign currency liabilities. As long as the public is willing to keep their liquidity in a domestic bank, i.e. there is no concern over the bank solvency, domestic banks can simply convert their liabilities in foreign currency. In a fixed exchange rate regime it should make no difference to a domestic bank whether its assets (for example loans) are denominated in a domestic currency while its liabilities (deposits) are in a foreign currency. In the extreme, all bank deposits might eventually be denominated in foreign currency (what is normally

155

referred to as dollarisation). In time, most bank assets would also be denominated in foreign currency. This explains why a currency board applies well to countries which already have high levels of dollarisation (for example, following episodes of hyperinflation) and where there are no constraints on domestic holdings of foreign currency deposits. Note that this might be a good approximation of the situation of 'outs' after 1999, where it would be reasonable to expect some degree of 'euro-isation'. Note, however, that domestic banks in this scenario would assume considerable currency risk which could expose them to the risk of a devaluation.

If bank solvency is an issue, things could get much nastier. In fact, doubts over solvency would lead to mass withdrawals of deposits. People would not be satisfied with converting their domestic currency deposits into foreign currencies and holding them at domestic banks. They would shift their deposits to foreign banks (causing what is called capital flights) which is likely to lead to a severe banking crisis. The crisis would be greatly exacerbated by the fact that, in a currency board regime, the central bank cannot act as lender of last resort. As described above, the central bank cannot offer credit unless this is backed by foreign currencies. The most likely outcome would be for the currency board system to be abandoned and the currency devalued.

Is the system feasible?

The case of Argentina attracts interest because it involves a large country with a reasonably sophisticated financial market. Argentina had two characteristics which made it an ideal candidate for such a currency regime: the financial system was already largely dollar based, with a high level of substitution between peso and dollars. The 1991 Convertibility Law also eliminated most restrictions on dollar based financial transactions. In considering whether the currency board is feasible it is important to specify its main sources of weakness relative to the specific characteristics of a country.

Main sources of weakness

Higher real interest rates   The main sources of fragility of a currency board system are similar to the risks run by any system which limits foreign exchange flexibility. However, the extreme rigidity imposed by the currency board system makes it particularly vulnerable. Suppose that the market starts to doubt that the country can sustain the currency link. A consequence of this, as described above, is a rise in domestic interest rates. This increase could be potentially very significant with dire consequences on the real economy. Increased business borrowing costs are likely to depress both investment and consumer demand leading to an abrupt slowdown in economic activity. Increased borrowing costs for the government and the economic slowdown might worsen the country's fiscal position. The 'dollarisation' of the economy could limit this effect somewhat, but it is unlikely to prevent it altogether. Moreover, dollarisation may increase financial exposure to currency risks which could prove damaging if the final outcome is actually a devaluation.

Non-bank assets Developed financial markets also make the story more difficult, particularly if there is a high level of diversification in portfolios and a large number of assets competing with bank loans (as in advanced financial markets). If the public or institutional investors such as pension funds decide to sell their assets for foreign ones, the consequence would be a sharp drop in bond and equity prices (with potentially adverse effects on wealth and on the banking system) and a rise in interest rates. The alternative would be an increase in monetary base by the central bank which would imply a *de facto* abandonment of the currency board system.

Case study: Is it feasible for Italy?

The currency board system has many desirable properties for Italy. It is, in fact, attractive for a country which is willing to give up monetary sovereignty, in a move which would be seen as temporary, ahead of full participation in EMU. Moreover, it is likely that, if Italy is out of EMU, it will undergo some degree of euro-isation. Due to its favourable characteristics, currency board proposals have already been voiced (among others, see Gros 1996). A closer analysis of currency boards, however, has led us to the conclusion that this regime contains risks which appear to outweigh by far the potential benefits.

In practical terms, Italy has some features which would make a currency board possible:

1   The amount of forex reserves in Italy is currently IL110 trillion. The monetary base is around IL170 trillion. The difference is not very large so that, with a further increase, Italy should be able to back its monetary base with forex reserves
2   The reserve requirement in Italy is still relatively high, at least compared with other European countries. It stands now at around 15 per cent of assets subject to the requirement. Note that, in Argentina, the reserve requirement stands at 30 per cent
3   Italy has experienced a significant current account surplus over the last few years (IL 57 trn trillion and IL 71 trn trillion in 1994 and 1995).

A number of other considerations sketched below suggest that a currency board would be vulnerable and would leave Italy's financial market exposed to a considerable risk:

1   The link between monetary base, M1 and M2 is fairly strong. The ratio is 3.1 and 6.1. This compares to around 1.1 and 1.4 respectively in Argentina (ratio between M1 and M2 and forex reserves)

2   The history of 1992, when the lira was forced out of the ERM, teaches a number of lessons. The Bank of Italy spent its entire stock of reserves in an attempt to defend the Lira. In a currency board, the effect on the real economy would have been devastating. Note that not even Sweden, which for a time kept short term interest rates at 500 per cent, survived the speculative attack; the krona was devalued

3   The stock of bad bank loans is relatively high at around 15 per cent. Also, the banking system has high and rigid fixed costs and it is exposed to public debt instruments

4   Banks' foreign exposure increased steadily ahead of the 1992 crisis (from IL51.8 trillion in 1990 to IL187 trillion two years later). It has narrowed to IL130 trillion since then. A currency board would have exposed banks to an even higher foreign currency exposure. The low level of foreign indebtedness of the public sector (foreign currency debt is roughly 5 per cent of the total) lowers the incentive to defend the currency regime

5   The stock of public debt is very high (over 120 per cent of GDP) so that a confidence crisis might have large effects both on real activity and on the soundness of financial institutions

6   The amount of financial assets not intermediated by the banking system is high; households, mutual funds and insurance companies own the vast majority of the public debt (banks only own 19 per cent and the central bank another 11 per cent)

7   The Italian political situation is always exposed to sudden crises of confidence and changes of direction. These could undermine faith in the willingness to maintain the strict currency regime, particularly because such a regime would be unlikely to obtain cross party support

Conclusion

The need to consider the fate of those countries which will not be able to join EMU in the first wave has spurred a debate on possible options. Here we have briefly reviewed possible currency regimes. We focus on proposals for the ERM, which appear to be very similar to the current ERM. We then analyse the possibility of a stricter form of currency pegging, the introduction of a currency board. We conclude that this introduces excessive risks to the stability of the financial system. As a result, we suggest that there is little in between a viable, but weak ERM, and full participation in EMU. This partly justifies the insistence of peripheral countries on inclusion in the first wave.

11

THE UK AND EMU

> Between the mainland and the high seas, we shall always choose the high seas.
>
> Winston Churchill

Political indecision: Thatcher and Major on Europe

The Thatcher legacy

The Thatcher government's long rule allowed a stronger hold on the Conservative party by its more Euro-sceptic elements. Unfortunately, John Major had to cope with that legacy and did little to shift the balance of the party. The Conservative party's more Euro-sceptic attitude towards Europe has therefore dominated the last decade and a half, and has defined much of UK policy and tone in European negotiations. It is difficult to say whether this is a good representation of public opinion, and it often seems that Euro-sceptic attitudes have dominated the political debate, as well as the Conservative party, thus shouting down other voices. EMU is still a divisive issue amongst both political parties, but splits over Europe were much more evident within the governing Conservative party in the 1980s and early 1990s. As Lynton Robins illustrates so well, the Conservatives catalogue of disarray over all things European makes quite a remarkable history.

> in addition to the agonising which accompanied the decision on whether or not Britain should enter the ERM ... the political dramas which will be remembered from the Thatcher years have had European plots and sub-plots. The 'Lawson affair' which ended with the resignation of the Chancellor, resulted from his policy of sterling shadowing the deutsch mark as a prelude to EMS entry; the 'Westland affair' involved rival European and Atlanticist rescue bids for the beleaguered helicopter company from two Cabinet ministers, Michael Heseltine and Leon Brittain both of whom resigned ... Finally, of course, the 'Thatcher affair' in which the EC was the key which prompted the resignation of her Deputy Prime Minister, Sir Geoffrey Howe and the events which followed, resulting in her own resignation. . . . Can it be possible

159

that twenty years of thinking about Europe has resulted in so little change in British politics?

(Robins 1992: 244)

Margaret Thatcher's downfall was a direct result of her isolation in Europe and of growing splits in the Conservative party. These splits appeared to widen in the 1990s with John Major's leadership less astute at clamping down on ideological disputation. Thatcher left Major with a party already divided over Europe, but with substantial power in the hands of the Euro-sceptics. Thatcher had cultivated a Euro-sceptic faction amongst the party's elite. This left Major requiring to humour this hard-core group by continuing (to some extent) the anti-European rhetoric.

Although splits in the party of government always appear wide, there is evidence to show that the Conservative party was more split on EMU than the Cabinet suggested. An *Observer* poll (May 1994) showed that although Conservative ministers were equally divided 44/44 per cent, Conservative backbenchers were 61/30 per cent against the process. This explains much of Conservative government procrastination and confusion with Europe. These splits ran deep and took over from any previous ideological debates. Apart from everything else, it was a real vote loser, making the party seem confused and ineffective. Even a couple of months before the general election of May 1997 when Health Secretary Stephen Dorrell stated that Britain would not join EMU in 1999, contrary to Cabinet policy that EMU membership in 1999 was unlikely but possible, indicating the depths to which the split on Europe was bubbling under the surface, at a time when the desire to look like a cohesive government should have been strong. To add insult to injury the Conservative backbencher John Redwood (who challenged John Major in a leadership contest in 1996, but lost) published, at the beginning of the election campaign (March 1997), a book arguing against the single currency. Britain has been all too keen to defer the responsibility of a decision on EMU until the latest possible date. In appearance it seems that the majority of Labour and Lib-Dem MPs favour British entry to EMU. In contrast, it is said that many on the right-wing of the Conservative party openly discuss the possibility of leaving the European Union. Though views vary on why the Conservative party lost the 1997 election by such a large margin, splits on Europe remain a common explanatory factor.

ERM membership

Thatcher's tough line on EMU, was largely to do with the advice of her right hand man of many years, Alan Walters. As the closest economic adviser of an autocratic leader, Walters' opinions, and fears about closer ties with Europe defined government policy. The 'Walters Critique', stated that in a pegged exchange rate system where exchange rates are expected to be fixed for, say a year ahead, interest rates would have to be set equally between countries in the system. This would mean that the interest rate would either be too low for high-inflation countries (which need high interest rates to get inflation down), or too high for low-inflation countries which would consequently suffer from deflation and unemployment.

Reluctance to join the ERM was generally due to worries about losing some degree of autonomy on interest rate policy. But in the UK's particular case, there was also a prevalence of theoretical arguments about the petro-currency status of sterling, the role of London as an international financial centre, and a predominance of political arguments regarding loss of sovereignty. After much dragging of feet, the UK eventually joined the ERM in October 1990, with a 6 per cent margin of fluctuation. British membership of the ERM lasted less than two years, ending in September 1992. The exit from the ERM was seen as a major policy defeat. The political consequences were entirely negative. The Conservative government had broken both its promise not to raise taxes, as well as its exchange rate policy. The devaluation of the pound helped exports while lower interest rates encouraged growth and gave an impetus to domestic demand. When the British government regained autonomy over its interest rate after leaving the ERM in 1992, it was then able to cut interest rates to below those of Germany. The low was at 5.25 per cent, contrary to its declaration on 'Black Wednesday' that it was going to raise the bank base rate to 15 per cent. The exchange rate plummeted, at one point to 25 per cent below its previous central ERM parity.

The Major years

Prior to the 1992 election, the 1991 party conference had to face the issue of Europe, in light of the renegotiation of the Maastricht Treaty due at the end of 1991. Major tried to do a balancing act, alternating between declarations that Britain should be 'at the heart of Europe' and saying that Britain could strike 'the right balance' between closer co-operation and a proper respect for national institutions and traditions. Major's indecision was necessary in a way, given the party's split over EMU and the Social Chapter, it also made it easier for him to negotiate the upcoming election. Major secured opt-outs on the Social Chapter, and the third stage of EMU. These helped secure some peace with the backbenchers. But it did not last long.

After the election victory, Major's position on Europe still remained blurred, but he appeared more sympathetic to Europe and tried to stand up to the party's Euro-sceptics more forcefully. After securing the ratification of the Maastricht Treaty in the summer of 1993, however, he again pursued a position of seeking to appease the Euro-sceptic right. Britain's central parity in the ERM of DM2.95 was Major's decision as Chancellor, and when sterling came into difficulties, the Euro-sceptics had a field day. The pressures of ERM membership mounted through the summer of 1992, and Lamont announced the departure of sterling from the ERM on 16 September 1992. This severely damaged Conservative popularity and market confidence in the government. The episode undermined confidence in the Conservatives ability to handle the economy, especially given Major's reiterated declarations that all would be well.

The 1992 party conference proved problematic. Lord Tebitt asked delegates in his speech whether they wanted to be citizens of the European Union and they replied with a loud 'no'. Even the pro-European Douglas Hurd rejected a European super state in his conference speech. The government still had difficulty in passing the Maastricht Treaty through the House of Commons in 1992 due to opposition party dismay at the opt-out to the Social Chapter. The Tory rebels also created disarray, clubbing together with Labour to produce an opposition amendment declaring that ratification should not take place until the government accepted the Social Chapter. A confidence vote was eventually called, and won.

Differences seemed most pronounced at the May 1994 party conference. The former Chancellor, Norman Lamont, asserted that Britain could leave the EU. Former Foreign Secretary Sir Geoffrey Howe alleged that this would be electoral suicide.

> Howe attributed the Euro-sceptical attitude to a residual nostalgia for Thatcher, a contempt for bureaucracy, and an outdated patriotism. He believed that for 'a great nation to remain a great power' it must wield influence; and only by affecting European decisions would Britain be able to maintain a voice in Washington.
>
> (Evans and Taylor 1996: 250)

Major's party conference speech, on the other hand ignored Europe and seemed to bring the party back together. The issue came to embody Conservative failings and Major's use of the veto to prevent the appointment of Jean-Luc Dehane as Commissioner of the European Union managed to re-unite the party (temporarily) over Europe around the concept of a multi-speed EMU.

The BSE beef scandal which reached its height in 1996 looked to be the first opportunity to gain the public advantage against all things European. With British farmers losing out, John Major's policy of non-co-operation was an attempt to both please the Euro-sceptic factions of the Conservative party and to gain public support as a PM standing up for British interests. The issue came to embody Conservative failings, however, and Major's policy of non-co-operation looked a too convenient way of killing two birds with one stone.

Labour in opposition: the European record

The Labour party opposed Britain's first application for entry to the EEC in 1961–2. While in government however, in 1967, an application was made. With Labour out of government, there was, once again, opposition to entry, particularly from trade unions. Support in the parliamentary Labour party was much stronger and a compromise was arrived at where the party supported the principle of entry, but opposed the terms reached by the Heath government. This caused some splitting of the Labour party, with Roy Jenkins' resignation (he was deputy leader at the time), along with David Owen, Bill Rodgers and Shirley Williams later. In 1974 with the Wilson government, a referendum was held on British membership and in this a majority of the Cabinet canvassed for a 'Yes' vote though many of the influential unions supported withdrawal. The result of the referendum was a majority of almost two to one for staying in. This issue was a difficult one despite this however, as the anti-EEC MPs continued to make it difficult for the government to wholeheartedly support any European initiative.

When Roy Jenkins, David Owen, Bill Rodgers and Shirley Williams left the Labour party to form the Social Democrat Party (SDP) this considerably reduced support for the EEC within the Parliamentary Labour party. With Michael Foot at the helm, the 1983 manifesto was considerably more left wing than its predecessors, especially on foreign and security issues. The manifesto called for British withdrawal and the introduction of a more projectionist economic policy, the so-called Alternative Economic Strategy, to help British industry. This included withdrawal from the European Community.

After the disastrous defeat in the 1983 election, Michael Foot was replaced by Neil Kinnock. The policy on Europe also changed, now focusing on getting the best deal for Britain within the EEC. This change reflected a softening of the Trade Union Congress (TUC) stance on the issue. The TUC started to support the EEC more strongly from 1985, when Jacques Delors (the French socialist) became Commission President. Delors sought and secured the support of the British trade unions for his desire for a social aspect to the single market. By 1987, there were few signs in the Labour party of support for withdrawal. During the Thatcher years the Labour party leadership increasingly allied itself with Europe over a range of issues, especially on the Social Charter and the environment.

Differences in policy (1997)

Going into the 1997 election, the Labour and Conservative parties seemed to have more common ground on Europe than differences. The notable difference seemed to be emphasis (or not) on the nation state and sovereignty. The Conservatives stressed the need to maintain the latter, whilst Labour seemed to emphasise the need to be in Europe to shape its progress. Comparing the party manifestos, both parties pledged that they would not introduce majority voting for the EU's Common Foreign and Security Policy. Both supported the enlargement of the EU to the east, though Labour was less enthusiastic on flexibility of policy (more opt-outs by different countries as the Union grows). Both parties promised to give larger countries such as Britain more votes in the Council of the European Union. Labour however said it would seek to open up some Council procedures to the public. Labour wanted majority voting for some social, environmental, industrial and regional policies that then required unanimous decision making. Labour promised to give a bigger say to the European Parliament on the farm budget and an equal say with the Council of the European Union, on all laws that ministers settle by majority vote. The Conservatives pledged to limit the powers of the European Court of Justice (which has notably enforced several important court rulings e.g. on sexual equality and employee rights), whereas Labour said it would leave it alone. On the Social Chapter, Labour said that they would sign it, though the Conservatives said they would not (see below). Though the Labour party have also emphasised the need for national social measures. They argue that the Chapter has not led to many laws, and therefore would only have a small and limited impact anyway.

Both Labour and the Conservatives pledged to try to extend the single market and to reform the Common Agricultural Policy. Labour promised to switch spending from farms to training, industry and infrastructure. On EMU, the Conservatives leaned towards Euro-scepticism (see below), though the party line was that it would be possible to join EMU, though they would not do so without a national referendum. Mr Major said that it would be very unlikely for a Conservative government to join EMU at the start. Labour also said that they would not join without a referendum though they appear generally warmer towards the process.

Britain as an EMU member?

For the future, and as progress towards EMU reaches its inevitable conclusion with the birth of the union, the UK can no longer afford to sit on the fence. It becomes no longer a question of the pros and cons of EMU, but of the pros and cons of being left out when the rest go ahead. In searching for a new role after loss of empire, Britain has no other feasible partnership than that within Europe. Politically it may be preferable for the EMU process to include Britain, to counter the political weight of Germany. France alone in this role would be insufficient. Federalist fears are better dealt with in the union rather than by avoiding the process altogether. Britain does have allies in this. During the Maastricht negotiations in 1991, it was France that sided with Britain against the idea of a federalist Europe.

The main problem with trying to assess the costs and benefits of EMU membership for Britain is that it is very difficult to assess how well the union will work, how large it will be, and how businesses will react to the change. It is difficult to predict future behaviour from what we have seen in the past, although the initial indications appear to be good. British exports of goods to the EU rose from 9.3 per cent of GDP in 1980 to 10.6 per cent in 1994, as a result of the internal market. We can see in Figure 11.1 that after a fairly indistinguished performance in the late 1980s, 1994 saw a strong rise in exports (particularly in comparison to countries such as France and Germany). This was partly to do with the advent of the single market in 1992. This one-off benefit was however eroded by falls in exports in 1995.

Although the UK has seen a relatively good export performance, this was marred by a sharp increase in export prices in 1995 and 1996 due to sterling's strength. 1993–6 saw a fairly poor record on export prices (see Figure 11.2) in the UK. Sterling strength in 1996–7 kept export growth moderate then too. It is precisely these swings in national currencies which EMU would guard against, and therefore the UK could potentially perform much better in a single currency, without this added instability.

Britain would also gain in terms of increases in investment. Given that the UK's record of rate of return on capital is fairly dismal compared to that of France and Germany (see Figure 11.3), the loss of investment that might be incurred by staying outside the single currency could be huge. Even if investment is now attracted to the UK due to competitive labour costs, wages may have to be even *more* competitive to maintain investment interest in the UK.

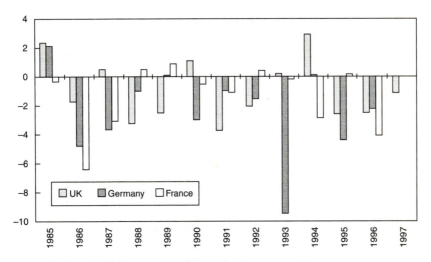

Figure 11.1 OECD measure of export performance for total goods
Source: OECD *Economic Outlook*, June 1996, Paris
Note: 1996–7 figures are OECD projections

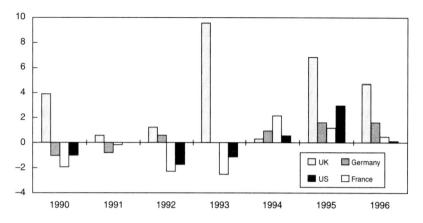

Figure 11.2 Export prices (average unit values)
Source: OECD *Economic Outlook*, June 1996, Paris
Note: 1996 data is an OECD projection. Data is for total goods, percentage changes, national currency terms

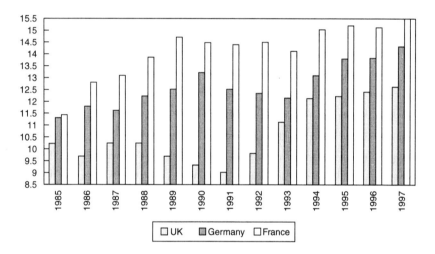

Figure 11.3 Rates of return on capital in the business sector
Source: OECD *Economic Outlook*, June 1996, Paris

This is because there would obviously be an extra currency risk when investing in the UK as opposed to an EMU country. Since the 1960s, labour productivity rates have not fallen as much in the UK as in Germany, France, Japan or the US. Relative unit labour costs have fallen dramatically compared to Germany in the 1990s, and are much closer to US costs. This position is enviable, but not joining EMU could mean throwing away many of these benefits. These facts all point to a strong case for UK membership, as the benefits for the UK in this area could be even higher than for other countries.

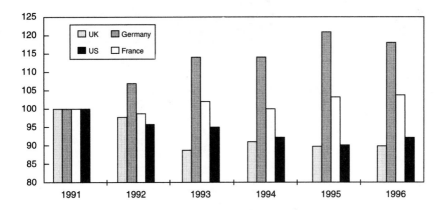

Figure 11.4 Competitive positions: relative unit labour costs (1991=100)
Source: OECD *Economic Outlook*, June 1996, Paris
Note: Indices are expressed in a common currency and concern the manufacturing sector. They take into account both export and import competitiveness

The UK is a leading country in terms of its global foreign investments. In fact it is the third biggest earner of foreign investment income after the US and Japan. It is also one of the most popular destinations for foreign investment from other countries. It is the second most popular recipient in the OECD, with US$200 billion or 17 per cent of the total of foreign investment. Such investments cover the gamut from direct investments by firms and businesses, as well as stock and bond investment by pension and insurance funds. The net returns from UK investment abroad and foreign investment in the UK are positive, amounting to about £3–4 billion.

This could all change if the UK stays out of EMU. The lack of exchange rate risk of investing in another EMU country will deter EMU member countries from investing in non-EMU countries. Much of the inflow into the UK in the 1990s has been from multinationals seeking a base from which to export to the single market. The UK has been favoured due to its lower labour costs (one argument against the UK's adoption of the Social Chapter, see Figure 11.4). If it does not join the single currency, concerns that multinationals were losing out by investing in a non-EMU country would lead to relocation of investment to within the Union. New investment would also fall back. Some investors would remain, as the UK's advantages of lower wages and a less regulated business environment could outweigh the costs of location outside the Union for some businesses. Of course the ability of sterling to devalue against the euro would also be an advantage as this would make goods exported from Britain cheaper, but this would be countered by the lower asset value of revenues which made their way back to the home country from the UK when converted to the home currency.

Another large area of benefit for the UK is via the reduction of nominal interest rates. It is estimated that if nominal interest rates fall by 1 per cent

Table 11.1 EU trade (per cent of
GDP i.e. degree of integration)

Belgium	49
Ireland	41
Netherlands	32
Portugal	25
Greece	19
Denmark	16
Germany	15
Spain	13
UK	13
France	13
Italy	12

Source: European Commission no. 58,
1994.

and real interest rates by the same amount, that capital spending could also go up by 1 per cent of GDP, causing GDP growth to increase by 5 per cent over a period of about 10 years. This could add about 0.5 per cent to the UK's long-term growth rate. The London Business School model indicates an even bigger reaction of 0.75 per cent a year, though the UK Treasury model shows only 0.2 per cent per year. The lack (until recently) of an independent central bank did tend to mean that the UK was perceived to be more of an inflation risk, in fact inflation rates in the UK have been more volatile than other comparable countries (see Chapter 6) but the record has improved in the 1990s.

The economic benefits of EMU increase proportionally with the degree of integration the country has with the union. The degree of integration is derived from both the importance of trade as a per cent of GDP and the per cent of trade done with the other EU members. The proportion of GDP traded is a function of the size of the country. Small European countries trade between one-third and two-thirds of GDP, larger EU countries trade between 22–28 per cent. With economic benefits to membership of EMU inversely proportional to size (as well as the foreign policy benefits of being a member of such a vast monetary union) it is not surprising that smaller countries tend to be more eager to join. The UK is an exception, as we have discussed above, its integration may actually be larger than is embodied in the 13 per cent figure, as services provide a large part of UK exports. Though the UK is one of the larger EU members, Bayoumi's rationale for EMU membership does not apply.

The incentives for a region to join a currency union are different from the incentives to admit a region into a union. The entrant gains from lower transmission costs on trade with the entire existing union, while the incumbent regions gain only on their trade with the potential entrant. As a result, a small region will always have a greater incentive to join a union than the union will have an incentive to admit the new member. A corollary of this is that even if a country would prefer a free float across all regions, it may still have an incentive to join a currency union with other regions if it is going to be formed. This is because most of the welfare losses from the nascent union will occur whether or not the region decides to join. This set of incentives may explain why some countries in the EU who are not particularly convinced of the merits of EMU are also worried about being relegated to the second division of a two-speed EMU.

(Bayoumi 1994)

Lastly, the problem of the UK's structural differences compared to continental Europe usually dominate any debate about its membership of EMU. Structural differences are often cited as evidence that membership of EMU would have different effects on the UK than continental Europe. Therefore justifying arguments that the UK may benefit from staying out of the union. Changes in monetary policy in the UK are regarded as having different, and a different magnitude, of effects. How fast and how much central bank policy rates filter through into market interest rates and bank loan rates differs greatly between countries. This may result from dissimilar competitive pressures between the banking sectors. Estimates by the Bank for International Settlements (BIS) showed that in the UK, changes in policy rates were quickly and fully translated into changes in market interest rates, more so than in Germany or France. A paper by the Bank of England has concluded that these results may not be the result of a large structural difference:

> estimates of this sort often fail to identify genuine structural differences, because they take an average of temporary and persistent interest rate changes. So a country that has experienced more temporary changes to policy rates will probably ... appear to have a smaller pass-through from policy to market interest rates.
>
> (Britton and Whitley 1997: 153)

Their paper argues that the high level of gross indebtedness seen in the UK should be associated with weaker rather than stronger real interest effects on expenditure. They suggest this is primarily to do with an absence of liquidity constraints. The UK's high rate of home ownership is also often cited as one reason why the UK may be more sensitive to monetary policy rate changes than its European counterparts. But, as Britton and Whitley argue, if variable rate owners do not experience constraints in their ability to borrow, this should not affect their consumption dramatically in itself. Therefore, what are normally seen as structural differences in the monetary transmission mechanism, may not be so at all. Given doubts about the structural nature of these differences, policy and time may bring the UK and continental Europe closer together in terms of interest rate reactions.

British EU gripes

An escalating Community budget

In 1975 the EU budget amounted to ECU6.5 billion, of which ECU4.5 billion went to the European Agricultural Guidance and Guarantee Fund (EAGGF). By 1980 the figures were ECU16.2 billion and ECU11.5 billion, and by 1985 they had risen to ECU28.4 billion and ECU20 billion. It was widely accepted that the budget should continue to be readjusted towards regional and social spending (see Chapter 2), and within the EAGGF towards structural support. There was a problem as the Common Agricultural Policy was the only mandatory element in the Community budget, and the Council of Agricultural Ministers, backed by business and agricultural interests, had a strong interest in maintaining that situation. The package put forward by Mr Delors however included a proposal to double the Regional Fund and Social Fund by 1992. The summit called in February 1988, forced Britain, under the leadership of Margaret Thatcher, to make certain concessions. It was agreed that the EAGGF growth rate would be limited to 74 per cent of the annual growth of the EU GNP in volume terms; that the budgets should be no more than 1.2 per cent of EU GNP; that the VAT base of each member state would be capped at 55 per cent of its GNP, with the continuation of the ceiling of the 1.4 per cent of VAT proceeds to be given over; and that a fourth source of revenue should be introduced based on shares in GNP. The rate required was to be that which (given all other revenue) would balance the budget.

Structural funds have become an increasingly difficult issue (see Chapter 2). Especially after the signing of the Maastricht Treaty. The four poorest signatories demanded an additional transfer of resources from the richer members on the grounds that the latter would be the main beneficiaries of the Treaty. This transfer, called the 'Cohesion Fund', was to be incorporated into the new five-year plan commencing in 1993, known as Delors II. Delors II proposed the increase of structural funds by about 60 per cent. Also, the funds allocated to external action were to be doubled. These proposals caused the budget to increase to ECU87.5 billion. It was therefore proposed that the 'own resources' ceiling be raised from 1.2 to 1.37 per cent of EU GNP.

As a net contributor to the Community budget.

In 1975 the European Council agreed on a corrective mechanism for net contributors, which was to apply for an experimental phase of seven years until 1983. This however proved to be insufficient since the net debit was not really eliminated, and the growth in size of the UK's net deficit balance continued. By 1979, the situation had worsened considerably. In 1980 it was agreed that the net UK contribution for 1980–1 would be reduced from an aggregate of ECU3,924 million to 1,339 million. This reduction was financed by the other EU members, partly by direct payments to the UK Treasury and partly by generous extra payments from the Regional Fund. This was still unsatisfactory to the British government of the time. This issue dominated every summit until it was finally resolved following the Fontainebleau summit (June 1984). This summit led to an agreement on agriculture spending, and to a system of budget correction for those countries with excessive budget burdens, with a specific formula for the UK. These corrections were subtracted from the next year's VAT payments. The UK's gain, however, placed an extra burden on other EU countries as they had to pick up the short-fall by paying a larger amount.

VAT contributions

It was decided in 1970 to make VAT the chief source of the Community's own revenue, but it was not until the 1980 budget that every member paid its full VAT contribution. The members agreed to give the Community up to 1 per cent of a uniform basis of assessment of VAT. This was increased to 1.4 per cent in January 1986 after the Fontainebleau summit. There was pressure to raise the figure again, but opposition from the UK and Germany deterred this. VAT was chosen as a sixth source of revenue after the VAT Directive of May 1977 harmonised the VAT systems. The tax is paid by all EU citizens and its revenue supposedly closely reflects the economic capacity of each Member State. It is not dependent on the VAT rates which vary quite widely between members, instead the amount paid is based on a uniform level of assessment, defined as the sum of all taxable supplies of goods and services to the final consumer in the Community.

1992 saw an attempt to 'harmonise' VAT rates. In 1991 a compromise was reached whereby a 15 per cent minimum standard rate of VAT by 1 January,

Table 11.2 Contributions to and receipts from the European Community budget 1993 (£ billion)

	Contributions	Receipts	Net Contrib.
Germany	14.9	5.6	9.3
France	9.0	8.2	0.8
Italy	8.0	6.8	1.2
UK	5.9	3.5	2.6
Spain	4.0	6.5	−2.5
Netherlands	3.1	2.1	1.0
Belgium	1.9	1.9	0
Denmark	0.9	1.2	−0.3
Greece	0.8	4.0	−3.2
Portugal	0.7	2.6	−1.9
Ireland	0.5	2.3	−1.8
Luxembourg	0.2	0.3	−0.1

Source: Court of Auditors Report 1993

1993 would be implemented until the end of 1996. The UK was against har-monisation because it would have had to impose the tax on items then exempt, notably children's clothing and food. 1988–9 saw some extensions of VAT in the UK to items such as opticians' services, and some construction items. In 1990 it raised the standard rate of VAT to 17.5 per cent. In 1994, VAT was introduced on domestic fuel, though the last stage of the phasing-in was abandoned in favour of other tax increases, so an 8 per cent VAT rate remained on domestic fuel. The French were also averse to full harmonisa-tion as it would imply lowering many of their VAT rates, and finding alterna-tive sources of revenue.

The UK opt-out from Stage III

The UK's involvement in the EMU process is defined by an attitude of drag-ging its feet. The opt-out from Stage III is the defining element of this. The protocol to the Maastricht Treaty states that the UK shall notify the council whether it intends to move to the third stage, and that unless it does, it will be under no obligation to do so. If no date is fixed for the beginning of Stage III, the UK may change its notification before 1 January 1998. The UK will retain its powers in the fields of monetary and exchange rate policy and be free to negotiate international agreements for itself, but will have no rights to participate in the appointment of the president, vice president and the other members of the executive board of the European Central Bank. If the UK changes its mind after the commencement of Stage III it may notify its desire to join, but must meet the necessary convergence criteria and pay its dues in terms of capital subscriptions and the transfer of foreign reserve assets to the ECB.

The Social Chapter

The ideal behind the Social Charter is to unify Member States on social stan-dards as well as monetary and economic standards. It is also intended to even out the elements of competition which are based on inadequate social pro-tection. Though the setting of minimum standards is not a bad thing, and countries with unjust practices should have those practices changed, there are also some economic grounds for attempts to create a unification based not just on currency but on social and labour standards. As we have pointed out before (see Chapters 2 and 3), labour mobility is one of the safety valves which could facilitate a stable currency union. Greater labour mobility in Europe, however, requires some smoothing out of legal standards. There is also another argument in favour of greater social cohesion. The stability and continuance of a currency union, if it cannot rely on a high level of labour mobility (which has been stubbornly low in Europe), must rely on a willing-ness of one country's population seeing flows of funds into another country for some time. This is made much easier if there is some sort of social cohesion. Governments however cannot legislate this cohesion into existence, the Social Charter is in one sense, an attempt to nurse it. As Goodhart points out:

> any attempt to impose an exchange rate union on set of areas without an underlying social unity can lead rapidly to disaster. If the members of the more prosperous regions should object to providing a potentially large flow of funds for an indefinite time period to the less prosperous regions on the grounds that these foreigners are different and should be content with different treatment, then the adjustment costs and separatist pressures with the single-currency area could easily become intense. The 'optimal' currency area is a function not so much of geography but rather of social psychology.
>
> (Goodhart 1989: 422)

The concept of a 'social charter' was initially mooted by the Belgium Minister Hansenne in 1987. The concept was greeted with enthusiasm by the European Commission as well as most national governments: Germany, Greece, Spain and France, though there was strong opposition from the UK. The Social Charter was officially adopted by the European Council in Strasbourg in December 1989, though the UK abstained. This marked the beginning of a string of actions taken without support from the UK.

Box 11.1 The Impact of the Social Charter

The Charter is based on the fundamental principles relating to 12 main themes, or rights:

1 Free movement of workers based on the principle of equal treatment in access to employment and social protection
2 Employment and remuneration based on the principle of fair remuneration; that is a decent basic wage, receipt of a fair wage, and fair treatment for part-time workers
3 Improvement in living and working conditions. This is concerned mainly with working hours, holiday entitlement, shift working, rest periods and redundancy procedures, among other things
4 Social protection based on the rules and practices proper to each country. (It is this section that makes the controversial reference to a guaranteed minimum wage and to social assistance to those who lack adequate means of subsistence although there is not an intention to impose a minimum wage across the board.)
5 Freedom of association and collective bargaining

6 Vocational training. This refers to the right to continue vocational training throughout one's working life, including the right to have leave from work in order to undertake such training

7 Equal training for men and women. This aims at the equality of access to employment, social protection, education, vocational training and career opportunities

8 Information, consultation and participation of workers. This has proved to be a very controversial proposal because it aims particularly at those employed in transnational companies. It intends that they be given the right to be informed and even consulted about major events affecting the company that may influence working conditions and employment

9 Protection of health and safety in the work-place. This area has led to the issue of several directives following the issue of a Framework Directive in 1989. These are an attempt to create union-wide standards of good practice. The fishing, mining, and construction industries are the major targets for improvements in health and safety practices but people working in offices have also been affected by the legislation on, for example, the use of display-screen equipment

10 Protection of children and adolescents. This aims at a minimum working age of 16 with youth employment being subject to labour regulation geared to the needs of young people. It also intends to establish the right to two years of vocational training after the end of compulsory education

11 The elderly. This asserts that those reaching retirement, or early retirement ages are entitled to a pension which provides a 'decent' standard of living. Those not entitled to a pension should be given a minimum income, social protection, and social and medical help

12 The disabled. This aims at giving every disabled person the right to benefit from measures for training, rehabilitation, and social and occupational integration

(Source: Goodman, 1996: 247)

The Charter was a non-binding political declaration. Included in it were the principles of freedom of movement, the safeguarding of living and working conditions, freedom of association and collective bargaining, and equal rights for men and women. Though these are not particularly controversial measures, the Commission was at pains to play down any element of federalism. The common problem with legislation of this sort however is that it is all too easy to whip up emotional reactions against the idea of losing legal control/power to 'Eurocrats' in Brussels. The UK's opposition to the Social Chapter of the Charter meant that it was removed from the EMU Treaty at Maastricht, into a separate protocol enabling the other EU states to continue with the Social Charter's proposals. The opt-out works so that though the agreement of all fifteen members is still sought, agreements made under the protocol will continue to be taken within the framework of the Community's institutions which will be 'on loan' to the fourteen members. If the UK cannot accept a particular proposal it will opt-out of discussions and decisions. The UK's opposition to the Social Chapter illustrates, to a great extent, what has been their attitude to Europe over many years.

Box 11.2 The Application of the Qualified Majority Vote to Social Policy: summary table of the chief legal bases for social policy instruments, Protocol No 14 on Social Policy, EC Treaty.

Qualified Majority possible
Article 2 (1)

- Improvement of the working environment to protect the health and safety of workers
- Working Conditions
- Informing and consulting workers
- Equal opportunities - labour market and treatment at work
- Integration of persons excluded from the labour market

Qualified Majority possible
Article 49: free movement of workers
Article 54: right of establishment
Article 57: mutual recognition of qualifications
Article 125 (new): vocational training
Article 127 (new): vocational training
Article 118a: health and safety at work
Article 100a, Article 75: agriculture, Article transport

Unanimity (14 states) required
Article 2(3)

- Social security and social protection for workers
- Protection of workers in the event of termination of employment contract
- Representation and collective defence of workers' and employers' interests, including co-determination

- Conditions of employment of nationals of non-member countries residing lawfully in the Community
- Financial contributions for promotion of employment and job-creation

Unanimity (15) required
Article 51: social security (measures needed for free movement)
Article 100: internal market
Article 130d: tasks, priority objectives and organisation of Structural Funds
Article 235

Explicitly outside Community powers
Article 2(6)

- Remuneration
- Right of association
- Right to strike
- Right to impose lock-outs

Source: Intergovernmental Conference 1966, Commission Report for the Reflection Group, Annex 14 (Luxembourg: Office for Official Publications of the European Communities, 1995).

Further divergence in social legislation is to be expected if the opt-out on the Social Chapter works as it was intended to. This is already occurring: the Works Council Directive first discussed in 1972 went through in November 1994 under the agreement of the other fourteen EU states. The European Directive came into being in September 1996. The directive means greater information and employee consultation about, for example, plant relocation, closure and collective lay-offs. The procedure has to be initiated by a request from at least 100 employees from two different countries (or their representatives). It applies to enterprises and groups which employ at least 1000 people in fourteen countries, with at least two establishments each of which employ 150 people, in two EU countries. Despite the opt-out, many UK firms announced their plan to comply with the directive and to set up works councils. Among these were Marks and Spencer, BP, United Biscuits, ICI, Courtaulds Textiles.

Continental based multinationals with plants in the UK will undoubtedly establish Works Councils or the equivalent. In practice, such councils are simply institutionalising established methods for consultations and exchanging information. The most common method of doing this in the UK is the Joint Consultative Council (JCC) of employees and employers' representatives. The UK's worry about the directive is the extra costs these measures would impose, and that these higher labour costs could mean an increase in unem-

176

ployment. The UK government may also be worried about the potential costs to them of social provisions. The counter argument cites the sharp increases in productivity that can be obtained with job security and a secure workforce.

Labour measures

The labour market is resistant to change as productivity differentials and other differences in economic conditions make legalities somewhat meaningless in everyday life. Though one would expect these issues not to be overly debatable, some issues have proved to be more disputable than expected. The conflict between work welfare measures such as the minimum wage, and the need to maintain flexible labour markets became a crucial sticking point. Many governments protested fiercely against loss of labour market flexibility in the face of legislation on minimum standards in terms of social security, health and safety protection, holiday and training entitlements, limits on overtime hours and the protection of pregnant women. This opposition, in many instances led by the UK, in effect means that qualified majority voting has been extended to working conditions, the information and consultation of workers, equality between men and women, and the integration of the unemployed back into work. More recently (November 1996) Britain again tried to block plans for closer EU integration after a European Court ruled that it should accept EU limits on the working week (to forty-eight hours only). The UK government argued that the forty-eight hour limit qualified as a 'social issue' and therefore it could use its 'opt-out' (secured in the Maastricht Treaty).

Conclusion

Britain's relationship with Europe has always been a difficult one. Some of the political friction however has been blown out of proportion by political posturing and bravado. Britain's attitude to the EU, and to the possibility of EMU, has been characterised by sitting on the fence, justified by a 'wait and see' approach. This policy has stultified valuable public debate on the EMU issue. Though the Conservative party has been split on the issue of Europe from the start, the new Labour government has also found its own 'European' path a rocky one. With EMU seeming more like an inevitable step as 1999 creeps closer, the question of UK entry becomes more clearly defined. The debate should no longer be whether it is right to be in EMU or not, but how much the UK will lose out when everyone else goes ahead. As EMU widens out to include more countries, it will become more expensive for Britain to remain outside of the process. The competitive gains the UK has made in recent decades in unit labour costs, productivity and inflation could be negated by staying out of the single currency. Initial indications on the Euro-X Council suggest that the UK will have little input into what is likely to be the main forum for European discussion.

12

ITALIAN INSTITUTIONAL REFORMS
Reaching for stability

Introduction

It is often recognised – in economic policy and other areas of politics – that future gains require some degree of short-term pain. Economic theory has placed much importance in the last few years on how institutions affect economic outcomes. For example, fighting inflation implies some short-term output sacrifice. The long-term gain of greater efficiency and long-term growth implies the short-term effort to control budget deficits and lighten state presence in the economy, whilst also increasing the efficiency of that state presence. It seems hard, therefore, to expect these policies from countries with a very high turnover of governments. In taking difficult decisions there is always a temptation for parties to 'opt-out' of coalitions when a decision implies short-term unpopularity. In Italy's case, it is not by chance that among the three biggest pieces of economic reform in the last five years (the massive 1993 budget, the July 1993 labour agreement and the 1995 pension reforms) were all approved by technocratic governments, where parties can hide behind the technocrat character of the Prime Minister and not take full responsibility for unpopular decisions.

The need for Italy to give each of the two political wings the chance to enjoy a relatively long spell of power is easy to recognise. Indeed some historians go as far as identifying the lack of alternating majorities as Italy's primary problem since its unification in 1861. The argument is that in all regimes since then, the party in government has defended its power on the grounds that the other side was not fit to govern. Counterbalancing this, the opposition has traditionally promoted a radical programme. This caused corruption and malpractice in government, prevented the development of a full liberal democracy and meant that necessary political changes were belated and tended to be associated with profound regime crisis. The international scenario has since changed. Both the fall of communism and the end of the juxtaposition between western and eastern blocks have changed the terms of confrontation. The Communist party has transformed itself into a social-democratic party in line with other moderate left-wing parties in Europe. This has eliminated the role of the Christian Democrats, in government since the World War II, as a shield against the presumed left-wing threat. This has opened up the opportunity for Italy to turn itself, for the first time, into a democracy in which changes in the parties in power are natural, legitimate and take place within a set of institutions recognised by both sides. The election of 1994, won by a right-wing coalition led by media mogul Berlusconi, took place after a comprehensive anti-corruption enquiry, which had changed the political landscape and led to the downfall of the old Christian Democrats. The 1994 campaign was, however, again conducted in a climate of strong confrontation, with extensive use of the media and reciprocal accusations of secret, anti-democratic agendas. The resulting government was based on an unstable alliance between the right-wing Alleanza Nazionale (recently evolved from a neo-fascist party), the regionalist Northern League (originated from the North's unhappiness about Rome's rule and high tax burdens) and the newly created Forza Italia (the highly publicised creation of Silvio Berlusconi, the media tycoon, turned politician). The Berlusconi government had a short life and Italy faced a new spell of technocratic government, very similar to the phase between 1992 and 1994, during the transition to a new electoral system (see Salvadori 1996). The subsequent election of a centre left government led by Romano Prodi seemed to bring a new stability to Italy. The government considered further institutional reforms as one of its top priorities. (Probably the most interesting book on Italy's recent history in the English language is Ginsborg's 'A History of Contemporary Italy', 1990).

There is also a consensus that the old system, based on a parliament-centred system with proportional representation (as described in more detail below) was faulty. The system was designed in the post-war era in order to ensure, as typical with proportional representation, an even distribution of power and to help the integration of extreme parties and groups showing profound ideological differences. Proportional representation almost always results in coalition governments and generally increases the number of parties. In a proportional system, the voter only elects a parliament while in other systems the vote also implies a choice for the government. Parties should therefore declare in advance on which side they will be, so as to make it harder for them to change sides. The new electoral system has introduced elements of the 'first-past-the-post' form. Yet, we describe below how recent changes have led Italy only half-way through its political reform. The changes introduced, though certainly in the right direction, are not sufficient to lead to greater stability. In this sense, institutional reform remains in our opinion one of the single most relevant issues in the long term. Some history, proposals and future prospects are described briefly.

Origins

The need for institutional reforms was recognised early, with evidence that the old constitutional system did not produce stable governments, as shown by the high number of Italian governments (fifty-five) in the post-war period. A commission to study possible reforms was set up as early as 1983. The process accelerated significantly in 1990 with the foundation of the referendum movement (led by politicians such as Segni and Barbera) which proposed three referenda to change the electoral system. The first proposed changing the electoral law of the Senate towards a first-past-the-post system. The second wanted to eliminate the possibility of choosing candidates among a long list presented by each party. This was due to the choice of candidate often resulting in vote control in Mafia dominated constituencies. The third referendum intended to extend the rule used for small city councils, based on first-past-the-post, to all city councils. The Constitutional Court ruled out two of the three referenda on formal grounds, but declared the second one (on abolishing candidate preferences) admissible. The vote took place on 9 June 1991 with many mainstream old style politicians inviting people to boycott it. Despite this a respectable 60 per cent of the electorate showed up, 95 per cent of which voted in favour of the changes.

The reasons why the referendum on introducing first-past-the-post was declared unacceptable were mostly technical. Therefore, the referendum movement decided to propose it again in 1992. This time the Constitutional Court deemed it acceptable. However, it coincided with a general election and was therefore postponed to the following year. The vote took place on 8 April 1993, with those in favour winning 70 per cent of the votes. The vote, which coincided with dramatic developments in the anti-corruption enquiry involving many top 'old guard' politicians, signalled the electorate's desire for change. The referendum imposed a hybrid system by design, with 75 per cent of the seats allotted by first-past-the-post but the remaining 25 per cent by proportional representation. The new system was then extended to the Lower Chamber in the summer of the same year. Also in the same year, parliament approved a new law for city councils which implied the direct election of the mayor in a two-round poll. Interestingly, Japan also moved from a proportional system almost contemporaneously. Their system was 50 per cent majority and 50 per cent proportional.

The new national electoral system was tried for the first time in the general election on 24 March 1994. It was won by the alliance of the right-wing Polo della Liberta' and the Northern League with Berlusconi as Prime Minister. The result of the election immediately proved the system to be faulty as it delivered different majorities in the Senate and the Lower Chamber. Moreover, the newly elected government did not last long, as differences between the Polo and the Northern League led to Berlusconi's fall and to a technocratic government led by Dini. The right-wing alliance, forced to form alliances by the introduction of a majority system, failed to pass the test of actually governing together. The April 1996 election gave victory to a centre–left coalition led by Romano Prodi. Prodi appeared able to ensure some stability and effectiveness in government (it passed a huge 1997 budget to enable Italy to attain Maastricht targets), but this has not eliminated the need for reforms.

Institutional reforms: the base for discussion

Some common points

During this period, discussions continued in a number of Parliamentary commissions. The two sides seemed to agree on a number of general principles. These included:

1   Moves to differentiate the role of the two Chambers: currently, the Senate and Lower Chamber have the same powers and all pieces of legislation need the approval of both. This implies that every change made by one Chamber needs the approval of the other. The system was, again, an attempt to balance power between two institutions, but leads to complications and delays as laws often get sent back and forth between the two Chambers. The idea is, as in Germany, to give the Lower Chamber a wider role and relegate the Senate to a role of control and possibly of veto on some issues. Also, as in Germany and Spain, the Senate should have a regional bias
2   Some federalist reforms: all parties agree on the idea of strengthening the power of local authorities, though with very different degrees of intensity. The Northern League threatens secession unless a federalist state is promoted, the left is very cautious, and the Alleanza Nazionale strongly opposes any federalist proposal. There is also a controversy between Regional councils and City councils on which powers should be attributed to one rather than the other
3   Reduction of the number of MPs: currently the Lower Chamber has 630 MPs and the Senate 315. A significant reduction is generally considered a good idea
4   The name of the head of the government and/or President should be agreed for each of the political groupings before the general election: the characteristic of a system in which the name of the President/Prime Minister would be known beforehand were not defined

Areas of contention

The agreements on the above left two main issues unresolved: the Constitutional form, i.e. the relation between government and parliament, and the electoral system. The two camps supported two very different proposals.

The left supported a Chancellor-based system, similar to Germany. In Germany, people vote for a party, the leader of which is assumed to become the Prime Minister if that party wins. The Prime Minister needs the support of parliament (one of the key issues for the left) and, in fact, can be changed by parliament (as when the Liberals dropped the Social-democrat-led Schmidt government and installed Kohl in 1982). The system is not overly different from the current Italian one, apart from 'constructive no confidence' (i.e. a no confidence vote must contain a proposal for a new government). The other main innovation for the left is the introduction of a new electoral system. The left proposed, as a stability enhancing measure, the introduction of a two-round election. There are different possible two-round systems: the French one, for example, implies that many candidates participate in the first round and whoever wins the absolute majority gets elected. If no one does, everyone who obtained 12.5 per cent or more of the votes can either join the second round or withdraw. At the second round whoever obtains the largest number of votes is elected. The two-round system has considerable advantages both in forcing alliances and keeping the electorate closer to more moderate parties. Also, it allows smaller parties to survive, but forces them to join coalitions. Apart from serving the purpose of being more likely to deliver stable majorities, it has also specific advantages for the Italian left, which has an extremist fringe (the Communists) and several small, but vociferous parties.

The right presented several different proposals, with an insistence on the fact that the President/Prime Minister (depending on the case) had to be elected directly by the people. The proposals went from a US presidential system, where the President is also head of the government and cannot be changed by parliament (an essential feature of the presidential system); to the Mayor of Italy proposal where the Prime Minister is elected directly in a two-round system and cannot be changed by parliament. The problems here would emerge in the case where parliament and President/Prime Ministers belonged to different sides with the risk of a political impasse (in 1995 this situation led to government shutdowns in the US three times in a few months, a similar Italian situation could have been disastrous).

A possible agreement: the French system

The two sides came very close to an agreement. Such agreement was based on a French style semi-presidential system, introduced by the Fifth Republic in 1958. This was ideal as it contained elements of the systems sponsored by both sides and ways to smooth out conflict if it arose. Semi-presidentialism has the following characteristics (e.g. see Sartori 1995):

1   The President is directly elected by the people for a particular period of time

2   The President is involved in the running of the government, although it divides this task with the Prime Minister
3   The President is independent from parliament, but cannot govern alone. His directives need to be mediated by the government
4   Conversely, the Prime Minister and his cabinet are independent from the President, even though the PM is nominated by the President, to the extent that they are subject to the confidence of Parliament

In this system, the right obtains the direct election of the President by the people. Also, the President nominates the Prime Minister, and is thus involved in setting the government agenda. The left also gains, with the government needing the support of parliament and the fact that the election is run under a two-round electoral system. Notably, many argue that the French system has the flexibility to work as a presidential system (ensuring a more effective government) when President and parliament belong to the same side, and as a parliamentary system when they do not. During the French 'cohabitation', for example, the Socialist President Mitterrand shared power with right-wing Prime Minister Chirac in the late 1980s and again between 1993 and 1995 with Balladur. In these periods the right-wing dominated parliament very much set the agenda, with Mitterrand exerting some control, but limiting his intervention mostly to foreign policy (where the French President maintained a certain independence of action).

The debate focused on the main attributes of the President in the French system (listed below). It was quite widely accepted that the President, as in France, would be able to nominate a Prime Minister and have the power to dissolve parliament. However, there was disagreement on other attributes, such as the French President's control over magistrates and the military and the fact that he can assume emergency powers or call referenda. The details were also open to debate on whether to allow a direct involvement of the President in foreign policy. The prospect of the government being able to present policy proposals and to issue decrees on a 'take it or leave it' basis to parliament, are also an area of debate.

Main attributes of the French President:

- To appoint the Prime Minister
- To chair the cabinet
- To dissolve parliament
- To sign international treaties
- To supervise foreign policy
- To be heavily involved in defence policy
- To chair the Magistrates Council
- To call referenda
- Can take emergency powers
- To appoint top civil servants

Semi-presidentialism

The French semi-presidentialist system was introduced with the foundation of the Fifth Republic between 1958 (when the new Constitution was introduced) and 1962 (when the French introduced the direct election of the President of the Republic). Typically, semi-presidentialism is associated with the French experience. It is based on the idea that there needs to be two centres of powers, able to balance each other. A fundamental characteristic of semi-presidentialism is that the President has enough power to limit the action of parliament. This role is exercised via a number of prerogatives: as in the case of France, these normally entail the ability to influence the action of government, the power to nominate and suspend ministers, some powers on the process of legislation (such as a veto), the power to assume extraordinary powers in cases of emergency and, finally, the ability to dissolve the Chambers. These prerogatives, together with the fact that, generally, the government still finds its legitimisation through parliamentary approval, very much define a semi-presidential system.

Early experiences of semi-presidentialist regimes were present in the Constitutions promoted by Finland (in 1919) and Austria (1929). The Weimar Republic (1919) also had a semi-presidentialist structure. Ireland and Portugal also have similar regimes and, since the early 1990s, Poland. In the latter two cases, the introduction of semi-presidentialism accompanied the transition to democracy. They represented useful ways to mediate the need to maintain stability and the need to allow new political forces to organise and consolidate. In fact, one positive feature of the semi-presidentialist system is that it ensures an equilibrium of powers. In practice, semi-presidentialist regimes often tend to oscillate between a purely presidential system and parliament based system, depending on circumstances. This flux can add flexibility to the system, but might also make the system vulnerable. In the case of the Weimar Republic, it is well known that Germany experienced severe political instability which, eventually, in those particular historical circumstances, led to dictatorship. Between 1919 and 1933, Germany had twenty governments, with an average life of seven months. On the other hand, in France, the flexibility of the semi-presidentialist system allowed it to work under very different circumstances (as in the case of the cohabitation mentioned above). Historical conditions are obviously the real determinant of whether the system works properly or whether it deteriorates into undesirable outcomes. Nevertheless, constitutional design can help to make the system more stable. Apart from the prerogatives of the President, the electoral system plays a significant role. In the case of the Weimar Republic, for example, the proportional system, coupled with a very large number of parties, was partly responsible for the weakness of parliament. Electoral systems which promote the formation of two alternative blocks, such as a two-round system, normally increase the ability of parliament to take decisions.

This tends to make the system more balanced. Finally, constitutional engineering can only go so far in ensuring that a system works properly. Practical, day-to-day politics makes the rest. Based on the Austrian and Portuguese experiences, some voiced concern that limiting the attributes of the President would create a system in which the President is directly elected, but commands little power. Finally, for the Italian case, there was also a general agreement to co-ordinate the elections for parliament and the President (unlike in France) to minimise the risk of 'cohabitation' (see Ceccanti, Massari and Pasquino 1996).

Conclusion

Constitutional reforms in Italy are an important further step after the changes introduced in the electoral systems over the last few years. Italy's recent history has highlighted the need for greater political stability and for a system of government which allows all parties to have the chance of experiencing a spell in government. Greater political stability is also seen as crucial, together with other reforms, to allow Italy to uproot its endemic corruption problem and construct a more efficient public sector. In this sense, the debate over constitutional reforms is of great importance. It is also important in light of Italy's hard-nosed attempt to be in EMU as early as possible. In the search for new rules, the French semi-presidentialist system seemed a positive compromise between the views of the two political camps. However, disagreements on implementation led to a failure to finalise a deal and to an early election in April 1996. New impetus for reform progress has been given by the establishment of a two Chamber all-party commission to look into the issue (the commission was established in early 1997 and in June gave preliminary backing to a semi-presidential system – though a final decision is still some way off). The reforms remain of great importance to increase chances of greater political stability and to expand the average life of Italian governments.

13

CONCLUSION

Europe can be seen from a multiplicity of angles. We have identified four. The *first* angle – probably Europe's biggest challenge in the years to come – is the launch of monetary union. A *second* angle is to look at oft-mentioned European economic difficulties. These might be better understood by considering Europe's apparent low level of innovation and of economic dynamism. Other economies, such as the US, seem to have performed more successfully in areas with high technological turnover such as computing, or at creating jobs in the service sectors (many of which, admittedly, of pretty low quality – the so-called McJobs). Europe seems to have lagged behind, with the result that it is now faced with a high and dramatic level of unemployment, employment practices considered too rigid and welfare provisions – previously a reason for pride – which need to be scaled down as they become too expensive to maintain. All these problems are epitomised by Europe's high and persistent rate of unemployment. *Thirdly*, there is the larger theme of how to deal with the consequences of Europe opening eastwards following the fall of the Berlin wall. Eastern countries are knocking on the door of the Western world for recognition and integration into their economic order. Development issues have emerged in the transition from command to market economies. The transition has often resulted in success stories, but also at times has caused areas of stress. Western Europe is faced with the need to help make the transition smoother and, when possible, to help to reduce conflicts or political tension. In prospect, the issue of how to widen the European Union and the timing and characteristics of such widening, must figure prominently in every European political agenda. Key issues include 'variable geometry' – groups of countries going ahead on single issues on which they agree – or multi-speed Europe, a much discussed hypothesis for EMU. *Fourthly*, Europe also faces a constitutional challenge concerning the reform of its decision-making structure. Economic integration was represented, from the beginning, by the three original communities: the European Coal and Steel Community, the European Atomic Energy Community (Euratom) and the European Economic Community (EEC). More recently, and particularly since the 1993 Treaty on the European

Union, new initiatives have been launched on new areas of great political relevance, the so-called second and third pillars. The second pillar is represented by further steps towards the development of a Common Foreign and Security Policy (CFSP). The third pillar corresponds to the area of Justice and Home Affairs (JHA) where greater co-operation is slowly developing. Important choices regard the level at which decisions have to be taken, moves towards federalism need to take into account the general consensus that the principle of subsidiarity – according to which decisions must be taken at the lower possible level – should be applied. Altogether, these developments, via greater harmonisation of rules and an increasing number of common decisions, will probably lead towards deeper political ties (on this, see, among other books, Goodman 1996).

In this book, we have focused on the first angle: getting monetary union off the ground. This is obviously interlinked however with many of the key political and economic issues which are currently facing Europeans. Therefore, we have also often addressed the second angle, the problem of economic dynamism. Monetary union cannot be seen in isolation. Firstly, because of the sheer size of the operation. It involves the over 350 million inhabitants of the European Union and would create a currency area which could potentially be the largest in the world, in terms of economic and financial power. Secondly, many deep-rooted economic problems have been brought to light by the process towards monetary union. All EU countries are potentially involved in the process. Monetary union will unite their destiny and has therefore forced them to look more closely at each other. This partly justifies the importance of the Maastricht criteria. The criteria have highlighted the need for economic convergence before any step towards monetary integration is undertaken. Attention has focused mainly on those economic characteristics which could damage more virtuous countries once EMU is launched, for example, the deficit and inflation criteria. This explains why there are no explicit employment criteria: EMU could penalise a country with an unemployment rate considerably higher than the others, but on the other hand, EMU is unlikely to have a long-term adverse impact on unemployment for more virtuous countries. On the contrary, large budget deficits and high inflation rates could have adverse effects on the entire currency union. The former, in particular, increases the overall level of borrowing and leads to higher interest rates in the entire union. High inflation in one country could spill over to other countries or damage the stability of the newly created currency.

All of these – deficits, inflation, unemployment – are crucial problems in themselves. They are at least as urgent, with different intensity, in all other areas of the industrialised world. In the US, the *deficit* problem is at the top of the political agenda and has spurred various attempts over the last ten years to balance the budget. As in Europe, the health and social security sectors are, in some cases, on the verge of bankruptcy. *Inflation* has kept quiet in the current decade in most countries. In spite of a large institutional debate on the nature of inflation and on the best way to keep it under control, it remains a threat in the eyes of policy makers and financial markets. Inflation opponents have learnt that a short-term approach to monetary policy is a dominant cause of inflation and that establishing independent wardens of monetary virtue could help solve the problem. Since then, independent central banks have flourished almost everywhere. *Unemployment* is a very European problem. European unemployment is not only high, but rising and persistent. It has unpleasant social features (it often leads to long-term unemployment and discouragement). It is also very costly as the unemployed need income supplementation. The problem has been identified as one of institutional nature: a too rigid labour market sometimes combined with oppressive regulation. However, such characteristics reflect Europe's preference for protective labour regulation and a dislike for large US-style wage differentials. How to address the problem therefore becomes a difficult political balancing act.

Unemployment, deficits, inflation do not directly stem from monetary union itself but EMU is the occasion for Europe to address such problems. We have based our discussion on the idea that Western Europe has already reached a level of economic and cultural integration for which it is beneficial to address such problems jointly. In this book, we have followed a line similar to the debate in Europe: looking at monetary union, but also at all the other topics attached to it. We have also tried to distinguish the items which are directly linked to the introduction of a single currency and those that are associated with it, but which exist beyond monetary union.

EMU as designed in the Maastricht Treaty is based on the implicit, but important, assumption that monetary union is possible and sustainable without political union. The latter is still not an issue in Europe. The decision process is complex: the Maastricht criteria needed unanimity – as most other important decisions – and had to be ratified by Parliaments in each of the EU countries. Obviously, revisions are very difficult as they imply that the whole process must be repeated all over again. Moreover, while the European Parliament maintains a largely consultative role, the day-to-day running of European affairs is in the hands of the European Commission and the Council of the European Union – the latter formed by ministers from each country. So, the Council is formed by representatives of elected home governments, but they are not directly elected as European representatives. The system of qualified majorities – on which, for example, most steps towards monetary union are conditional – allows a relatively small coalition of countries to form blocking minorities. Some progress has been made by the 1986 Single European Act which has removed an individual country veto power on decisions that require qualified majority, but the decision process remains cumbersome. The union has often been forced to progress at the slow speed imposed by the most reluctant or intransigent members (a phenomenon often referred to as Eurosclerosis – a popular expression, at times used for

Europe's constitutional difficulties and at other times, as elsewhere in this book, to define its economic plights). We are not arguing here whether Europe's current decision-making process is good or bad. This is part of the *fourth angle* and it is beyond the scope of this book. The point we stress is that *as it stands* political union is very far, while monetary union seems close to becoming a reality.

Monetary union without political union implies the idea that monetary matters are really not decisions of day-to-day politics. It implies, for example, that monetary policy is not to be used actively to promote economic growth. It is based on the view that monetary stability must be pursued under any conditions and that this can be done via an independent body, acting upon technical indicators. In this sense, one should not underestimate the link between central bank independence – which is posited with great emphasis in the Maastricht Treaty – and the European version of monetary union. The two largely go together. Central bank independence has been a seemingly unstoppable trend world-wide over the last decade. Academics are almost unanimous in arguing that it is the most effective weapon against inflation. Most European central banks – until recently with the notable exception of the UK – are independent (for an interesting book on the recent history of European central banking see J.B. Goodman 1992). Still, it is important to stress that the idea that monetary policy should not be used by elected politicians in day-to-day running strongly underlies the Maastricht Treaty. This opens up a number of questions which do not relate directly to monetary union, but become very relevant for Europe as a consequence of it. These include the accountability and transparency of central banks, how the European central bank will run monetary policy and which indicators will be used (given that monetary targeting is out of fashion and inflation targeting poses a number of problems). The Maastricht criteria, particularly those referring to deficits and debts, also implicitly set limits on the ability of governments to use fiscal policy. The focus on attaining the Maastricht criteria before EMU in order to qualify for the decision on who joins (i.e. in 1997), has blurred the original intention of the criteria to provide guidelines to ensure the stability of the union after its birth. The Stability and Growth Pact will quickly re-focus minds however, with fines for those countries which exceed the deficit levels after EMU is introduced (and few exceptions). This implies that countries are no more able to freely spend their way out of recessions, accumulating debt. Similarly to monetary policy, deficit-financed expansionary fiscal policy is very much out of fashion everywhere. Fiscal restraint is the recommended policy by all international organisations and supranational lenders to both developing and developed countries (the so-called 'Washington consensus' on economic reforms in developing countries puts reducing budget deficits at the top of key policy actions, see Williamson 1994). On top of this, financial markets act as guarantors of fiscal orthodoxy, another element making the reduction

189

of budget deficits largely an obligatory choice. The Maastricht criteria simply make this trend more explicit.

The concept of monetary union has a long history and was already a distant final target when the European Community was first founded in the post-war period. The motivations are varied: political and economic. The former are perhaps prevalent. It was not entirely chance that the decisive step towards monetary union – the Maastricht Treaty – was agreed just after German unification at a time when both Germany and its neighbours felt strongly about deepening European integration among European Community countries. A strategic alliance between France and Germany to increase their role in the international arena is also present in the plans of the promoters of EMU. Monetary union is a key step towards this because it is largely irreversible. The southern European countries view monetary union as a step towards political integration and this represents much of the appeal to them. The contrary attitude is prevalent in Britain and other Nordic countries. They appear, at times, persuaded by the economic rationale for EMU, but are strongly opposed and often horrified by the fact that it might be a precursor to greater political integration. The economic motivations are strong but somewhat evanescent, as benefits are difficult to measure with precision. They must also be viewed along with a number of risks and disadvantages.

Monetary union has two main advantages: it reduces transaction costs and protects business from the uncertainty due to exchange rate fluctuations. Despite pegged systems and the Exchange Rate Mechanism (which was designed to limit exchange rate movements) exchange rate fluctuations have at times been large. Such advantages for business must be considered in light of the very significant trade integration among the EU countries. In this sense, it appears, monetary union is a natural and useful complement to the common market. Particularly, some would argue, in an environment in which technology rewards companies with direct access to large potential markets. This is the case in telecommunication and information technology industries. Furthermore, there are some direct macroeconomic advantages. The main one is that the countries participating in EMU may share the anti-inflation credibility of the Bundesbank and enjoy a stable currency, with low inflation expectations and low interest rates. These advantages must be weighed against disadvantages such as the loss of the monetary policy tool to limit fluctuations in output, and the loss of the use of temporary adjustments in the exchange rate. Regional imbalances could be difficult to correct: the case of Germany's unification (discussed in Chapter 3) represents a warning. Political considerations suggested that an early monetary union between the two Germanies was desirable, but the costs of economic integration turned out to be a lot higher than most people anticipated. The experience has further highlighted the possibility of adverse shocks which may hit particular regions within the EU. The role of the EU budget and the possibility of higher solidarity transfers within the Union will gain greater relevance and might even turn out to be critical to the success of EMU. The risks mentioned suggest caution, but do not seem to have deterred most political parties from considering monetary union as a beneficial move. The process has, it seems, become almost unstoppable. Without underestimating the risks involved, the reasons for monetary union seem pretty convincing.

It is important to emphasise two other factors. Firstly, there seems to have been progress in building a stronger European cultural identity. This is particularly true for core European countries, but it probably also applies to the periphery. This might make the move towards monetary union easier. It is true that monetary union does not score very well on the popularity contest in opinion polls throughout Europe (with some notable exceptions). The Germans in particular appear a little sceptical, but this may be due to their experiences with unification. The opinion polls, however, seem to reflect more a dissatisfaction with the political leadership and with the policy measures associated with EMU. We have argued that most of these measures, particularly deficit reductions, were probably necessary regardless of EMU. We do not think that public opinion at large will be an obstacle to continued progress towards greater integration (though it plays a large role particularly in the case of the UK, which is discussed in chapter 11). On the contrary, we detect a sense of inevitability about the course Europe has taken. In light of past history this is reassuring.

The second factor which should be emphasised is that EMU is also the fruit of a convergence of interests. Most countries willing to participate have their own particular reasons to see EMU go forward. In Germany, EMU is seen as an effective way to protect German competitiveness *vis-à-vis* the rest of Europe. Germany has suffered from bouts of Deutsche Mark appreciation which have damaged its economic growth prospects. Monetary union would insulate Germany from future, sudden losses in competitiveness. France sees monetary union as a way to share German *de facto* domination on European monetary matters. It is a reality even now that the Bundesbank plays, willingly or not, a role as European central bank. The Euro is also seen as a European counterweight to the world-wide role of the US dollar. Southern European countries, but also France and the UK, are attracted by the low interest rate environment which would follow monetary union. They perceive this as being beneficial both for economic growth and for public finances, as it lowers the cost of servicing public debts. Finally, southern European countries also look to core Europe with its greater political stability and more efficient public sectors, and believe that they could indirectly benefit in those areas from greater integration. The case of Italy's recent political changes is closely linked to the country's fear of being left behind as core Europe progresses. This fear might have provided impetus to the corruption clean up of the early 1990s and to the drive towards political reforms (as discussed in Chapter 12).

Most countries have individual incentives for EMU, but most also have individual fears. Germany is worried that – faced with Europe-wide monetary discipline – some countries might be tempted by fiscal profligacy. Large budget deficits might lead to higher interest rates throughout the currency area and cause damage also to the countries which enforce fiscal restraint. On the other hand, with monetary policy unavailable, countries facing domestic difficulties may want to have some fiscal policy leverage. This explains the intense discussions on the Stability Pact at the end of 1996, to which we refer throughout the book (see particularly the appendix of Chapter 4). Another aspect – the main worry of the less virtuous countries – is how to deal with the failure to reach the criteria in time. What happens to the currencies which are not allowed in EMU from the start? The issue has so far been addressed with the somewhat unsatisfactory solution of a second edition of the Exchange Rate Mechanism (ERM II). Finally, as EMU approaches, much discussion takes place on technical issues, some of which often underlie pretty substantial questions on what EMU should look like. Among recent steps, the EMI's paper on the introduction of the euro, 1995, (Chapter 2) and the European Monetary Institute's Operational Framework (January 1997) – see the appendix of Chapter 6 – are among the main official documents detailing various aspects of monetary union.

Last, but not least, changing international financial markets are playing a significant role in shaping monetary union. Given the increased globalisation of economies, it appears that the most durable exchange rate regimes are at the two ends of the spectrum: either free floating or monetary unification (as discussed in Chapters 9 and 10). Everything in between contains flaws and risks which could undermine stability in the long run. The increasing size and efficiency of currency markets also means that countries, particularly smaller ones, are finding that their economic wealth and success is inextricably tied to exchange rate fluctuations which often only partially reflect economic fundamentals. Mis-pricing in exchange rates are often sustained for years, so that there might be many advantages for groups of countries, particularly those which belong to the same trade zone, to fix their exchange rates to form larger currency areas. Large countries like the US, Japan and Germany – and Europe as a whole after EMU – will continue to float one against the other, whereas smaller countries will seek to establish durable pegs with the larger trading partners. Such arrangements would also make it easier to promote international policy co-ordination in both macroeconomic management and trade agreements. This implies that we are moving towards a world of three currency zones – dollar, yen and euro. The roots of such system are already very much in place and EMU is just another, albeit very significant, step forward.

REFERENCES

INTRODUCTION

Bank of International Settlements (1996) *66th Annual Report.*

Kapstein, E.B. (1996) *Governing the Global Economy,* Cambridge, MA: Harvard University Press.

Krugman, P. (1994) *The Age of Diminished Expectations,* Cambridge, MA: MIT Press.

North, D. (1990) *Institutions, Institutional Change and Economic Performance,* Cambridge: Cambridge University Press.

Popper, K. (1945) 'The open society and its enemies', in D. Miller (ed.) (1993) *Popper Selections,* Princeton, NJ: Princeton University Press.

MONETARY UNION: TO BE OR NOT TO BE?

Balassa, B. (1961) *The Theory of Economic Integration,* New York: Richard and Irwin.

Committee for the Study of Economic and Monetary Union (1989) *Report on Economic and Monetary Union in the European Community* (the Delors report), Luxembourg: Office for Official Publications of the European Communities.

European Commission (1990) 'One market, one money', *European Economy* No. 44, October 1990.

European Commission (1992) *Official Journal of the European Communities,* C224, Vol. 35, 31 August 1992.

European Commission (1995a) 'The impact of currency fluctuations on the internal market', *Communication from the Commission to the European Council,* (document requested by the European Council at the Cannes summit October 1995).

European Commission (1995b) *Green Paper on the Practical Arrangements for the Introduction of the Single Currency,* 31 May 1995.

European Commission (1996a) *The Community Budget: The Facts in Figures,* 1996 edition SEC(96) 1200 – EN, Luxembourg: Office for Official Publications of the European Communities.

European Monetary Institute (1995) *The Changeover to the Single Currency,* November 1995, Frankfurt.

Financial Times (1995) 27 November.

Halwood, P. and MacDonald, R. (1986) *International Money*, Oxford: Blackwell.
Kenen, P.B. (1995) *Economic and Monetary Union in Europe*, Cambridge, Cambridge University Press.
Krugman, P. (1989) 'Increasing returns and economic geography', National Bureau of Economic Research, Working Paper, Washington, DC.
Marsh, D. (1994) *Germany and Europe*, Oxford: Heinemann.
Myrdal, G. (1957) *Economic Theory and Undeveloped Regions*, London.
OECD (1996) *Economic Outlook*, June 1996, Paris.
Süddeutsche Zeitung (1990) 27 November.
Tsoukalis, L. (1993) *The New European Economy – The Politics and Economics of Integration*, second revised edition, New York: Oxford University Press.

Further reading

Eichengreen, B. (1993) 'European monetary unification', *Journal of Economic Literature*, Vol. 31, 1321–57, September 1993.
European Commission (1996b) 'Secondary legislation for the introduction of the euro and some provisions relating to the introduction of the euro', *Proposal for a Council Regulation (EC) Communication of the European Parliament, the Council and the European Monetary Institute*, Brussels, 16 October 96 COM(96) 499 final.
European Commission (1996c) 'On the strengthening of the surveillance and coordination of budgetary positions', *Proposal for a Council Regulation (EC)* and 'On speeding up and clarifying the implementation of the excessive deficit procedure', *Proposal for a Council Regulation (EC)*, Brussels 16 October 1996 COM(96) 496 final.
European Commission (1996d) 'Reinforced convergence procedures and a new exchange rate mechanism in stage three of EMU', *Communication from the Commission to the Council*, Brussels, 16 October 1996 COM(96) 498 final.
European Monetary Institute (1997) 'Specification of the operational framework', *The Single Monetary Policy in Stage Three*, January 1997, Frankfurt.

3 GERMAN UNIFICATION AND EMU

European Commission (1990) 'One market, one money', *European Economy* No. 44, October 1990.
European Commission (1994) 'The economic and financial situation in Germany', *European Economy*, No. 2.
Corker R., Feldman, R.A., Habermeier, K., Vittas, H. and van der Willigen, T. (1995) *United Germany: The First Five Years, Performance and Policy Issues*, May 1995, Occasional Paper 125, International Monetary Fund, Washington, DC.

4 SOLVING THE DEFICIT PUZZLE

Banca d'Italia (1995) *Relazione Annuale Appendice Statistica*.
The Economic Report of the President (1996) Transmitted to Congress February 1996, Washington, DC: United States Government Printing Office, p. 69.
The Economist (1996) 9–15 December, 'The etiquette of merging currencies', p.108.

REFERENCES

European Commission (1992) *Official Journal of the European Communities*, C224, Vol. 35, 31 August 1992.

European Commission (1996a) 'On the strengthening of the surveillance and coordination of budgetary positions', *Proposal for a Council Regulation (EC)* and 'On speeding up and clarifying the implementation of the excessive deficit procedure', *Proposal for a Council Regulation (EC)*, Brussels, 16 October 1996 COM(96) 496 final.

Federal Reserve Bank of Kansas City (1995) symposium on 'Budget deficits and debts', August 1995.

Feldstein, M. (1994) 'A personal view' in *American Economic Policy in the 1980s*, Washington, DC: NBER.

Jackson Hole Conference (1995) conference on 'Reducing unemployment: current issues', August 25–27, 1995, The Federal Reserve of Kansas City.

Auerbach, A.J., Gokhale, J. and Kotlikoff, L.J. (1994) *Journal of Economic Perspectives*, Vol. 8, Winter 1994.

Ministero del Tesoro (1995) 'Documento di programmazione economica et finanziaria (DPEF)', Rome.

OECD (1996) *Economic Outlook*, June 1996, Paris.

Poterba, J. (1991) 'Budget policy', National Bureau of Economic Research, Washington, DC.

Sheffrin, S.M. (1991) *The Making of Economic Policy*, Oxford: Blackwell.

International Monetary Fund (IMF) (1996) 'Focus on fiscal policy', *World Economic Outlook* May 1996, Washington, DC.

Skidelsky, R. (1995) *The World after Communism*, London: Macmillan.

Further reading

European Commission (1996b) 'Reinforced convergence procedures and a new exchange rate mechanism in stage three of EMU', *Communication from the Commission to the Council*, Brussels, 16 October 1996 COM(96) 498 final.

Masson, P. and Mussa, M. (1995) *Long Term Tendencies in Budget Deficits and Debts*, IMF Working Paper 95/128, December 1995, Washington, DC.

5 IN BUNDESBANK CLOTHES

Alesina, A. (1988) 'Macroeconomics and politics', *NBER Macroeconomic Annual 1988*, Washington, DC.

Blinder, A. (1995) 'How to run a central bank', *The International Economy*, Sept/Oct 1995.

Castello-Branco, M. and Swinburne, M. (1991) *Central Bank Independence: Issues and Experiences*, IMF Working Paper 91/58, Washington, DC.

Cuckierman, A. (1992) *Central Bank Strategy, Credibility and Independence: Theory and Evidence*, Cambridge, MA: MIT Press.

Deutsche Bundesbank (1982) *The Deutsche Bundesbank, its Monetary Policy Instruments and Functions*, DB Special Series No.7, Frankfurt: Johannes Weisbecker.

European Commission (1992) *Official Journal of the European Communities*, C224, Vol. 35, 31 August 1992.

Fischer, S. (1993) 'The role of macroeconomic factors in growth', *Journal of Monetary Economics*, Vol. 32.

Grilli, V., Masciandaro, D. and Tabellini G. (1991) 'Political and monetary institutions and public financial policies in the industrial countries', *Economic Policy*, October 1991, pp. 139–49.

International Monetary Fund (IMF) (1996) 'The rise and fall of inflation', *World Economic Outlook* October 1996, Washington, DC.

Levy, A.D. (1995) 'Does an independent central bank violate democracy?', *Journal of Post-Keynesian Economics*, Vol. 18.

Lucas, R. (1973) 'Some international evidence on output-inflation trade-off', *American Economic Review*.

Newmann, J.M. (1992) 'Reflections on Europe's monetary constitution', *Central Banking*, Vol. 3.

Posen, A. (1995) 'Declarations are not enough: financial sector sources of central bank independence', *NBER Macroeconomics Annual 1995*, Washington, DC.

Rogoff, K. (1985) 'The optimal degree of commitment to an intermediate monetary target', *Quarterly Journal of Economics*, Vol. 100, pp. 1169–89.

Walsh C.E. (1995) 'Recent central bank reforms and the role of price stability as the sole objective of monetary policy', *NBER Macroeconomics Annual, 1995*, Washington, DC.

6 CENTRAL BANKS GET ECLECTIC

Deutsche Bundesbank (1995) *Monthly Report,* January 1995, Frankfurt, p. 23.

Dicks, M. (1996) 'Rules as tools: an investigation into the usefulness of policy rules', *Lehman Brothers International Economics*, August 1996.

The Economist (1996) 'Monetary policy, made to measure', 10 August 1996.

European Commission (1992) *Official Journal of the European Communities,* C224, Vol. 35, 31 August 1992. Article 105 on Monetary Policy.

European Monetary Institute (1997) 'Specification of the operational framework', *The Single Monetary Policy in Stage Three*, January 1997, Frankfurt.

Federal Reserve (1995) *The Rise and Fall of Money Growth Targets as Guidelines for US Monetary Policy*, Washington, DC: Federal Reserve System.

HMSO (1980) *Financial Statement and Budget Report 1980–81*, London: HMSO.

International Monetary Fund (IMF) (1995–7) *World Economic Outlook* various editions, Washington, DC.

Mussa, M. (1994) 'Monetary policy' in *American Economic Policy in the 1980s*, Washington, DC: NBER.

OECD (1994) *Economic Survey Annex I*, Paris.

Reuters (1996) *News 2000*, 29 April 1996.

Reuters (1996) *News 2000*, 11 October 1996.

Padoa-Schioppa, T. (1995) *Bank of Italy Bulletin*, June 1995, Rome: Bank of Italy.

7 EUROPEAN UNEMPLOYMENT

Bank for International Settlements (1996) *66th Annual Report*, June 1996.

Barell, R., Pain, N. and Young, G. (1994) 'Structural differences in European labour market' in R. Barell (ed.), *The UK Labour Market: Comparative Aspects and*

Institutional Developments, London: The National Institute for Social Research, Cambridge: Cambridge University Press.

Bertola, G. and Ichino, A. (1995) 'Wage inequality and unemployment: United States versus Europe', *NBER Macroeconomics Annual 1995*, Washington, DC.

Centre for Economic Policy Research (1995) 'La disoccupazione: scelte per l'Europa' London.

European Commission (1993) *Growth Competitiveness, Employment: The Challenges and the Way Forward for the 21st Century*, Brussels, December 1993.

International Labour Organisation (ILO) (1996) *World Employment Report 1996/1997*, Geneva: ILO.

Krugman, P. (1994) 'Past and prospective causes of high unemployment', in Proceedings from the Symposium on *Reducing Unemployment: Current Issues and Policy Options*, Jackson Hole, Wyoming, August 1994.

Maddison, A. (1995) *Monitoring the World Economy 1820–92*, Paris: OECD.

Malinvaud, E. (1994) 'Are macroeconomic theories challenged by the present European recession?', *Labour*, Vol. 8, No. 1.

OECD (1994) *The OECD Job Study: Facts, Analysis, Strategies*, Paris.

OECD (1996) *Economic Outlook*, June 1996, Paris.

Ormerod P. (1996), 'Unemployment: a distributional phenomenon'. Paper prepared for the conference *Unemployment and Policies Towards It*, April 1996, European University Institute, Florence, Italy.

Reich, R. (1991) *The Work of Nations*, New York: Simon and Schuster.

Robinson, P. (1996) *The Role and Limits of Active Labour Market Policies*, London: Centre for Economic Performance, London School of Economics.

Simonazzi, A. and Villa, P. (1996) 'Employment, growth and income inequality: some open questions', Università di Trento, discussion paper 1/96.

8 GERMAN UNEMPLOYMENT

Layard, R., Nickell, S. and Jackman, R. (1991) *Unemployment – Macroeconomic Performance and the Labour Market*, New York: Oxford University Press.

OECD (1996) 'Germany', *Economic Surveys,* Paris.

9 BUBBLES, CRISES AND INTERVENTIONS

Bonser-Neal, C. (1996) 'Does central bank intervention stabilize foreign exchange rates?' *Federal Reserve Bank of Kansas City Economic Review* Vol. 81, No. 1, Q1 1996, pp. 43–59.

Dornbusch, R. (1976) 'Expectations and exchange rate dynamics' *Journal of Political Economy*, Vol. 84, pp. 1161–76.

Dornbusch, R. (1983) 'Flexible exchange rates and interdependence', IMF staff papers, Vol. 30, No. 1, March.

Dornbusch, R. (1987) 'Exchange rate economics: 1986', *Economic Journal*, Vol. 97, No. 385, March.

Edwards, S. (1992) 'Trade orientation, distortions and growth in developing countries' *Journal of Development Economics*.

European Commission (1995) *The Impact of Currency Fluctuations on the Internal Market,* communication from the Commission to the European Council, document requested by the European Council at the Cannes summit October 1995.

Fama, E.F. (1984) 'Forward and spot rates', *Journal of Monetary Economics,* Vol. 14, December.

Frankel, J.A. and Froot, K.A. (1986) in 'Understanding the US dollar in the eighties: the expectations of chartists and fundamentalists', *Economic Record,* Vol. 62, Supplementary issue pp. 24–38.

Frenkel, J. (1981) 'Flexible exchange rates, prices and the role of the news: lessons from the 1970s,' *Journal of Political Economy,* Vol. 89, pp. 665–705.

Goodhart, C.A.E. (1988) 'The foreign exchange market: a random walk with a dragging anchor', *Economica,* Vol. 55, pp. 437–60.

International Monetary Fund (IMF) (1996) *World Economic Outlook,* May 1996, Washington, DC.

Isard, P. (1978) 'Exchange rate determination: a survey of popular views and recent models', *Princeton Studies in International Finance* 42, Princeton: International Finance Section, Department of Economics, Princeton University.

Krueger A.O. (1978) *Foreign Trade Regimes and Economic Development,* National Bureau of Economic Research, Washington, DC.

Krugman, P. (1988a) 'Louvre's lessons – let the dollar fall', *International Economy* Vol. 1, pp. 76–82.

Krugman, P. (1988b) *Target Zones and Exchange Rate Dynamics,* NBER Working Paper 2481, Washington, DC.

Mussa, M. (1979) in 'Empirical regularities in the behaviour of exchange rates and theories of foreign exchange rates' *Carnegie-Rochester Conference Series on Public Policy* 11, pp. 9–57.

OECD (1996) *Economic Outlook,* June 1996, Paris.

Teunissen, J.J. (ed.) *Can Currency Crises be Prevented or Better Managed? Lessons from Mexico,* Forum on Debt and Development (FONDAD, Netherlands), 1996.

10 LIFE OUTSIDE EMU

European Commission (1996) *Communication from the Commission to the Council, Reinforced Convergence Procedures and a New Exchange Rate Mechanism in Stage Three of EMU,* Brussels, 16 October 1996 COM(96) 498 final.

Goldman Sachs (1995) *Economic Research on Currency Boards.*

Gros, D. (1996) '*Towards Economic and Monetary Union: Problems and Prospects*', Centre for European Policy Studies Paper No. 65, for the CEPS Economic Policy Group, Brussels: CEPS.

International Monetary Fund (IMF) (1995) 'Evolving roles of exchange rate mechanisms', *World Economic and Financial Surveys, Issues in International Exchange and Payments Systems,* April 1995, Washington, DC: IMF, p. 18.

Rojas Suarez, L. and Weisbrod, S.R. (1995) 'Financial fragilities in Latin America', IMF Occasional Paper, October 1995.

Spaventa, L. (1996) 'Out in the cold? Outsiders and insiders in 1999', in *Banca Nazionale del Lavoro Quarterly Review,* Special Issue, supplement to No. 196, March 1996.

11 THE UK AND EMU

Bayoumi, T. (1994) *A Formal Model of Optimum Currency Areas,* discussion paper No. 968, June 1994, London: Centre for Economic Policy Research.

Britton, E. and Whitley, J. (1997) 'Comparing the monetary transmission mechanism in France, Germany and the United Kingdom: some issues and results', *Bank of England Quarterly Bulletin,* May 1997, p. 153.

European Commission (1996) *Intergovernmental Conference 1996, Commission Report for the Reflection Group, Annex 14,* Luxembourg: Office for Official Publications of the European Communities, 1995.

Evans, B. and Taylor, A. (1996) 'Conservatism and the 1990s' in *Salisbury to Major: continuity and change in Conservative politics'* Manchester: Manchester University Press.

Goodhart, C.A.E. (1989) chapter XVII, section 1 on 'Optimal currency areas' in *Money, Information and Uncertainty* 2nd edition, Basingstoke: Macmillan, p. 422.

Goodman S.F. (1996) *The European Union* 3rd edition (*Economics Today,* edited by Andrew Leake) London: Macmillan, pp. 247–8.

OECD (1996) *Economic Outlook* 59, June 1996, Paris.

Robins, L. (1992) Chapter 15 'Britain and the European Community: twenty years of not knowing' in B. Jones and L. Robins (eds) *Two Decades in British Politics,* Manchester: Manchester University Press.

12 ITALIAN INSTITUTIONAL REFORMS

Ceccanti, S., Massari, O. and Pasquino, G. (1996) *Semipresidenzialismo,* Bologna: Il Mulino.

Ginsborg, P. (1990) *A History of Contemporary Italy,* Harmondsworth: Penguin.

Salvadori, M.L. (1996) *Storia d' Italia e Crisi di Regime,* 2nd edition, Bologna: Il Mulino.

Sartori, G. (1995) *Ingegneria Costituzionale,* Bologna: Il Mulino.

13 CONCLUSION

Goodman S.F. (1996) *The European Union* 3rd edition (*Economics Today,* edited by Andrew Leake), London: Macmillan.

Goodman, J.B. (1992) *The Politics of Central Banking in Western Europe,* Ithaca, NY: Cornell University Press.

Williamson, J. (1994) *The Political Economy of Policy Reforms,* Washington, DC: Institute for International Economics.

INDEX

200